JESUS WANTS
YOU WELL!

ABOUT THE AUTHOR

DR. C. S. LOVETT

Dr. Lovett is the president of **Personal Christianity Chapel,** a fundamental, evangelical interdenominational ministry. For the past 41 years he has had but one objective—**preparing Christians for the second coming of Christ!** This book is one of over 40 of his works designed to help believers **prepare for His appearing.**

Dr. Lovett's decision to serve the Lord resulted in the loss of a sizable personal fortune. He is well equipped for the job the Lord has given him. A graduate of American Baptist Seminary of the West, he holds the **M.A.** and **M.Div.** degrees conferred *Magna Cum Laude.* He has also completed graduate work in psychology at Los Angeles State College and holds a **Ph.D.** in counseling from the Louisiana Christian University.

A retired Air Force Chaplain (Lt. Colonel), he has been married to Marjorie for 50 years and has two grown daughters dedicated to the Lord.

JESUS WANTS YOU WELL!

by

C. S. LOVETT

M.A., M.Div., Ph.D.

Director of **Personal Christianity**

author of

"HELP LORD—THE DEVIL
WANTS ME FAT!"
JOGGING WITH JESUS
SOUL-WINNING MADE EASY
DEALING WITH THE DEVIL
LOVETT'S LIGHTS ON REVELATION
LONGING TO BE LOVED

illustrated by LINDA LOVETT

published by:
PERSONAL CHRISTIANITY
Box 549
Baldwin Park, California 91706-0549

1992 EDITION
ISBN 0-938148-29-X

DEDICATED TO

the precious blood of the Lord Jesus
Christ which can cleanse the soul
of a man and make him brand new...

and

the wondrous blood of the human body
which cleanses and nourishes the organs
and tissues and makes them new

CONTENTS

The examples and illustrations used in this book
are based on actual cases. However, they have
been fictionalized to prevent the parties
from being recognized. The author has
sought to protect the identity of those referred
to in this book, except where permission
has been given.

THE PLAN FOR USING THIS BOOK

1. Read the entire book as fast as you can to get a picture of the overall plan. Don't try to learn or memorize the various points on your first reading.

2. Reread chapters four through nine paying particular attention to the summaries at the end of each chapter. This time try to fix some of the ideas in your mind.

3. Start using the healing technique, adapting it to your particular illness or affliction.

4. When you feel your determination starting to fade, reread chapters eight and nine, It will bolster your determination to realize you are working with fixed laws which must work when you meet the conditions.

5. Once you begin using the plan, carry an affirmation card on your person. You'll find 3 of them on page 300. Whenever your mind goes to your illness, let that be a signal to take out your card and use it per the instructions printed on the back.

JOGGING KEEPS DR. LOVETT AND
HIS DAUGHTER LINDA IN SHAPE FOR CHRIST. IT
IS A MATTER OF STEWARDSHIP OF THE BODY TO
GET THAT BLOOD MOVING EVERY DAY.

FOR DOCTORS ONLY

It is possible, doctor, that some of your patients may ask for your opinion of this book. I thought it might be helpful to devote a page to physicians, providing an overview of what I am seeking to do. The book deals solely with emotionally induced illness and presents faith healing as a reasonable approach. The method set forth is consistent with the writings of the following medical men:

The effects of emotional stress as outlined by:

Hans Selye, M.D., Dir. of Institute for Experimental Medicine, University of Montreal, Canada. **"The Stress of Life,"** McGraw-Hill Publications, 1956.

John A. Schindler, M.D., Chairman of the Dept. of Medicine, Monroe Clinic, Monroe, Wisc. **"How to Live 365 Days a Year,"** Prentice-Hall, 1954.

S. I. McMillen, M.D., **"None of These Diseases,"** Fleming Revel, 1963.

The Cybernetic approach as advanced by:

Maxwell Maltz, M.D., F.I.C.S., **"Psycho-Cybernetics,"** Prentice-Hall, 1960.

L. Gilbert Little, M.D., **"Nervous Christians,"** Moody Press, 1956.

The effects of nutrition on disease as reported by:

Roger J. Williams, Ph.D., Dir. Clayton Foundation Biochemical Institute at the University of Texas. **"Nutrition Against Disease,"** Pitman Publishing Co., 1971.

George Watson, Ph.D., Dir. Psychochemical Studies, University of Southern California. **"Nutrition and Your Mind,"** Harper and Row, 1972.

E. Cheraskin, M.D., D.M.D., and W. M. Ringsdorf, Jr., D.M.D., M.S., **"New Hope for Incurable Diseases,"** Exposition Press, New York, 1971.

The effects of exercise on health as advanced by:

Lawrence E. Lamb, M.D., Professor of Medicine, Baylor College of Medicine, Houston, Texas. **"Your Heart and How To Live With It,"** Viking Press, New York, 1969.

Paul Dudley White, M.D., Emeritus Professor of Medicine, Harvard Medical School, as quoted in **"Atherosclerosis—the Silent Killer,"** Executive Health, 1969.

William J. Bowerman, Professor Physical Education, University of Oregon and W. E. Harris, M.D. **"Jogging,"** Grosset & Dunlap, New York, 1967.

When the works of these men are considered together with all that the Bible has to say about the relationship of the mind to the body, a series of laws emerges amenable to the concept of faith healing. The faith, of course, is faith based on REASON as well as promises. These laws have been fully demonstrated in the labs and clinics of our universities. Arranged in order, they offer a plan for regulating the health of the body. This book presents that plan.

The author sees no conflict between this approach and the medical approach. Both use the same laws. A doctor may set a bone, but he cannot heal the break. He relies on the healing principle in the human body to do that. He may remove a physical blockage, but again he must trust the healing laws to make his patient well.

The psychiatrist also depends on these laws. He may remove a mental block, but healing must still follow a lawful pattern. True, he works with laws governing the relationship between the mind and the body, nonetheless he must wait on the healing principle to restore his patient to health.

The author feels that the spiritual approach has been overlooked. Some religionists have abused the laws to the place where medical men cringe at the mention of faith healing. But should we throw out the baby with the bath water? The author believes the spiritual approach to these same laws, PROPERLY APPLIED, deserves an equal place with the other disciplines.

In no way does this book prejudice the reader against seeking medical or psychological help.

PREFACE

An artist had just completed a new painting and was anxious for his friend to come and see it. When the friend arrived, he ushered him into a room that was pitch dark.

"What are we standing here for," asked the friend. "I thought you wanted me to see your painting?"

"I do," replied the artist, **"but if you'll sit down in this chair and be patient for a bit, I promise you won't be sorry."** In a few minutes he clicked on the light over his painting.

"It's beautiful," exclaimed the friend, "and what fantastic colors!"

"I thought you'd like it," beamed the artist, **"but you would not have appreciated these colors had I let you see them with the glare of the street still in your eyes. That's why I kept you in the dark. I wanted your eyes to be able to enjoy the full effect of the painting!"**

I WAS IN THE DARK ABOUT HEALING

For some months I had a painful disorder that didn't improve. After each examination the doctor would say, "Everything looks okay." Yet I knew things were not okay, and I didn't like it. It made me nervous. So I went to God about it. I thought to myself, "If the doctor isn't going to help me, maybe God will." I learned later that doctors have no successful treatment for my problem and prefer to put off surgery until they feel the patient's health is in danger.

Well, asking God about healing was new to me. Until this problem arose, I had no reason to be concerned.

My health has always been good. I hadn't paid much attention to faith healing. "Sure God can heal, why not?" That was my attitude when I heard the testimonies of people who had been healed. I just never had any reason to look into it for myself. But now I was interested.

When I began to think about healing, I found I was in the dark. I had been for years. So I made up my mind to find out what faith healing was all about. I put myself in the Lord's hands and got set for an unbiased, unprejudiced look at His Word as well as His working in my body.

"Click." The light went on. Wow! Did He have a surprise for me!

SURPRISE . . . !

I suspected healing might be AVAILABLE in Christ today. After all, the Lord Jesus is The Healer. His record includes thousands of healings of men's bodies and souls. Besides, isn't Christianity essentially a healing religion? Sure. Everywhere the gospel goes, healing of some sort always follows. So I wasn't too surprised to learn that physical healing is available in Christ. What did thrill me was HOW God accomplishes it.

We receive it via fixed laws.

Through a series of experiences and studies which I would have never considered apart from my disorder, the Lord exposed me to some VALID LAWS which regulate the health of the body. I say "some" for there must be others waiting to be discovered. While many of the healings in the New Testament and in bodies today are easily explained by these laws, not all of them are.

I can't tell you how excited I became when those

laws started surfacing. I felt as though I had discovered an original manuscript of the N.T. I began listing them one by one. When I put them all on paper, they were beautiful. I felt like the artist's friend staring at the new painting. I had been in the dark all right. But from out of that darkness I was able to behold something dazzling from the Lord.

As I worked with those laws and began arranging them in different ways, the Holy Spirit showed me a definite order. That's when the surprise came. A PLAN for healing emerged. It was so simple. I wondered why it hadn't been announced sooner. But like many of God's wonderful truths, it was hidden on the surface. I didn't discover it until I tripped over it.

This plan is different. It is quite unlike anything that comes to mind when you think of faith healing. This is faith based on **fixed laws** supported by the promises of God. After the Lord showed me the healing laws and the logic behind them, it was up to me to decide whether I would put my trust in them or not. Seeing them on paper made my faith rise to the place where I was ready to watch them work in my body. I decided I would accept them as from the Lord and put my trust in them.

THE APPROACH WAS SOUND

I tried the plan the Lord gave me.

The laws were absolutely valid.

My body was healed.

After discovering this HEALING PLAN and having it work in my body, and others who have used it since, I knew the Holy Spirit didn't give it to me for myself alone.

14

That's why this book is in your hands. You are about to learn a method of healing based on your ability to work WITH Jesus. It adheres to the admonition, "Without Me ye can do nothing" (John 15:5). As you learn the laws and see how they operate, you may be tempted to think the Lord's part is too small. But it just isn't so. Underneath the operation of the laws is the solid truth that Jesus is the only Healer. We are merely His agents. The plan you are about to learn is for self-healing. You are going to administer those laws to your own body as the Lord's agent.

So get set for a new experience, a new adventure in faith. Before you have read very far, you will be convinced that. . .

JESUS WANTS YOU WELL!

INTRODUCTION

READY FOR A MIRACLE . . .?

 I asked that question of my congregation to kick off a series of messages on faith healing.

My people were wide-eyed. They knew of my experiments in faith healing. There was some excitement in the air—inasmuch as a number of Christians had been healed. I hadn't said much about the work I was doing, feeling it best to be silent until the Lord finished teaching me. But now it was time to share what I had learned with my people.

When I said, "Are you ready for a miracle?" they were sure I was going to bring some sick person from the audience onto the platform. They expected to see the power of God at work before their eyes. But that didn't happen. Instead my hand reached inside the pulpit and brought out a transistor radio. Then I announced, "This is the miracle!"

I held the radio near the microphone and turned the dial. Sounds from a number of stations went over the PA system. As I looked on the faces of my people, I could tell they were disappointed. After all, listening to a transistor radio was hardly a miracle to them. "Don't you think this is a miracle?" Some shook their heads in reply. No, they didn't think it was at all miraculous. Then I explained.

"To appreciate this miracle, we have to go back to the days of Peter and Paul and TAKE OUR RADIO WITH US! Are you ready to GO?"

16

APPRECIATING THE MIRACLE

Imagination is a great thing. We can go anyplace and do anything we like simply by picturing it in our minds. So let's flash back over the centuries to New Testament times and put ourselves in Syrian Antioch. There's Paul now. He's speaking to a group of believers gathered about him. He's sitting on a large rock. He beckons us to join the group.

As we reach the spot, we turn on the radio. The sounds blare loudly. A look of consternation comes over everyone's face. Then we set the tiny receiver on the rock near Paul. He stares in bewilderment. Can you picture those disciples walking slowly around the rock, wondering what kind of a box it is that speaks!

"It's a magician's trick!" says one.

"It's a miracle!" says another.

The apostle Paul cautiously picks it up. He's reluctant to call it the devil's work, but the thought enters his mind. He was familiar with the amazing things the Eastern magicians could do. As he turns it in all directions, the voices continue to come from inside. Then he puts it to his ear. No, it's not a ventriloquist's trick. Those sounds are really coming from the box. He sets it down. "Yes," he says, "I don't understand it, but it's a miracle."

Paul was right. It was a miracle—to him. That's the only way he could explain it. He had no knowledge of transistor radios. Such things weren't invented then. But is it a miracle to us? Of course not. Transistor radios are commonplace in our time. We know about radio waves and the laws of electronics. We understand them and use them. Yet those radio laws aren't new. They were just as true in Paul's day as they are now. The difference is, **we know about them.** Time has allowed us to discover the laws and remove the mystery. Consequently, what was once considered as miraculous is now regarded as rather ordinary.

IT'S LIKE THAT WITH HEALING

The healing laws were at work in Jesus' day, but He didn't establish them at His advent. They were ALREADY in existence. He simply USED them. They were just as true in the days of Noah, only no one knew of them. Had they, they could have performed "miracles." We would have called them that. That's the way they appear to us. Do we not look on the healings performed by Jesus as miracles? Sure we do. Why? Because we don't understand the LAWS behind them. Just as a transistor radio would be a miracle to Paul, so do the New Testament healings seem miraculous to us.

But knowledge removes mystery. Thus, when we learn the laws of healing and how they function, certain types of healings no longer seem miraculous. They can even become ordinary. As you read this book, you are going to learn a number of healing laws. God has been pleased to let us discover some of them. But please note that I said SOME. We do not know ALL of the healing laws. Some of the healings in the New Testament are definitely a matter of authority over ANOTHER PERSON'S BODY. Those which have to do with the healing of others apparently involve laws as yet unknown to us. At least they are unknown to me. And there are certain types of healings I can't explain either. It is probable that some of God's Laws could not be used even if we did know them.

> **NOTE.** In the course of reading this book you are going to find THREE kinds of healing mentioned: (1) automatic healing, (2) faith healing, (3) command healing. Automatic

healing is the natural process doctors rely on to mend the body after they have done their work. Faith healing has to do with using certain laws which govern the relationship between the mind and the body. The healing process can be triggered when these laws are invoked by faith. Command healings are those which the Lord Jesus and the disciples performed on certain occasions when it was obvious that no faith was present. Jesus delegated authority for command healings to His disciples (Luke 10:1). At various points throughout the book I will be referring to all three types of healings. But the technique you will be learning has to do with faith healing.

● What you are about to read is NOT a plan for healing others. The approach is based on your ability to rise in faith where you can trigger God's healing laws in your OWN body. You will be healed, but you will **not** be able to heal others by the same process. Why? There is no way to **substitute** your faith for someone else's. Each person has to climb the faith ladder for himself. Of course there is nothing to keep you from sharing the insights of this book with others and encouraging them to rise in faith also. If they reach the place where they too can activate the healing program, you will have brought them healing indirectly.

> **NOTE.** Even though I have just said this book does not offer a plan for the healing of others, I do not wish to limit God in any way. On one occasion Jesus said, "All things are possible to him that believeth" (Mark 9:23). I am being careful to say that I simply do not know the laws which govern the healing of others, and am presenting a PLAN based on laws I do know. Most readers will have their hands full reaching the degree of faith needed to activate them. But that won't be true of all who read. You might be one who could GO BEYOND what is needed for this approach and trigger unknown laws. It's not impossible. Tremendous things happen when we rise in faith. I should be most pleased if this book became your stepping stone to HIGHER FAITH.

When we plant seeds in the ground and wait for the harvest, we are using known laws of God. Yet to this day we do not know how life comes from a seed. There are some secrets about living things remaining to be discovered. But within the limits of what we do know, we use God's laws to grow crops. So it is with the healing laws. Within the limits of what we do know, we are privileged to use them. I am confident there are MORE healing laws waiting to be discovered. What I have done in this book is to apply those laws which God has been pleased to reveal. I am not attempting to explain all the different kinds of healings that have been known to occur. But I do insist that these laws can be used to secure healing. The believer who uses them will be obliged to PRAISE THE LORD as surely as if he had received a "supernatural touch."

LET ME BE FRANK ABOUT THIS

I am NOT writing this book merely to teach people how to get well. My motive is deeper than that. Healing for its own sake does not deserve that priority, to my thinking. There are too many well Christians refusing to serve the Lord. Health and devotion to Christ are not partners. Sickness is more apt to make a man get serious about Jesus than is good health. Therefore I am writing for people willing to let their sicknesses draw them close to Christ.

There is no way to be truly well unless one is close to the Lord. His own counsel at this point is, "Seek ye first the kingdom of God and ALL these things will be added to you" (Matt. 6:33). This is the golden rule for the Christian. Healing for our bodies is included in the ALL THINGS package. For the man ready to put Christ first, this book is going to prove a fantastic blessing. He is going to see his faith produce astonishing things in his body. That's the man I'm interested in.

Such a person truly seeks to exalt Jesus above himself or his family and his faith is likely to go beyond the requirements of this book. If you have set your heart on honoring the Lord Jesus by faith, this book could introduce you to the supernatural. See now why I asked if you were . . .

READY FOR A MIRACLE?

Chapter One

JESUS WANTS YOU WELL

"Whenever anyone gets well, it is because he has employed a method of healing that cooperates with the law of health."

Come with me into the back yard. Here's a small tree. We break off a branch. Some weeks later we return to this same tree and examine the wound. What do we see? The tree has healed itself. A burl has formed at the point where the branch was removed. From within the tree itself has come new material to build a thick wood tissue about the break. Who told the tree to do that? No one. Yet the healing took place. Why? There is a healing principle in operation throughout the world.

One animal breaks a leg. Another is torn in a fight. Wounded animals retire for a time to await the healing that always comes when the wound is not too serious. Again, no outside help is needed. Why? There is a law of health which operates in all living things. Wherever there is life, the law of healing is **constantly** at work.

A man is shaving. He nicks his face. Does he panic? No. He knows it will heal. How do we explain this. "Nature heals it," says one person. But let's be more precise and say, "It is healed according to the law of nature." Yes, there is a natural law which has to do with healing. There are natural laws which govern everything in the universe—including our bodies.

NOTE. God designed this world to operate according to law. To create living things and then turn them loose without laws to regulate their behavior would make Him the author of confusion. Without laws, this world would

22

be like a busy intersection with no traffic signals—one huge jam. Since God is Himself a lawful person, everything He does is lawful. A perfect God cannot establish an imperfect creation. Neither could He impose imperfect laws for its maintenance. To author a law of imperfection (such as a law of sickness) would be a contradiction to His own nature. Therefore, we must assume that God's laws are intended to maintain the PERFECTION of His universe.

It is one of God's wonderful laws that our bodies begin to heal as soon as an injury occurs. His laws seek to sustain the perfection built into the animal kingdom. Therefore we observe this:

> **"When a person becomes sick, he has in some way violated the law of health. For a person to get well, he must cooperate with that same law.**

GOD'S LAWS ARE IMPERSONAL

While God has established laws to benefit mankind and preserve the perfection built into our physical beings, those laws are quite impersonal. That is, they have no feelings about us, one way or another. Laws can't think. Neither do they make judgments. If we obey them, they prosper us. If we violate them, they punish us.

Here is the law of gravity. Because of it we move about the earth's surface easily and safely. Without it, we'd have no control over our position and would fly off this globe. By means of gravity our streams and rivers flow and we harness them for electrical power. Life would be unbearable without gravity to keep things in place. But suppose you get too close to the edge of a cliff and lose your balance. That same law will take you to your death on the rocks below and have no feelings about it. Because it is a law, it simply does its job.

23

● A mother is bathing her infant son. While her back is turned, he reaches out to the electric heater and is electrocuted. A gurgling sound causes the mother to turn around. She sees her dead child. In anguish she tries to fix the blame. "If there is a God," she cries, "how could He let this awful thing happen?" But you see what she is doing. She is blaming God for giving us the law of electricity. That is like blaming Henry Ford for all the auto accidents that take place. It is what we do with God's laws that determines whether they are a blessing or a curse.

> **NOTE.** It matters not to the laws that we are ignorant of them. Because they are laws, they do what they are established to do, regardless of our reasons for using or violating them. Laws cannot make allowances for our mistakes. This may seem cruel at times, but natural laws MUST penalize us when we break them. What law is to blame when someone leaves the gate open to a swimming pool and a toddler is drowned? God's law says no one can live with his lungs full of water. Cooperating with that law by locking the gate would have saved the child's life. It is man's responsibility to acquaint himself with God's laws, particularly those which have to do with health and survival.

DOCTORS DEPEND ON THE HEALING PRINCIPLE

"The doctor dresses the wound, but God heals it."

No physician, psychologist, evangelist, or witch doctor ever healed anyone. There is but one Healer, the Lord Jesus Christ. He is the One Who established the healing principle (Col. 1:16). Whenever healing occurs, it is because men have somehow aligned themselves with His law. Every healer of any kind must cooperate with the healing principle in some way. Healing CANNOT occur apart from it. As one doctor put it:

24

"No intelligent physician of any school claims to do more than assist the natural forces of the body to restore a person to health."

 One man goes to his surgeon. A blockage is removed and he is sewed up. The doctor has done all he can do. If he is a Christian, he will say, "Now it is up to the Lord." Once his work is done, all any doctor can do is wait for the healing principle to finish the job. The point? No human agent can heal. The healing occurs only because the Lord has established a lawful healing process in the body.

Here's a man with a doctor's prescription. He goes to the pharmacist. He takes the medicine and gets well. Another man seeks relief through a chiropractor. His problem is solved and he too gets well. Then there are those who are ministered to by the "healing" evangelist. The methods can vary from consulting hypnotists, witch doctors, psychics, and visiting famous shrines. Yet they all have one thing in common—THEY WORK. Why? At some point, they cooperate with the healing principle.

Consider the witch doctor. A patient is brought to him. Watch as he dances about in his weird garb. He shakes his rattles and pronounces his incantations. Then he applies blood and cow dung to the injury. Does he have any idea as to what is really taking place? Of course not. Yet, if he should say the right words, words to which his patient can respond with faith—the victim's own faith can trigger the healing process in the body and he will get well.

Does it surprise you that a witch doctor can produce a genuine healing? The more so when I have just said

25

the Lord Jesus is the ONLY healer? The witch doctor knows nothing of the Lord, much less any laws at work in the human body. How then is he able to get this healing? BY ACCIDENT. If, by chance, his words cause the victim to BELIEVE he is going to get well, his own FAITH will activate the healing program. Now that same law works the other way too. If the witch doctor tells his patient he is going to die—AND THE MAN BELIEVES IT—he will die. That is the basis of voodoo.

> **NOTE.** Healings are not only performed by witch doctors, but by spiritualists as well. In his book, I Talked With Spirits, Victor Ernest says, "In nearly every session where the demons ministered, there were healings." Those of the religious science cults, who in no way acknowledge the healing power of the Lord Jesus, are also able to obtain "miraculous" healings. They are a lot more sophisticated about it. They have learned some of the laws which regulate the health of the human body and have discovered how to harness them for healing. Their work is valid, but they give no credit to the Lord Jesus, the Author of those laws. Also they forfeit the privilege of working WITH the Lord to obtain the healings.

● The law of health doesn't care **who** cooperates with it or how crudely it is set into motion. It is the nature of the healing principle to do its job regardless how one performs the steps necessary to trigger it. A visitor to Lourdes, the famous healing shrine of France, who truly expects to throw away his crutches, is as likely to be healed as the man stretched out in surgery. It doesn't matter that believing pilgrims have no understanding of psychology or medicine. When they exercise the kind of faith that activates the healing principle, they get well regardless.

If men can **accidentally** or **knowingly** discover the principles regulating the body's healing mechanism, think how much more wonderful it is to have the Lord Jesus teach us these principles Himself. Beyond that, consider the joy and glory of working WITH the Great Physician to trigger these lawful processes in your own body. Not only does it bring you closer to Him, but it adds to the reality of His presence. That's the purpose of this book. Not only will you learn the healing laws, but you will learn to use them—**with Christ.** If the cults can heal without Him, think what we can do WITH Him!

DESIGNED FOR HEALTH

Insofar as we can fathom our animal house, it furnishes concrete evidence that God means for us to be well. When we study the development of the human body and the ingenious program God has installed for its maintenance, we become convinced He never intended for man to be sick—ever! We are NOT designed for sickness.

Let's make a quick survey, beginning with the instant of conception.

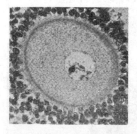
A female egg unites with a male cell. That tiny speck starts off as a fertilized ovum. Wrapped up in that infinitesimal particle of jelly-like stuff are complete instructions for the body that is to be. That's amazing. This means that at the instant of conception, all the characteristics of the fully developed creation are already written in that cell. The complete know-how for shaping the splitting cells into a human body is coded into the new organism in a split-second. What's so remarkable is that it includes such things as the color of the hair, eyes, skin, tone of voice, as well as all the traits and mannerisms that can be inherited from parents.

We'll call this growing speck, Johnny's body. At the moment it is one cell. Scientists tell us that a com-

27

plete blueprint of the future body—as well as every function scheduled to be a part of it—is already programmed in that first particle of life. How can so much information be crammed into that microscopic cell? Today's child learns that it contains a remarkable substance known as deoxyribonucleic acid. I won't hit you with that big word again. The textbooks simply refer to it as DNA. The DNA contains the genetic code of Johnny's body.

The drawing above represents a DNA molecule with its six foot long strands. In reality, this molecule is so small it cannot be seen except with an electron microscope with 1000 times the resolving power of the most powerful light microscope. This infinitesimal substance is crammed into the first tiny cell of our bodies. All of the information needed for the development and maintenance of our bodies is contained in those threads. When scientists discovered DNA a few years ago, they cracked the "code of life." It is now believed that God gives life to things by way of the DNA.

You can find this information in any encyclopedia not over 10 years old. Only a few years back, investigators were racking their brains trying to solve the mystery of living nature. Then DNA was discovered. It consists of molecular threads so thin they can only be seen under a high powered microscope. Yet, when stretched out, each of these strands can measure up to six feet in length. Imagine how tiny they must be! Yet the smallest details of the future body and its operation are written there. The storage capacity of these molecular threads is unbelievable. And they are all compressed into that first cell.

If all the instructions impressed on the DNA of that original cell could be translated into words, they would fill THOUSANDS of BOOKS. Yes, even the maintenance program for Johnny's body is written there. With all that programming, isn't it unthinkable that God would design ANY animal with no plan for keeping it well? Of course. In every living creature the law of health is written in the body itself—right there in that first cell.

AS THE BODY TAKES SHAPE

As Johnny's earthly house begins to grow, the first thing that happens is the division of that first cell. That's the way all living things grow—by cellular fission. A cell splits into two. Then the daughter cells divide again and there are four. The four become eight and so on. With each division, the number of cells doubles until the process has produced billions upon billions of cells. Along with the production of cells, various organs take shape. In time the whole new organism appears. Yet the entire formation follows the DNA blueprint in that first jelly-like cell.

29

NOTE. The first organ to start developing is the brain. We think of it as a living organism, and it is. But in reality it is a MACHINE. It is a sophisticated computer, yet it is alive. It is the most complex piece of machinery on earth, far more intricate than anything ever conceived by man. It is composed of 10 billion cells (neurons) that never sleep. This living computer has more than 500 trillion connections in its circuitry called synapses. It works with its own computer language, receiving and interpreting electro-chemical impulses. This computer (brain) is developed according to the specifications in the DNA of the first cell. All of the instructions of the DNA go into the computer which then takes over the responsibility of seeing that they are carried out. This makes the brain the master of the body. The law of health is in the computer along with all the know-how for healing any part of the animal. It may be difficult to picture your brain as a computer, but that's exactly what it is. It is a machine. And it works as impersonally as any of God's laws.

REPAIR AND DEFENSE

Consider the blood stream. Did you know that more than 100,000 miles of tubing lace through your body. Some of the vessels are so small their existence wasn't known until the microscope was invented. Life of the body depends on the circulation of the blood which begins eight months before birth. Inter-woven through all the tissues of the body is this vital system which supplies oxygen and food to the organs and carries off wastes. So dense is this system, that if it were possible to dissolve away all flesh and bone, a fragile but recognizable model of the body would remain. If all the arteries, veins, and capillaries could somehow be held in place, a person would be able to make out the human figure complete with ALL of its organs.

The blood stream is also a repair system. It is able to rush red and white cells to any part of the body in fantastic numbers. One of its maintenance marvels is its ability to produce more than 10,000,000 red cells EVERY SECOND. Even more white cells are created and pass away in the same interval. If there were some way for us to see the trillions of cells that are constantly being created and passing away, we'd behold our bodies as **dynamos of creation!**

● Scientists tell us that the creative force of the human organism is so great, that we get a brand new body every ELEVEN MONTHS! That is, every cell in the body (except the brain cells) is replaced in that time, so that no organ is more than 11 months old. All of this creative activity goes on silently and effortlessly without any awareness on our part. Those trillions of cells are continuously rebuilding organs by replacing old cells with new ones. The brain directs the entire operation automatically, unconsciously.

> **NOTE.** The average child is born into this world in brand new condition, with all of its organs working perfectly. This is as God intends, which indicates that perfect health is the NORMAL condition. He has provided the body with amazing powers of recreation, all aimed at keeping the organism in the peak of condition. Therefore it is ABNORMAL to be sick. Sickness is a violation of the principle of life and growth. Can we be sure of that? Where, in all of creation, has God ever designed anything to mature in the direction of sickness and corruption? To get sick, a person has to OVERCOME the massive resources of health God has installed in the animal. This explains why serious diseases take a long time to develop in the body. It also indicates that the normal condition of the body (perfect health) can be restored with less effort than it takes to induce abnormal conditions in the first place.

When we see this vast repair system at work, we are further convinced that Jesus wants us well.

THE DEFENSE SYSTEM AT WORK

The paring knife slips. You accidentally cut your finger. Are you overly upset? No. You know the bleeding will stop and the wound will heal. It's a chilling nuisance, but there's nothing traumatic about it. It will repair itself. Ah, but are you conscious of the healing process? Is there anything you can CONSCIOUSLY do to assist the brain in its work?

Yes, you can clean and dress the wound. I don't mean that. Can you do anything about producing new cells to replace the damaged ones? Can you consciously call on anything in your body to mend the slice? Indeed you cannot. Neither can your doctor. He is unable to manufacture a single cell. If you went to the world's greatest scientists they couldn't help either. So what do you do? You wait. Your body, under the direction of the brain, silently and easily performs this simple task which is beyond man's power to duplicate.

> **NOTE.** I don't mean to imply that you shouldn't go to your doctor with your complaints. Nothing in this book will even hint that doctors are not God's servants. The Lord gives gifts to men, among them the ability to cooperate with the law of health. A good doctor can do a lot to assist the forces at work in your body. Here I am speaking of the healing process itself which is beyond the skill of any man. If your doctor had to HEAL your wound, you'd be wearing a bandage on that sliced finger the rest of your life. The Lord has designed the body's repair system and backed it with an intelligence and power so great, no man can duplicate it.

Do you tell your blood stream to rush the materials to the wound on your finger? You can't. The whole process takes place AUTOMATICALLY according to the program that was in the DNA of that first cell. As soon as the brain received the news flash that a cut had occurred, it UNCONSCIOUSLY ordered the healing program into effect. The machinery went into action without any CONSCIOUS effort on your part. When it comes to the healing process itself, there is nothing anyone can do but trust the law of health written in his brain.

 You break your leg. Your body is programmed to cement the joint back together. It is NOT programmed to reset the bones. You have to go to a doctor for that. And it is marvelous that he knows how to set broken bones and support them with slings and casts. Without his help, the healing process would knit the bones however they happened to come together. So it is a blessing that doctors can straighten limbs and help them mend as they ought. Yet, when it comes to growing the bones together, the doctor cannot help. Only the brain, using the body's resources can do that. Since it made the bones in the first place, it knows how to knit them together.

You catch a cold. It turns into pneumonia. What will your brain do about that? Once a virus becomes active in your body, the signal is flashed to the computer and your defensive forces are organized for a fight. All of the body's various factories are ordered to begin making antibodies. In about nine days (that's how long it takes for the body to complete its preparations) the organism is ready to make an assault on the invader. You have nothing to do with this. You don't even know what is going on. While you are lying there with a thermometer in your mouth, your body forces move to the attack right on cue.

When the two foes meet, the battle that follows is called "the crisis." If your system has been able to produce plenty of antibodies, the invader will be destroyed.

● I could list dozens of ways in which the organism defends and repairs itself according to the law of health written in the computer. But this is sufficient to show that healing is a NATURAL function of the body. God has installed a healing program in the brain via the DNA. But nowhere has He installed any kind of a program that moves in the direction of sickness or disease. The mere fact that the healing program is built into our bodies is proof that God does NOT want us sick. If he did, He would have designed us differently. Therefore no reader needs be puzzled as to whether or not it is God's will for him to be healed. Jesus wants us well.

> **NOTE.** I don't mean to imply that God doesn't USE sickness. Indeed He does. It is surely His favorite form of discipline. When their bodies are in pain, people tend to get serious with the Lord. It is one time when He really has their undivided attention. And it is a time when they are usually ready to make the changes God wants in their lives. But the point is—HE DOESN'T SEND sickness. He doesn't have to. We bring it on ourselves by the way we react to people and circumstances. It's true that God does manipulate circumstances, but He does NOT attempt to control our reactions to those circumstances. He allows us to act as we choose. But HOW we react, determines whether we stay well or get sick. Once the illness occurs, God is pleased to make the most of it. If His people are to suffer, He wants it to count. But as for WANTING anyone sick, that is out of the question. His design of the human body is proof that He does not.

THE PSALMIST WOULD AGREE

When David said, "I am fearfully and wonderfully made,"* he didn't tell the half of it. If these bodies were

---

*Psa. 139:14

wonderful to him, how much more wonderful are they to us who can appreciate that God has designed them for perfect health? When we behold the vast creative energy resident in the blood stream and the intelligence built into the brain / computer system, it's hard to believe there is any condition which cannot be corrected. The POWER for healing IS IN our bodies, no question about it. The forces in us are so great, they can easily heal ANY disease, whether cancer, diabetes, arthritis—anything. To us, healing should never be a miracle. Sickness is the miracle. It has to occur in the face of all that God has done to insure perfect health for His creatures.

● Do I make it sound as if ALL healing comes automatically? You could get that idea. But that's not the case. Some healings are automatic. We've mentioned the cut and the bruise and the healing which follows the doctor's work. There are other healings which come when we eliminate destructive emotions from our lives. If the answer to all healing were the removal of harmful emotions, our book could end right here. Unfortunately, there is more to it than that. We not only make ourselves sick with lustful and vicious emotions, we can introduce SICKNESS PROGRAMS into the body's computer system. (I explain this system in another chapter).

Did you get that? When we persist in unhealthy thinking, we run the risk of installing a SICKNESS PROGRAM in the computer. This sickness program, then OVERRULES the law of health. We not only get sick, we **stay sick** even after we have abandoned the harmful emotions causing our illness in the first place. We are then programmed for the illness. Therefore our book cannot end with AUTOMATIC healings. We must go on and discuss another kind of healing—FAITH HEALING.

> **NOTE.** Wonder why I now mention the two kinds of healing: faith and automatic? I wanted your mind free to behold

the POWER God has built into our bodies. You see it best in terms of automatic healing. We have all watched automatic healing work. We know a cut will heal. Therefore we have no trouble accepting the idea of a healing program that is on the job 24 hours a day. But we also know that some illnesses are NOT automatically healed. What do we do about those? They have to be approached another way. Once you are convinced that healing is NORMAL—and that God Himself WANTS us well—we are ready to consider the other approach. The idea of faith healing follows logically once we realize the extent of the healing power in our bodies. It also follows, that if God really wants us well, He must have a way of using the body's power for dealing with those illnesses that are NOT automatically cared for.

Dr. Alexis Carrel, after making a study of many healings occurring at Lourdes, wrote down his personal observations. He said the only explanation he could make, as a medical doctor, was that the body's OWN NATURAL HEALING PROCESS, which generally takes a normal amount of time to bring about healing, was somehow "SPEEDED UP" under the influence of intense faith. He considered it all the result of the SAME POWER (in the body) whether the healing took two minutes, two weeks, or two months.

I agree. The approach you are going to meet in the chapters ahead will show HOW the healing process is speeded up. But it will be according to laws God has provided. We have discovered a number of His laws which have to do with the mind / brain / body relationship. We will be using these to trigger the healing power He has built into our earth suits.

NOTE. When a Christian comes to the realization that the Lord really WANTS him well, it does something to his spirit. It changes his attitude toward healing. One of the most convincing things is to discover that the body is

36

designed for health, not sickness. When a man realizes that, he prays differently. There are many who half heartedly talk to God about healing, because they don't really expect to be healed. They think they DESERVE to be sick or that God is DISCIPLINING them. That, of course means that God would rather have them sick than whole. But it just isn't so. It is utterly foreign to His nature to want anything but perfection for His creatures. Again, this doesn't mean He won't USE sickness once it occurs. He does, but He prefers His people be well.

It is not enough to know that God wants us well and has provided laws and power for healing our bodies. There is someone who wants us sick. That someone has the power to make us sick as long as we remain ignorant of his operation. It is not God's will for us to be helpless before this scheming monster. Consequently our approach to faith healing must also include insight into the way the devil works to bring about illness and disease. We come to that—next.

● **REVIEW AND REMEMBER**

1. When living things are wounded, healing starts quickly. There is a healing principle in all animals. God has established a law of health for all living beings. Sickness comes only as we violate this law. The law of health is impersonal. If we cooperate with it, it blesses us. If we break it, it punishes us. That's where sickness comes from. There is NO law of sickness in the universe. It is up to us to learn how to cooperate with God's law of health. Any approach to healing must work with the healing principle in some way.

2. The law of health is written in the DNA of the first cell. Those threads contain complete instructions for the growth and maintenance of the future body, including the healing process. The brain is charged with administering the healing program for the body. It is a program for

37

the AUTOMATIC control of the defense and healing forces. With resources which can produce more than 10 million red cells every second, the body has more than enough power to deal with any illness or disease seeking a foothold in the organism.

3. The amazing design of the human body, with its provision to replace damaged organs, convinces us God means for us to be well. His law of health was established to insure the perfect health of the animal we use for an earth suit. If the creature did not have the image of God living inside and using it, it would probably last indefinitely. It is the man using the body who makes it sick. He is the one who violates God's health law, not the animal.

NOTE. Even as God makes His rain to fall on the just and the unjust, so does He provide laws for the benefit of ALL mankind. Consequently unsaved people can discover the healing laws and use them. The Science of the Mind (Church of Religious Science, etc.) cults flourish because they have discovered some of these laws and know how to use them. Because God's laws are impersonal, they don't care WHO uses them. They always do their work when people cooperate with them. The cultists do get remarkable healings. Unfortunately they use them as PROOF of the validity of their blasphemous teachings. The unsuspecting and ignorant, unable to deny the fact of the healings, are induced to accept these false doctrines. Since they cannot come up with any better explanation for the healings, they submit to the false teachers and are drawn into the cults.

Chapter Two

SATAN WANTS YOU SICK

 Some months back, my wife Margie was on the platform of our church making an announcement to the fellowship. She had a clip in her hair. She meant to take it out before we left home that day. But she had forgotten it. It was the first thing everyone saw when she stood up to speak. A rumble went through the audience. Margie wondered what was up. She looked at me. I gestured with my hand. She reached to her forehead. There was the clip holding a curl in place.

Margie turned a beautiful shade of red. Nobody said a word. Not a soul touched her. Yet that color came to her face. She was embarrassed. What's the point? All it took was an IDEA. As soon as she realized the situation, powerful feelings arose within her. They triggered a reaction in her body. She blushed. Her brain ordered a supply of blood to her face.

Embarrassment is purely an emotion, but it produces a **physical** result. See? Mental processes can cause physical reactions. Embarrassment is a powerful feeling that automatically triggers the vasomotor nerves and causes the blood vessels in the face and neck to dilate. It is automatic because no one CONSCIOUSLY tells his face to blush. No one ever says, "I'm going to blush now, so I hereby order a big gush of blood to my head." The circulation system does NOT take orders from the conscious mind. The only conscious part in blushing is the IDEA appearing on the screen of the conscious mind. After that, everything else is automatic.

● Consider the powerful emotion—FEAR. It also triggers violent reactions in the body.

You are a lady school teacher. A youngster has hidden a rubber snake in your desk. The class is in on the prank. The students can't wait for you to come in and open that drawer. Here you come, not suspecting a thing. Your hand goes to the drawer. The movement of the drawer makes the snake wiggle. Your eyes spot the quivering reptile. The image flashes on the conscious screen . . . "a live snake!"

There's no time to make a true judgment about the snake. You instinctively assume it is alive. After all you saw it move. So the picture in your imagination is that of a live snake ready to strike. The fact that it is only a rubber snake has nothing to do with your reaction. It is what you BELIEVE that counts. You believe it is alive. That's all that is necessary. From there on, everything else is automatic—even your scream.

> **NOTE.** Will you observe that we have introduced a new element into our discussion, one we haven't talked about so far. That new element is BELIEF. Later on I will be referring to the LAW OF BELIEF. You are now meeting it for the first time. In our snake illustration, you BELIEVED the reptile in the drawer to be alive. That's what is important. It is the fact that you BELIEVE IT that causes your body to react to the picture. If you did NOT BELIEVE the snake was real, there'd be no reaction. The very same picture would flash on the conscious screen, but your brain would DO NOTHING about it. Thus belief or faith is the KEY to getting action out of the brain. That truth will become more apparent as we go along.

Once you believed you saw a snake in your desk drawer, you didn't have to decide which emotion you were going to feel. Fear came automatically. That fear set your entire defense system into action. You didn't tell your heart to beat faster, but it did. You didn't tell your stomach to stop working, but it did. A lot of things happened as part of an UNCONSCIOUS process. Once that picture of a moving snake appeared on the screen and you BELIEVED IT, your brain acted to handle the threat. All sorts of orders went to various parts of your body AUTOMATICALLY and UNCONSCIOUSLY.

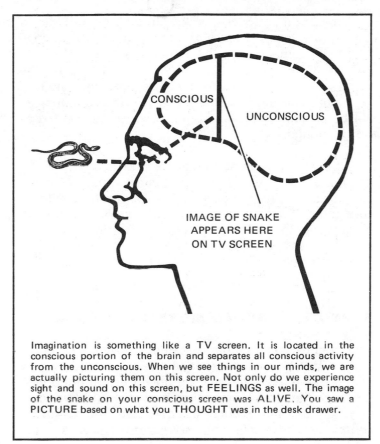

Imagination is something like a TV screen. It is located in the conscious portion of the brain and separates all conscious activity from the unconscious. When we see things in our minds, we are actually picturing them on this screen. Not only do we experience sight and sound on this screen, but FEELINGS as well. The image of the snake on your conscious screen was ALIVE. You saw a PICTURE based on what you THOUGHT was in the desk drawer.

● Now let's see the power of an IDEA in another way.

When I was in high school, we used to pull a trick on our classmates in the speech class. We'd have a sliced lemon ready. When one of our buddies would get up before the class to deliver his recitation, we'd pull out the lemon and begin sucking

41

on it. Our poor victim would see that lemon in our mouths and his own mouth would pucker in response. It would cause his saliva to flow so heavily, he couldn't go on with his speech.

Maybe you've never seen the lemon trick. But I have. It was pulled on me a couple of times and it really works. I had no contact with the lemon, but the IDEA OF EATING ONE appeared on my conscious screen. The scene was flashed there by my eyes. That was enough. My mouth puckered and the saliva flowed automatically. (I'll be explaining more about the conscious screen as we go along.)

I'll wager you've sampled the power of a yawn. I know you have yawned simply because you SAW someone else do it. Why? The suggestion of tiredness entered your mind. That's a very mild suggestion, of course, yet it works to produce a physical effect in your body. You don't say to yourself, "Now I'm going to yawn." You can't help yourself. You yawn whether you want to or not.

HYPNOTISM IS EVEN MORE CONVINCING

Hypnotism is an amazing subject. There's so much of it on TV now that most readers have some familiarity with it. If we ever doubted the power of the mind over the body, that doubt is dispelled by watching a hypnotist in action. I'm not endorsing hypnotism, but it has become a skill that is finding more and more uses in the field of medicine.

Those in the business of researching hypnotism claim every organ of the body can be affected by getting the right IDEA into a person's mind. Of course that's what hypnotism is, getting a subject to BELIEVE an idea. The more we know about hypnotism, the greater becomes our respect for the devil's power. It is by getting

42

us to believe his IDEAS that he damages our bodies. If he can get the right suggestion turning in our minds, he can make us sick.

The stage hypnotist has an impressive bag of tricks. Once he gets a subject into a hypnotic state, he gives instructions that are seemingly obeyed by the UNCONSCIOUS. The phenomena include such things as causing people to fall asleep, have their arms and legs become rigid, and perform all sorts of interesting feats.

A funny demonstration illustrates what we've been saying. The hypnotist holds a glass of water under the nose of an entranced subject and tells him it is an open can of pepper. When asked to smell it, the individual sniffs and sneezes. Now you know the water didn't make him sneeze. It was the IDEA of sniffing pepper. His mind accepted the idea and it was flashed onto the conscious screen. His brain took it from there. Since he BELIEVED it was pepper, his body mechanism reacted to the scene on the screen. He sneezed. The sneeze was PROOF that his brain was trying to get rid of an irritation in his nose.

Of course the irritation was not there. The nerves in his nose did NOT send that information to the screen. But they didn't have to. The man himself PUT THAT IMAGE on the screen. Since he BELIEVED IT, his body reacted accordingly. Sneezing is the body's way of ridding itself of nasal irritation. Even his lungs were involved. It takes air to sneeze. Here we have a perfect illustration of the mind exercising control over the respiratory system and causing an UNCONSCIOUS action to occur. Isn't that fascinating?

● People placed in deeper trances do even more remarkable things. I have seen a man break out in perspiration because he believed he was in a steam room, only to watch the same man develop a chill and goose

43

bumps when the hypnotist told him he was locked in a walk-in refrigerator. He made the switch from hot to cold on a command from the hypnotist.

NOTE. There is nothing magical about hypnotism. It works according to mental laws. God has designed us so that we do not believe everything we hear. That is, because we are thinkers, we can check, weigh, and evaluate what we hear and then decide whether or not we wish to believe it. Our minds are naturally suspicious. We tend to challenge things. We have the power to discriminate between ideas. We refuse to believe what we hear unless we have a good reason or want to believe it. All a hypnotist has to do is get us to RELAX these critical and examining powers of the conscious mind to the place where we accept what he says AS FACT. Once we do we flash the idea he gives us onto the conscious screen. Since we now BELIEVE IT, the brain takes over and carries out whatever function is demanded by the picture on our TV screen. I know that sounds simple, but that is the basis of hypnotism. Without some way to BYPASS the selective power of the conscious mind, hypnotism would not be possible.

The deeper the trance state, the more amazing the powers released in the body when the conscious accepts an idea from the therapist. When a subject is in a truly deep state, astonishing things can be done with his body—and his personality as well. People can give up smoking or over-eating when the personality is altered by ideas received into the brain / computer. Of course, you can put a person too deep. When you do, he no longer hears you consciously. He's asleep and his conscious operation shuts down. People are NOT asleep while in a hypnotic trance. They are in a state of suppressed consciousness. But they are definitely awake. They have to be in order to respond to the hypnotist's commands.

 The work of Dr. J. B. Rhine of Duke University has been well publicized. Many articles have been written telling of the startling things done in his psychological clinic. Research labs in other universities have reported equally amazing demonstrations. Students have been hypnotized and then told their fingers had just touched **a red hot poker.** Not only do their faces grimace with pain, but the lymph glands react as though actual contact had been made. Inflammation of the area and swelling occur. **Even blisters appear.** Think of that! Remember—these body functions occur wholly as the result of an IDEA received and believed by the conscious mind.

In other experiments, students in a hypnotic state were told they would develop a nose bleed at a later time. This is post-hypnotic suggestion. Sure enough, at the appointed time, drops of blood came from their nostrils. I personally know of a case where a man in a trance was told his back was being laid open with a knife. A piece of ice was drawn along the fleshy portion of his back. He developed all the symptoms of a man bleeding to death. The experiment was stopped for fear he would actually expire.

WHAT HAS THIS TO DO WITH SATAN?

I could tell of more fascinating experiments, but these are sufficient to show that symptoms of almost any disease can be reproduced in hypnotic subjects. Here's the point. If experimenters can do it, Satan can too. It's true that no one is going to voluntarily place himself in the devil's hands for this purpose, yet the evil one has other ways of accomplishing the same thing. He uses DECEPTION. Because he has DIRECT access to our conscious thinking, it is easy for him to get us to accept his thoughts as our own. Of course we still have to APPROVE them. But that task isn't as hard as most Christians suspect.

Why did I devote so much space to hypnotism? To show that ANY idea BELIEVED by the Christian can have an effect on his body. It doesn't matter whether that idea is true or not. As long as the person believes it, the brain will accept it as fact. That's tricky, isn't it?

● Let's return to the snake prank. You didn't take time to examine the thing in your desk drawer. You took one look and CONCLUDED it was a real snake. Your brain knew the proper reaction to make. You'd seen snakes before. All that was needed to get a reaction in your body, was for you to BELIEVE it was real. The wiggling caused by the movement of the drawer caused you to make that decision. Consequently the image on the screen of your mind was that of a LIVE snake.

Then came FEAR. It was a by-product of what you believed. The fact that the snake was NOT REAL made no difference to your brain. As long as you BELIEVED it was real, that was all that was necessary. To the brain it WAS REAL. The responses in your body occurred automatically.

Now that gives Satan something to work with. It means that the ideas he plants in your mind DO NOT have to be true. All he has to do is time them so that you will accept them as your own. That's a big edge. He can damage your body with FALSE ideas.

SATAN'S BIG EDGE

"I'm worried sick over this thing . . . " You've heard people say that. Well, they are correct in putting sickness and worry together. Worry, as you know, is concern over something that hasn't happened yet. The individual stews about something that MIGHT occur. It doesn't have to be true at all. It can be entirely FALSE and yet the person agonizes as though it had already happened. Worry is one of Satan's favorite devices for hurting God's people.

46

You've worried, I know that. You know how your mind can PICTURE THE WORST. Fear follows in the wake of that picture. If you've tossed and turned at night, stewing over a problem, you know how powerful those feelings can be. They produce so much activity in the nervous system, sleep is impossible. Yet, it is all caused by what you SEE on the conscious screen— **scenes which don't exist at all.** Satan merely drops those ideas in your mind and you take it from there.

But someone asks . . .

"Is it possible for the devil to cause illness in a Christian with carnal feelings? Can born-again people really have the kind of emotions that make people sick?" Indeed they can. Receiving Christ does not get rid of our old nature. When the Lord comes to indwell the believer, the adamic nature merely moves over. The believer has TWO natures, which the Bible calls "old man," and "new man" (Eph. 4:22,24). The devil is at home in the old nature and the Spirit of Christ dwells in the new. The believer, with his FREE WILL, can surrender to either of his two natures.

All the devil has to do is DECEIVE the believer into submitting to his old nature and up will come carnal feelings that can damage his body. Worry, by the way, has to do with the old nature. The Christian is told to "fear not." Worry is the devil's work in a man as surely as lust, greed, jealousy, or pride.

Sometimes it's a simple thing Satan uses.

I know a devoted Christian who allowed himself to become embittered against his neighbor over some chickens. The man next door started keeping two hens in the side yard next to the fence separating their properties. The city ordinance forbade such a thing, but this good Christian wouldn't dream

47

of making trouble for anyone, particularly a neighbor. He'd rather bear it himself.

Then came the flies. Somehow they conspired to meet at his back door. Every time he went in or out, a handful would buzz into his house. At first it was just an irritation. But Satan never lets an opportunity slip by. He fanned those feelings into full blown resentment. As long as he refused to speak to his neighbor about the chickens, Satan was able to use those mounting feelings against him. As the situation continued, the devil was able to drop damaging ideas into the Christian's mind every time he saw those flies.

Satan saw to it that those feelings rose higher and higher. Finally the poor man became bitter. Put resentment and bitterness together and you have an emotional combination the body can't absorb. Something has to give way in time. Well it did. He began having terrible headaches. They were so bad he went to the doctor about them. The first thing the doctor discovered was high blood pressure. His brain was directing those destructive emotions against his heart and head. Unknown to the man, his bitterness was damaging his system. The doctor's warning brought him to me.

When I heard the "fly story," which happened to come out during our interview, I knew where to begin. To me it was obvious that his symptoms were due to those damaging emotions raging against his body. The first step was clear. He had to go and talk to his neighbor about those chickens. But it wasn't easy to get him to do this, he was reluctant to bother others. But I insisted, offering to go with him.

NOTE. Right at that time I was conducting experiments in preparation for this book. This was an ideal case for watching the speed of healing once the bombardment of destructive emotions ceased. I made no secret of what

48

I was doing. I told the brother exactly what I was planning. Before we called on the neighbor I explained how his body was not equipped to discharge the harmful emotions building up within him. I promised that as soon as the problem was eased, his headaches and high blood pressure would disappear. I didn't see how I could miss.

We called on the neighbor together. He proved to be most gracious. To the surprise of my suffering client, he said he had intended to come over and see if the chickens were an annoyance. Once he learned of the fly problem, he said he would be glad to get rid of the chickens. It seems they weren't laying enough eggs anyway. Sure enough the chickens were gone the next day. And with them went my brother's problem. When he returned to the doctor two weeks later, his blood pressure was back to normal and his headaches were gone.

● What did Satan use this time? Pride. That's what really kept my friend from talking to his neighbor about the flies. It's disguised, of course, under the WILE of not making trouble for others, but it is pride. He didn't want the neighbor to think he was a complainer. Mixed in was some natural timidity as well. That's what made it easy for the devil to get away with his suggestion. The pride was foolish. The desire to be a good neighbor was admirable. Satan merely put the two together to create a destructive emotion in a gentle Christian. Had the situation gone unchecked, a vital organ of his body could have been severely damaged.

NOTE. Many sincere Christians work hard to free their lives from CARNAL ACTIVITIES, but they leave themselves wide open to CARNAL EMOTIONS. They proudly tell how the Lord has delivered them from drinking, smoking, stealing, and lying, etc., but they say nothing about ceasing to worry, banishing fears, and living free of anxiety. There are many who allow themselves to become distressed over

49

circumstances, when they should rest in the Lord. Parents fret over their children, workers resent their employers, some even hate the neighborhoods where they live. Husbands and wives often distress each other with bickering and nagging. Others become agitated with people and programs at church. These Christians may indeed put away a lot of evil practices, but a list of evil emotions is still very much a part of their lives. Nearly every believer has suffered some kind of sickness or disease by permitting Satan to make him the victim of damaging feelings.

DOCTORS AGREE

There was a time when doctors were primarily concerned with bacteria and infection. But more and more are turning their attention to those emotions which boil in the wake of stress. The popular name used to describe disorders which originate in the mind is **psychosomatic.** It comes from two Greek words: psyche (soul) and soma (body). Perhaps you've read some of the recent articles in Reader's Digest condensed from medical journals and magazines. J. D. Radcliff, a frequent contributor, gave one of his articles the arresting title, "Stress, the Cause of all Disease."

"Heart attacks," says one doctor, "can be triggered by anger." "Anxiety," says another, "places more stress on the heart than any other stimulation, including physical exercise." Dr. S. I. McMillen, in his excellent book, **None of these Diseases,** presents a list of disorders caused or aggravated by emotional stress. His list covers almost two pages. Significant among them are these:

ulcers	rheumatic fever
constipation	urological problems
diarrhea	headaches
high blood pressure	epilepsy
arteriosclerosis	diabetes
coronary thrombosis	nervous disorders

hay fever and allergies   infections of all sorts
backaches and muscle pains   eye and skin diseases

Others add cancer to the list.

If what the doctors say is true, and I'm convinced it is, think how easy it is for Satan to afflict God's people with sickness. Of course, we can't expect the doctors to acknowledge Satan's role in sickness. But it is as true as God's Word that he can make us sick with his suggestions. All he has to do is get an unhealthy idea into our minds and induce us to accept it. After that, the corresponding harmful emotion is AUTOMAT-ICALLY generated. Then the brain and nervous system have to dispose of the emotion somewhere within the body. If the emotion persists for any length of time, sickness or disease must result.

> **NOTE.** Satan may feed destructive thoughts in our minds, but his suggestions, **by themselves,** CANNOT make us sick. It takes our cooperation. We have free wills. We do NOT have to accept his ideas. If we learn to recognize them and resist them, there is NO way they can hurt us. But unfortunately we do accept them. And then FEED them. Why? It is natural to do so. The devil TIMES the planting of his ideas to coincide with distressing circumstances and events. So perfectly do his suggestions FIT the situa-tion, that we go along with them instinctively. We accept them as our own. Then we project the damaging image on the conscious screen. The harmful result is automatic.

HOW WE COOPERATE WITH SATAN

I had just finished a message on the devil's power to produce illness when a gentleman near the front couldn't contain himself. He jumped up from his seat and rushed up to the platform where I was standing. His wife had been a victim of arthritis for 30 years and he felt that, perhaps at last, he may

51

have stumbled on to the real reason behind her suffering. The questions literally gushed from him:

> "My wife's sixty now and doctors haven't been able to do a thing for her arthritis. Could Satan be responsible for her condition? Is there any chance of her being cured? If she learns to deal with the devil will she get well?"

I assured the man there was room for hope. We made an appointment.

He arrived pushing his wife in a wheelchair. We chatted and I probed. It came out that the man had a sister who lived in the same town with him and his wife. He had insisted that it be that way. He had a strange compulsion to take care of her and wanted her close by. He also made a ritual of visiting her twice a week.

At first this man's concern for his sister was not a problem for the wife. She admired his almost religious devotion to her. But as time went by, resentment crept in. We know the source of that, don't we? Gradually she began to be tormented by feelings of jealousy. Finally she spoke to her husband about it. But he was strong willed and wouldn't listen to her complaint. After that, her resentment turned to hidden rage.

The arthritis had already started. It was a gradual process. The resentment and rage had to be disposed of and this was the way her computer ordered it done. Her condition grew steadily worse. Finally it was impossible for her to walk. And now she was seated before me in a wheelchair. It took years to get her into this state.

The Devil's Dirty Work

To me it was obvious how Satan has used the situation to cripple this woman. I then explained to the pair how Satan plants ideas in our minds. And how his ideas match the circumstances so perfectly, we never suspect him. When he is successful in getting us to accept his ideas as our own, they will generate emotions which can damage our bodies. If those emotions persist over a period of time, illness and disease must occur. These dear people hadn't once suspected her arthritis was connected with her feelings of resentment. When I said, "Your mind can make you sick," the lady shook her head in dismay.

> "After all these years of suffering," she said, "and now to find it's all in my mind. I know worry can produce ulcers, but I didn't dream that bitter feelings could produce arthritis."

● Then I laid out a program for dealing with the destruction originating in her mind. I showed her how to work WITH the Lord to replace her evil feelings with ideas aligned with the LAW OF HEALTH. The promise of relief made her willing to try. I was glad. I knew she would be drawn closer to Christ in the process.

Later we'll discuss the actual technique I gave her.

Result

In a month's time the woman's arthritis had so improved she was able to walk. Her healing continued until the arthritis had disappeared completely. She gave her destructive thoughts and feelings over to the Lord. He worked with her to replace them with a healthy image in her mind. Thus the healing took place in her mind, first of all. Then her healed mind did its work to restore the body. What does that tell us? If our minds can make us sick, they can also make us well. The secret is learning to work with the Lord to establish the healthy image in our minds.

NOTE. If Satan could attack the human body directly, we'd all be dead by now. (Satan was given special permission to attack Job directly.) His working is entirely mental. If it were any other way, we could become the UNWILLING victims of his dirty work. God won't allow that. We have the privilege of deciding whether or not we will accept Satan's suggestion. So if he is to make anyone sick, he must do it through the victim's mind. This explains why the Christian's armor, as listed by the apostle Paul, is ALL MENTAL (See Eph. 6:11-17). None of it is physical. Every weapon of our warfare with the adversary is SPIRITUAL. Why? The battle takes place in our MINDS—no place else.

SATAN WANTS US SICK

Let's say you've got a crippling heart disease. Maybe it's a damaged nervous system or perhaps some vital organ is deteriorating. How much do you feel like serving the Lord? Not much at all. Too much of your energy is drained off trying to survive. You have your hands full adjusting to your affliction. This is exactly what the devil wants. He knows if we're sick, we won't be of much use to the Lord and a long way from enjoying the abundant life.

Therefore, he works around the clock to get his ideas into the believer's thought life. All he has to do is wait for some trouble or trial to come along and—BANG! He's right there with his suggestion. If the victim is ignorant of the devil's devices, he will accept his suggestion and sickness will follow. But the devil won't be to blame. The Christian has a free will. He can reject Satan's suggestion if he wants to. But sadly, most Christians are "ignorant of his devices." Consequently they yield to his influence totally unaware that their enemy is seeking to destroy them.

I know you've heard of this trick.

A group of office workers decides to play a prank on a fellow employee. When he comes into the office, the first one says, "What's the matter with you, John, aren't you feeling well?" He shrugs it off, claiming to feel fine. Then the next one says, "John, you don't look well. Are you sick?" He says, no. Then the third and fourth and fifth all take their turn at telling him how terrible he looks. After a good number of them say he looks awful, he begins to believe it. Before long he really is sick—and goes home ill.

Now that's a cruel thing to do to another person, but it has happened and more often than you'd suspect. Now consider this: if a group of people can do that to a man with just a few words, think what the devil can do to us with his direct access to our minds. I think we have underrated the power of our adversary, don't you?

The whole business of Satan making us sick by suggestion is mysterious, isn't it? Just what kind of a body do we have that it can be damaged by what we think? And why would God give us a body that could be made ill by IDEAS alone? We ought to look into this. There should be some valuable clues for healing in the relationship between the image of God and the body he wears. That's next.

● REVIEW AND REMEMBER

1. Ideas in the MIND, can produce responses in the body. This is demonstrated every time a person blushes. Ideas make people blush.

2. This truth is confirmed by hypnotic demonstrations. Hypnotism works solely with IDEAS. A subject is placed in a trance to bypass the discriminating powers of his conscious mind. In the trance he BELIEVES the suggestion

made to him by the therapist. Amazing demonstrations of mind over body can be performed by hypnotic experts and willing subjects. The science of hypnotism proves it is possible for others (Satan included) to affect our bodies with IDEAS.

3. If hypnotists can plant their ideas in the mind of a **willing** subject to produce amazing phenomena in his body, how much easier must it be for Satan to plant his ideas in the mind of a **deceived** subject? Whereas a hypnotist asks his subject to submit to his suggestions, the devil's access is INTERNAL. However, he too, must appeal to a person's will. No one can become the UNWILLING subject of any hypnotist or Satan.

4. Even though Satan can introduce ideas into our minds at will, they have to be ACCEPTED before they can do damage. Therefore, he times his suggestions to coincide with circumstances and situations so that our reaction to his IDEAS come naturally. Also, they have to be done in such a way that we think the ideas are our own. Because we have an old nature, it is easy for us to react to Satan's ideas with carnal (destructive) emotions.

5. Since a person does not challenge ideas which appear to be HIS OWN, the Christian tends to accept Satan's suggestions. They do NOT have to be true. All that is necessary is for the victim to BELIEVE they are true. Whatever the mind accepts as true, has an affect on the body. This relationship between the mind and the body is so amazing we must look into it. We do—next.

Chapter Three

YOU ARE NOT A BODY—YOU'RE GOD'S IMAGE!

This chapter takes us to a funeral parlor.

Before we head for the funeral parlor, let me prepare you. You are going to meet some startling truths. If you've never thought of them before, they might shock you. The first one is coming right up. It's the kind that sounds ridiculous at first, but as you weigh it before the Holy Spirit, it not only seems right—it becomes obvious.

Now let's go to the funeral parlor.

THE LESSON OF THE CORPSE

 We'll go down front where the casket rests on its stand. We'll gather in close so we can peer at the corpse. The body is that of a Mr. Johnson. He was (is) a fine Christian who died of a heart attack a few days before. His body has been prepared for a service to be held later in the day.

The funeral director is an obliging Christian. He knows we've come to learn the lesson of the corpse. He's given us permission to touch it if we want to. Don't turn pale. This is taking place in your imagination only.

Now why do we study a corpse? I want you to make sure it is ALL there, that it is a complete human body. See—nothing has been removed. It is complete, brain and all. Nothing is missing except Mr. Johnson. He is gone. What is more obvious than the fact that the man who used to live in that body has vanished. And yet, few people who observe this phenomenon catch the significance of it:

MAN IS NOT A BODY,
HE MERELY WEARS ONE.

Have you met this truth before? Then you're not upset by the idea that Mr. Johnson was merely WEARING that body. This is a whopping truth. It means that the body is wholly separate from the person who lives inside it. There is NO organic connection between a man and the body he wears. This means that the soul has a life of its own which is INDEPENDENT of the body. The Bible makes it perfectly clear that for the believer to be PRESENT with the Lord, he must be ABSENT from the body (II Cor. 5:8). They've got to be independent for that to happen.

> **NOTE.** Can you see what this does to the matter of dying? It is the body ONLY that dies. Physical death has NOTHING to do with the person who lives in the body. The body has its own life. The soul has its own life. The death of one has no affect on the life of the other. Where Mr. Johnson went, he DOESN'T NEED that old body. As far as he's concerned, people can take it out and bury it. Mr. Johnson himself remains alive in the spirit (spirit-world). Where Mr. Johnson went his physical body could not go.

WHY WAS MR. JOHNSON IN THE BODY?

That question is vital. If Mr. Johnson doesn't really need a human body to exist, what was he in it for in the first place? The answer takes us back to the garden of Eden.

God was not out of work when He made man. He was lonesome. When He said, "Let us make man in our image . . . '' it was to satisfy His need for company. He wanted people LIKE HIMSELF—those with whom He could have fellowship. It was God's NEED for eternal companions that led Him to make man.

NOTE. The appearance of Adam wasn't the first time God had created freewill creatures. Earlier He brought forth angels. But they were neither His image nor His likeness. Yet they were so designed they could bring Him joy. However, He did not put them on earth. He let them stay with Him in heaven, i.e., the spirit-world. But Satan, the most glorious of these creatures, used his freedom to lead a revolt against God. He saw the majesty of God and wanted it for himself. You've undoubtedly read how he presumed to assert himself over the Lord (Isa. 14:13). The day Satan fell he took many others with him. A host of angels was persuaded to join his attempt to seize God's throne. We now call them evil spirits or demons. This revolt introduced SIN into God's kingdom (Ezek. 28:15).

Was God Frustrated?

The fall of Satan was a sad thing, in one way. God was hungry for fellowship. But the satanic rebellion didn't frustrate His determination to have eternal companions. Now that SIN was present in His realm, He had the perfect means for getting what He wanted. With sin on the scene, He would USE it. So, in another sense, the fall of Satan was a good thing. It gave God the means of bringing forth a race of TESTED companions.

The second time God elected to bring forth freewill creatures, He would do more than create angels. He would give Himself SONS. The new beings would be HIS OWN IMAGE. See the difference? Those angels were NOT God's image. They were not made like

Him—**we are!** Now God could have those who could love Him as He longed to be loved. It would be a genuine love affair, a fellowship of equals. Equal in kind, that is, not in rank or being. Why? The created can never be the Creator.

● Also, God chose NOT to run the second program in heaven. He would not put His new creatures in the same position as Satan and tempt them with His throne. The only sure way of preventing another revolt was to put His people in ANOTHER environment, totally CUT OFF from heaven and His immediate glory. Thus it was that the first man appeared on earth. After he had successfully gone through a probationary period, during which he would be tested to see what he would do with his free will, God would then bring him into heaven.

> **NOTE.** Behold the wisdom of God! He did not destroy the devil after the revolt. You and I might have sent him into hell on the spot. But God didn't do that. He is too economy minded. He would now USE HIM to provide those made His image with a TEST of their wills. They would be able to choose between two gods—the God of glory and the "god of this world." (II Cor. 4:4). If the image of God chose to love the true God, even though he couldn't see Him, he would be eligible for heaven. If he chose the god of the flesh (Satan disguised as SELF), then he would fail the test and be disqualified for heaven. Such a thing wasn't possible until SIN was found in God's kingdom (Ezek. 28:15). Once people were tested and found to love the Lord FOR HIS OWN SAKE, rather than what they could get out of Him, God would have the companions He wanted. Those who chose to serve the devil (self) would be no different from Satan, and would share his fate (Matt. 25:41; Rev. 20:15).

God's image on earth

 Stand before a mirror. What do you see? A nice face? Yes, but can you see the person who lives behind that face? Can you really see yourself? No. Why? You are invisible. The real you is God's image. The Bible insists that we are the image of the INVISIBLE GOD. There is NO WAY for the image of God to be seen. Since God is spirit and therefore unseen, so are we (John 4:24). The image must be like the object. How shall we picture the unseen image? Let's do it like this:

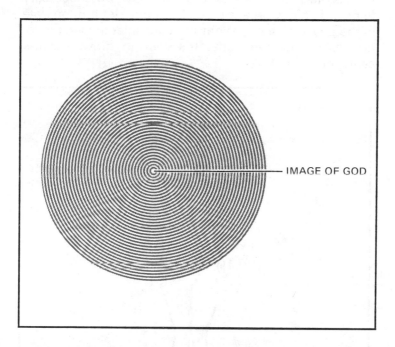

IMAGE OF GOD

We don't know what the image of God really looks like. No one has ever seen a spirit. Our eyes cannot see anything that doesn't reflect light. Since spirit is the opposite of matter, it cannot be detected by the human senses. But we do know that man is the image of the INFINITE God, therefore, we can represent him with a series of circles which expand ad infinitum. Circles are an adequate representation. They have no beginning or ending. The unseen image has to be as infinite as God Himself. How could there be ETERNAL fellowship unless this were true?

But what **do** you see in the mirror? You see a body occupied by God's image. This is all we can see when we look at people with our **physical** eyes. For a spirit being to function in time and space (life as we know it), he has to PUT ON some kind of a physical form. Without that, he couldn't be a part of this world. So for God to place His image on earth, it was necessary to provide him with a vehicle that would let him operate in the physical realm. What the Lord selected we recognize as the human body. It's easy to draw a representation of that:

When an astronaut goes into space, he needs a spacesuit. When a diver descends into the ocean, he needs a diving suit. When God's image comes into this world, he needs an "earth-suit." The human body is merely a creature the Lord designed to house His image on earth.

Now we see what God did in the garden of Eden. He took His UNSEEN image and placed it within a physical creature. The union was so remarkable that the person inside the body not only felt comfortable, the body seemed to be a part of him. When we put the two drawings together we have a picture of the amazing union of SPIRIT and FLESH, God's image in an earth-suit:

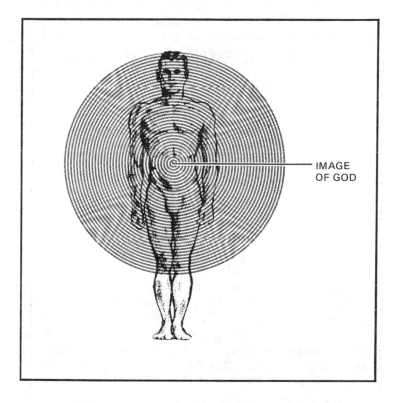

IMAGE OF GOD

NOTE. See how the circles extend beyond the body? There is no way to compress the image of God, which is infinite and eternal, inside a physical, corporeal body. Man is MORE than a body, much more. We're not aware of it, of course, but our BEINGS are not limited to the physical realm. We are also in the SPIRIT realm. This is why Paul could say that we "sit together in heavenly places in Christ Jesus" (Eph. 2:6). Those aren't idle words, they are facts. As long as we are in a body, OUR AWARENESS is limited to the physical. (For example we SENSE Jesus' presence within us, but we cannot apprehend him with the five senses.) It was God's strategy to place us in a FOREIGN environment. He wants us totally cut off from all awareness of heaven and His presence. That way we operate entirely by faith, and the test is genuine. With God's image isolated from the spirit realm, man could pass through an earthly probation. Even though he is a spirit-being, designed to live in heaven, he would be isolated from his natural habitat and limited to the physical world during the test period.

I know it sounds like a contradiction to speak of spirit and flesh as existing together. But God has done precisely that. He has taken His UNSEEN image and made it possible for him to live on this earth AS THOUGH he were a creature of the natural realm. It's an ingenius plan. When you see how the Lord accomplished it, you'll marvel at the wisdom which makes it possible for us to occupy these bodies and feel at home in them.

● Well that's why Mr. Johnson was in that body. God wanted him on earth. During the time of his earthly probation He would learn of God's plan to bring him to Himself. First of all, he would see nimself a sinner and take Christ as his only Savior. He did this BY FAITH, responding to the Spirit's witness in his heart. After that he began to grow in the knowledge of the Lord and the divine plan. Changes occurred daily as he sought to be like his Lord. That was God's plan for making him in His LIKENESS.

Finally the day came when God released Mr. Johnson from his body. We call the process, death. With his probationary period ended, the released Christian entered the real presence of God. But he couldn't take his earth-suit with him. That's not possible. ''Flesh and blood cannot inherit the kingdom of God" (I Cor. 15:50). There is no way for anything physical to enter the spirit realm. The two realms are mutually exclusive. A man can no more take his body into heaven than darkness can enter a lighted room. Body and spirit are two different worlds (John 3:6). Mr. Johnson's experience fulfilled that which is written:

> **"For we know that if the earthly TENT which is our house is torn down (physical death), we have a building from God (our eternal form) a house not made with hands, eternal in the heavens" (II Cor. 5:1).**

> **NOTE.** When our animal house dies, we are released from the brain and instantly at home in the spirit. What happens to the PERSON when the body expires is explained in detail in the author's book, **DEATH: GRADUATION TO GLORY.** Physical death is NOT the awful thing most people think it is. A wondrous release occurs when the image of God puts off the living straitjacket, which is his "earth-suit." That is one of the greatest adventures of life, but Satan has used the fear of death to terrorize people and blind them to the wonder of what is happening. Fear causes most Christians to dread that glorious moment when they shed this animal form and step into Jesus' presence.

● My point so far is that the image of God and his earth-suit are two SEPARATE creatures. God's image is a living being with his own life. The animal he occupies is also a living creature. However one is spiritual and the other physical. Yet the animal is so subject to the man inside that it fits him like a glove. He looks in the mirror and sees a face. He rubs his hand over it. It feels like he's touching himself. That's close. The union is so intimate that when the animal is hurt, the man inside experiences the creature's pain.

> **NOTE.** I am using the term **"animal"** in its most glorious sense. Every creature that moves on this earth is a fantastic

65

creation of God, but the Homo sapiens (human body) is absolutely astonishing. Nothing can compare with it for displaying the glory of God's greatness in His handiwork. For the purpose of this book, the word "animal" is used in this highest and most noble sense. In no way would I suggest that it was inglorious. It is the "temple of the Holy Spirit" as far as we are concerned. It is, though, a creature of this world. God's image is not. That distinction is the whole point of this chapter. Whenever I use the term animal, in no way do I refer to man. Man is NOT an animal. He is the image of the invisible God. But God has honored this animal by putting His image in it.

PROOF OF SEPARATENESS

If you've never weighed the idea of people and their bodies as separate creatures, this may be startling to you. You might even be shocked. But I assure you the teaching is not new. Neither is it foreign to the Word of God. The Bible insists on complete separateness. If I mention several biblical situations which demand separateness, I'm sure you'll agree. Then we'll move on.

Three scriptural situations require complete separation between the body and the person inside.

❶ Consider the Lord Jesus. No Bible-believing Christian will deny the ETERNAL existence of Christ. He was the Son of God before the foundation of the world, i.e., before there was anything physical. How do we know? He made everything that exists:

"All things came into being through Him; and apart from Him nothing came into being that has come into being" (John 1:3).

. . . and again:

"And He is before all things, and in Him all things hold together" (Col. 1:17).

66

To be the Creator of everything physical, He had to exist BEFORE there were bodies of any kind. Therefore, He did not have any kind of a body (as we know bodies) before His incarnation. It would be impossible to be the Creator and not exist BEFORE your creation. Once we accept the pre-existence of the Lord, we must conclude He donned an earth-suit for His appearance on earth. The Bible says one was actually prepared for Him:

"Therefore when He comes into the world, He says . . . a body thou hast prepared for Me" (Heb. 10:5).

If the Lord existed BEFORE His earthly body was prepared, then His person and His body have to be two separate things. He did NOT become a Person when His body was formed in the virgin Mary. The fetus developing in her womb was in no way connected to Jesus' eternal existence. It merely supplied Him with a two-legged vehicle. By it, He was able to enter the human stream and participate, as do we, in human experience.

NOTE. I do not mean to imply that the incarnation was the first time Jesus appeared on earth in a physical body. In old testament times He appeared as the "Angel of the Lord." He was then wearing a special, two-legged creation which theologians call a THEOPHANY. Just as He appeared in the whirlwind and the burning bush, so did He appear in a human form (Gen. 18:1,2). But those bodies were fashioned by DECREE. That is, God spoke and there they were. They did not come as the result of being BORN in the human line. It was not until Jesus became the son of Mary that He took on a body that had descended from Adam (Luke 3:23, 38).

❷ Consider the apostle Paul's statement on death. He says, "We . . . prefer rather to be absent from the body and to be at home with the Lord" (II Cor. 5:8).

67

From this we conclude that it is impossible for a Christian to be with Jesus as long as he is confined to a physical body. If he is to be WITH Christ (in the spiritual realm), he must be detached from the body, i.e., be absent from it. True, there is going to be a bodily resurrection at the Lord's return, but in that day we will be wearing bodies again. The Lord will too. For the moment, though, it is absolutely necessary for a person to be released from his body in order to be face to face with Jesus. This, of course, would be impossible if the life of the soul were in any way linked to the life of the body. They are two SEPARATE ENTITIES, each with its own individual life.

❸ A third point is the matter of our redemption. Did you know that the redemption of our SOULS and of our BODIES are two separate matters, occurring at two different times? That's right. Only the **souls** of Christians have been redeemed so far. Our **bodies,** which belong to the physical creation, still await redemption. Paul says a day is coming when ''the creation itself will be set free from its slavery to corruption (Rom. 8:21). In that day, our bodies will be redeemed. Paul states this specifically:

> **"We too groan within ourselves eagerly waiting for our sonship to be manifested, that is, the REDEMPTION of our bodies!"** (Rom. 8:23).

NOTE. According to that wonderful passage in Romans, a glorious day awaits the believer. It is clear that we are GOD'S SONS RIGHT NOW (I John 3:2). Our souls have been redeemed, but this fact has been hidden from the world. However, when Jesus returns in glory, we will appear with Him—in glorified bodies (Col. 3:4). The creation also awaits that day. God cursed the earth the day Adam fell (Gen. 3:17). It's in Satan's hands this moment. But in that coming day, it too will be redeemed. When it is, our bodies will also be redeemed, for they are PHYSICAL and also under the curse. So here's the point to observe:

68

how can our souls be redeemed independently of our bodies UNLESS THEY ARE SEPARATE? If they were in any way connected the soul couldn't be redeemed without also redeeming the body.

● Further proof of the separateness of body and person, is found in Paul's statement on the difference between the OUTWARD man and the INWARD man:

" . . . though our OUTWARD man (body) perishes, the INWARD man (soul) is renewed day by day" (II Cor. 4:16).

Could this be possible if one were linked to the other? The body is dying while the soul is steadily renewed. Such a thing demands complete separation. It would be impossible for the body to die if it were in any way joined to an eternal soul. Let's put the finishing touch on this truth. One more word from Paul should settle it:

"The things which are SEEN are temporal; but the things which are NOT SEEN are eternal" (II Cor. 4:18b).

There—that should do it. Our bodies are SEEN. They belong to the temporal creation. Our souls are UNSEEN, they belong to the eternal. You cannot mix that which is temporary with that which is eternal, any more than you can mix thoughts with sand. They belong to two different realms. It is as Jesus said to Nicodemus, "That which is born of the flesh is flesh; and that which is born of the spirit is spirit" (John 3:6). The physical world and the spirit world are undeniably separate.

Have I labored this? Perhaps. But it is necessary to see that our bodies belong to the animal creation and we do not. The average Christian simply does not stand before a mirror convinced that what he sees has nothing to do with him as a person. I don't know what it takes to persuade a person that he is looking at an

69

animal which God has provided as a temporary dwelling. However, this fact needs to be clear before we can understand the real cause of sickness and God's provision for it.

Where are we headed? We're going to see that the health of the animal depends wholly on the person who uses it for an earth-suit. You already know that worry can produce ulcers. Yet worry is a function of the man. Bodies don't worry. How is it that beings can indulge in certain IDEAS and bodies suffer? Apparently the "union" between a man and his body is so close one affects the other. But how can that be? We've already said that spirit and flesh don't mix. Yet somehow God clothes His image, which originates in heaven, with a body which originates on earth—and does it in such a way that the two function as one. Just how God has done this, we're going to learn next.

● REVIEW AND REMEMBER

1. Man is NOT a body, he merely WEARS a body.

2. Man, like God, has his own separate life, which is eternal. The body, on the other hand, has its own animal life, which is temporary.

3. God chose to put man in an animal body that would fit his person like a glove and allow him to participate in human experience while totally cut off from his natural environment (heaven). The body so marvelously fits the man, that the distinction between the two must be seen by faith. It is natural to assume that the person and his body are one.

4. The human body is properly called "Homo sapiens," for it is indeed an animal and belongs to the animal kingdom. Since it is occupied by the image of God, and in the case of the Christian, also by the Holy Spirit, it

is truly a holy vessel. In no way should we deprecate this glorious earth-suit. It is so marvelously designed we almost hate to refer to it as an animal. Yet, for all its glory, that's exactly what it is.

5. To establish that body and soul are SEPARATE living creatures, we observed the following:

a. The lesson of the corpse. Mr. Johnson was definitely gone from the body, which means he is able to exist without it. If he can do this, then the life of his PERSON has to be distinct from the life that was in his body.

b. Our Lord existed BEFORE He came to this earth. He did not put on a physical body until He was ready to enter the human stream. Yet He was a COMPLETE person. The acquisition of a body did not add to His person in any way, neither did the shedding of His body subtract from His person. He was and is the same God.

c. We have the statement of the apostle Paul that a person must be ABSENT from the body to be AT HOME with the Lord. The death of the body is necessary to release the man using it. Since "flesh and blood cannot inherit the kingdom of God," bodies cannot go into heaven (I Cor. 15:50). The life of the soul has to be separate from the life of the body for people to BE ALIVE in heaven WITHOUT their earthly bodies. If it were otherwise, a man would die when his body died.

d. At this point in God's REDEMPTION program, only the souls of men have been redeemed. The physical creation has not as yet been redeemed and our bodies belong to that creation. If the body and soul were somehow inseparable or in some way depended on each other, it would be impossible to redeem them at different intervals.

71

e. The apostle Paul declares specifically that the inner man is eternal while the outer man (body) is temporary and perishable. There can be no possible connection between the body and soul if one is dying and the other exists forever.

The inescapable conclusion is that bodies and souls are separate creatures, each independent of the other. Each has its own life and can exist apart from one another. When we consider that the life of the body is temporary and the life of the soul is eternal, we are forced to acknowledge their separateness.

But HOW can God place His invisible image in a visible animal and make him feel at home? Ah, that's our next exciting mystery.

Chapter Four

YOU'RE NOT A BRAIN EITHER

 Remember back in school what we called the really bright student? A brain, right? To us the fellow with an exceptionally high IQ was a walking brain. Now I have to correct that illusion. He wasn't a brain at all—HE WAS A MIND. Oh yes, there was a brain, but it belonged to his body. He, himself, was not a brain. People do NOT have brains. Brains belong to bodies.

In chapter three we distinguished between the person and his body. Now we're going to see the difference between his brain and his mind. We will find that while the brain belongs to the body, the mind belongs to the person. We can see a brain. It belongs to the physical creation of which our bodies are a part. But we can't see a MIND, because it is associated with the invisible image of God. Since I can't describe God's image, I won't be able to describe his mind. All we know is that man is like his invisible God.

While we can't describe God's image, there's one thing we can put our finger on. Both God and man are THINKERS. God thinks. This ingenious earth with its precise plan is proof of that. And you and I think. The technological advance of man is proof of this ability. But when it comes to the animals, they do not think. They have brains, but they don't think. It takes a thinker to do that.

ANIMALS DON'T THINK

Here's a cat. He wants to cross the road, but there's a car coming. He takes a quick look, then makes his move. He dashes across the street without getting hit. How was he able to judge the speed of the approaching car and measure it against his own ability to cover a given distance? What made it possible for him to compute the problem in a flash? The animal has a brain. That brain works like a computer. Does the brain work by itself? No. The cat uses it—BY INSTINCT. The reasoning is all done for the cat. All he has to do is decide whether or not he wants to cross the road. If he does, his computer calculates the risk.

In animals the brain functions like a computer. It is already programmed when the creature is born. This is why you don't have to teach a horse to walk, fish to swim, or birds to fly. The knowledge is already in the computer. God put it there. Then, as the animals grow and encounter various situations, the increased knowledge also goes into the computer. Animals learn by experience and repetition. What they learn goes into the computer. The more sophisticated the brain, the more knowledge that can be stored. The chimpanzee has a sophisticated brain. He can be taught remarkable things. At times he can perform as though human. Yet he functions entirely by instinct.

Take a hawk diving on a sparrow. He literally works out an intercept problem. Yet it is all done for him automatically. His eye follows the sparrow's flight path. His brain then computes the little bird's speed and gives him the right course for a perfect intercept. The mathematics (we'd call it that) are all worked out by the computer in the hawk's brain without any thinking on his part at all.

NOTE. Animals do remarkable things which seemingly require thought. Consider a bee colony. Have you noticed how organized they are? There is an intelligence behind their programming, but the bees don't come up with it. God builds it into their tiny computers. How do spiders weave those intricate webs? It's all accomplished by instinct and their little computer. Without any planning on his part, the salmon returns to the right river, and the swallows find their way to Capistrano on the precise day. These creatures function entirely by means of the instinct-operated computers in their physical organism. Animals never do anything imaginative, even though Lassie appears to figure out problems and come up with creative answers on her TV series. Animals just don't think. They react, but they don't think. At least not as we know thinking.

● Remember the demons who went out of the demoniac into the herd of swine? Those demons were thinkers. They were originally created for God's pleasure, so they had to be more than animals. If they are not people in the sense we are, they're close to it. Those demons could think. The pigs could not. It was simple for the demons to use the brain activity of the pigs and cause them to rush into the sea where they drowned (Mk. 5:1-17).

NOTE. Some Bible students do not believe the demons drove the pigs into the sea, but that the pigs themselves chose drowning to playing host to foul spirits. This would give the pigs "more sense" than some humans. It would mean they were capable of moral judgments, able to distinguish between good and evil. Besides, wouldn't it be a remarkable coincidence to have all 2,000 of those pigs get the same idea at the same time? Pigs are instinctual beasts. Demons are INTELLIGENT beings. An intelligent being can easily RULE a beast when he has access to the animal's mental system. Demons would have no joy from indwelling pigs. The only possible thrill would be the kick they'd get out of destroying them. Demons are destroyers by nature. After killing the pigs, they would be free to go anyplace they chose. Had they not received this permission, Jesus might have sent them to "their own place."

Now demons in pigs is an arresting idea. It shows that spirit beings can enter animals and USE their brains. They can exercise CONTROL over the animal. Why is that so interesting? That's exactly what happens with us. At physical birth, God places us in an animal. At first we function entirely by instinct—the instinct of the creature. That's why we cry for food, etc. And then, as we learn to think, we take over and USE the animal. Ah, but look what we are controlling—animal bodies that also have a brain with a computer. Our bodies, for the most part, are regulated by the computer God has placed in our heads.

> **NOTE.** Like the God Who made us, we too are spirit beings. We enter an animal form (perhaps at conception or when the mother feels life) and gradually take over the control of a creature which is already computerized and designed to operate BY INSTINCT. If we were not in these bodies, using them as time-space vehicles, they would function nicely as the highest form of animal life on earth. They would not be able to think as we know thinking, but they could survive. And do so very well. The brain that comes with the human animal is truly remarkable. It contains a fantastic computer. As THINKERS, we use this brain to make our animal function according to **our thoughts.** This fact will be significant when we come to the healing process.

MAN IS THE THINKER

Our bodies have brains. But like the brains of other animals, they don't think. Man is the thinker. He USES the brain that comes with his animal suit. It is a TOOL. It has nothing to do with him as a PERSON. It is NOT

76

connected with him in any way. If it were, he could not leave it behind when the body dies. The brain belongs to the dying, physical creation. Therefore, it can never be a part of thinking man who lives forever.

Man's ability to think is hard evidence that he is the image of God. We've already said that both God and man are thinkers. Ah, but notice this—they are thinkers whether they are in a body or out of it. Man does NOT need a body in order to think. Why? He has a MIND. Minds can work independently of a brain. In the last chapter we used circles to picture the image of God, but now let's add the word—MIND:

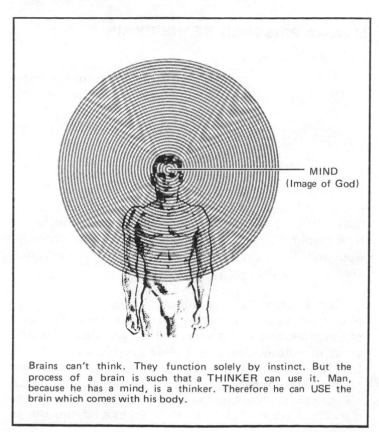

MIND
(Image of God)

Brains can't think. They function solely by instinct. But the process of a brain is such that a THINKER can use it. Man, because he has a mind, is a thinker. Therefore he can USE the brain which comes with his body.

● Does it seem blasphemous to suggest we were designed to THINK as God thinks? Don't struggle with that. Once we're outside the body, away from the limitations of an animal brain, I think we're capable of OMNISCIENCE—or close to it. How can God look forward to an ETERNAL fellowship with creatures who don't come close to His capacity for thinking? Anything less would make us mere pets. That wouldn't give God what He seeks from man at all. It definitely couldn't be called a fellowship. For the present, however, with our thinking limited to an animal brain, His thoughts are not our thoughts. Once we're released from these brains to operate at the MIND-LEVEL, it will be a different story.

MAN—A PRISONER OF HIS BRAIN

Let the doctors open a living body. Let them search for the PERSON. What will they find? NOTHING. There is nothing there but animal parts, including the brain. Man is invisible, he is spirit. Ah, but so are thoughts. No one can see a thought. And since man is a thinker—since he is a MIND—there is no way to find him. He doesn't dwell in the arms or legs. Neither does he dwell in the head. Yet he is a prisoner of the brain. How come? The point of contact between the image of God and the living creature he uses, is the brain. That's where the two meet.

Our bodies have awareness. They are conscious of themselves and what they are doing. They are aware of other animals and aware of their surroundings. The word to note is awareness. Now here's what I think God has done. He has taken His image and limited him to the **awareness** of a creature designed to serve as his earth-suit. Ah, but the animal's awareness has to do with a brain. That's true. Therefore, if the image of God is limited to the awareness of the animal, he is a **prisoner of the brain** that comes with his body.

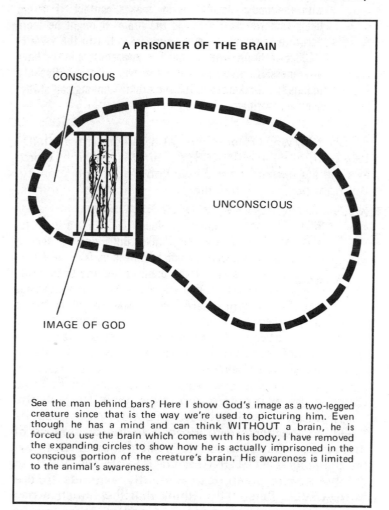

A PRISONER OF THE BRAIN

CONSCIOUS

UNCONSCIOUS

IMAGE OF GOD

See the man behind bars? Here I show God's image as a two-legged creature since that is the way we're used to picturing him. Even though he has a mind and can think WITHOUT a brain, he is forced to use the brain which comes with his body. I have removed the expanding circles to show how he is actually imprisoned in the conscious portion of the creature's brain. His awareness is limited to the animal's awareness.

NOTE. This truth is often demonstrated in surgery. If you give a man a local anesthetic, so that the lower part of his body is anesthetized, the man remains fully conscious. You cannot cancel his awareness by anesthetizing any part of his body from the neck down. But what happens if you anesthetize the brain? He loses ALL awareness. The brain then, is where the image of God makes contact with the body. Notice I said, makes contact. It is not likely that we even dwell in the brain. It might be more accurate to say that we are simply limited to the AWARE- NESS of a brain. The animal has awareness and we have awareness. God merely puts the two together. Because man is the thinker, he USES the brain. Thinking can always overrule instinct.

See now why I refer to man as a person with a MIND? Like God, he is a THINKER, so mind is the right word. Yes, he's a person, with all we know about personality. But right now we're dwelling on the fact that he thinks.

> **NOTE.** If man is a mind, he does NOT NEED a brain for thinking. It is MIND that thinks. But thinking involves AWARENESS. Since the animal brain is capable of aware- ness, the mind can USE the brain at the **awareness level.** I hope that doesn't sound too wild. This is God's ingenious way of isolating His image from the spirit world. He makes us prisoners by limiting us to the conscious awareness of a particular animal. When the creature's awareness becomes our awareness, then we act as though we were the creature itself.

A man puts a gun to his head. He pulls the trigger. Death occurs to the body. What happens to the person imprisoned in the awareness of the brain? He is released. He is still a thinker. But now his thinking is NO LONGER LIMITED to the ability of the brain. His awareness instantly expands to the MIND-LEVEL. Personally I think that the Christian has instantaneous awareness of God and all other beings in the spirit world in that moment. But that is specula- tion on my part. I really don't know what happens once we're released from the brain. In any event, it will be exciting. And it will be the TRUE mind expanding which is of God, not the titillating trips people take with drugs.

Now you have an idea of what I think of the mind of man. It transcends anything we know about the animal brain. Just as the person is more than a body, so is his mind MORE than a brain. Now let's picture what I have just said:

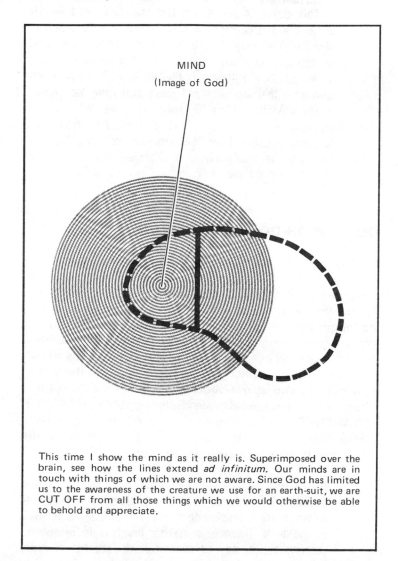

MIND
(Image of God)

This time I show the mind as it really is. Superimposed over the brain, see how the lines extend *ad infinitum.* Our minds are in touch with things of which we are not aware. Since God has limited us to the awareness of the creature we use for an earth-suit, we are CUT OFF from all those things which we would otherwise be able to behold and appreciate.

NOTE. In my opinion, if we were not operating in an animal body, limited to the capacities of the brain, we'd be aware of our true existence in the spirit world. I'm satisfied by God's Word, that we ALREADY have our existence in the spirit, but are simply CUT OFF from the awareness of it. This, again, is due to the fact that God has LIMITED us to the awareness of a brain which functions at the physical level only. I take as literally true the biblical proposition that born-again Christians are "IN CHRIST," a fact stated 39 times in the book of Romans. I am convinced that we "live and move and have our being" in the INVISIBLE GOD. Or again, that we "sit together in heavenly places in Christ Jesus" (Eph. 2:6). All of this is easily possible if we see ourselves as spirit, but cut off from the awareness of it. Nothing can change the fact that we are the image of God and He is Spirit (John 4:24).

OUR MINDS DO THE THINKING

Brains do not think—not even ours. We do the thinking. We USE the creature's brain. We THINK with it. We have to, because God has limited us to the brain for the moment. Once we're out of the body, that will no longer be true. But for now, as long as we're imprisoned, our thinking is limited to the capacity of the brain that comes with our body. God does not want us thinking BEYOND the capacity of the brain. Beyond the brain, you see—**is the spirit world.** And that's a "no no." Thus, while our minds are fully capable of SPIRIT AWARENESS, we are restricted to ANIMAL AWARENESS during our earthly probation. He does not want us in touch with the spirit world, yet.

NOTE. This truth answers an agonizing question. Here's a child with a damaged brain. It leaves him retarded, or worse. He is stuck with that brain as long as he lives in the body. Science is making progress in biogenetic surgery, but it may be some time before the problem

82

is licked. In the meantime it is comforting to know that the crippling is only temporary. Once the victim leaves the body, he escapes the damaged brain. When he is released to function at the MIND-LEVEL, there will no longer be any such handicap. The mind does NOT suffer damage because a brain is deformed. The brain is physical, whereas the mind is SPIRIT (John 3:6). Parents with a retarded child should be comforted by the fact that the crippling ends when the body dies. It does NOT follow a child into eternity.

INSIDE OUR ANIMAL HOUSE

I doubt if you have traveled under the ocean in a submarine. But you've seen them in movies. You know how isolated they are from the outside world. They have to get their information through devices. A periscope breaks above the water and turns this way and that. The commander peers through it. It is the eye of the sub. Subs have ears too. Sonar devices detect the sound of other vessels. Communication is made by radio. Should anything happen to these faculties and the sub be stranded on the bottom, it would be totally isolated from the outside world.

The same is true of us.

Put your hands over your eyes. Cover them tightly. Can you see anything? No. No more than a sub can see with its periscope covered. You are now cut off from visual contact with your surroundings. Now plug your ears. You're beginning to feel isolated, right? Next we'll plug your nose, letting you breath through your mouth. You can't smell a thing. Without anything in your mouth, there's nothing to taste. Next, I'll ask you to sit motionless to minimize the sense of touch. Yes, you'll feel the back of your chair. We can't create total isolation.

Can you imagine what it would be like for a person to lose his sight, hearing and touch, and on top of that be unable to taste or smell anything? That would be solitary confinement. He'd be alone in there, with nothing but his thoughts. I ask you to picture this to show that we are prisoners of the brain.

We live inside an animal house. All of the information from the world about us comes by way of the creature's senses. A brain cannot see, hear, or smell, etc. However, the body is equipped with eyes, ears, and nose. These are connected to the brain via the nervous system. But they are all physical. If your nervous system didn't work, you could bump into a chair, for example, and not know it. The BRAIN depends on the five senses for all of its information. Until the brain receives this outside information, YOU have no way of becoming aware of anything. The MIND depends fully on the brain and the nervous system for its information.

How do we see? You say with our eyes. No, that's not true. The eyes are optical scanners that pick up the sights about us, convert them to impulses and send them to the brain. The brain in turn, transforms those impulses into pictures and projects them onto a screen in the conscious portion of the brain. That's where WE see. We DO NOT see anything outside us. We read it off the **conscious screen.** The mind HAS NO EYES. It gets all of its information from the brain. The only way we see anything is to view it on the TV screen in our heads.

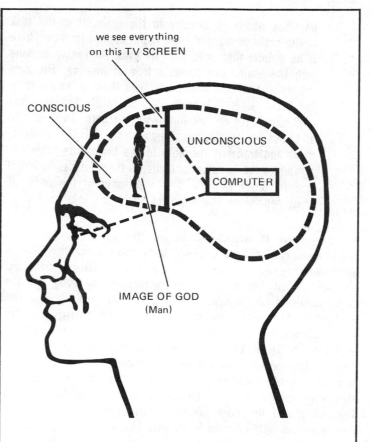

we see everything
on this TV SCREEN

CONSCIOUS

UNCONSCIOUS

COMPUTER

IMAGE OF GOD
(Man)

The eye of the body focuses on some external object. It converts
the scene into impulses which are sent to the brain via the optic
nerve. The computer unscrambles the impulses and projects the
same scene on the TV screen separating the forebrain (conscious)
from the hindbrain (unconscious). The image of God (man)
imprisoned in the forebrain views the scene on the screen. That's
how he sees. He uses the SAME SCREEN that the animal uses.
Until the computer projects the data on the screen, there is no way
for the image of God to behold anything.

NOTE. Every school boy learns that we do not see with
our eyes. Those amazing little orbs in the sockets of our
face are merely devices for scanning patches of light and
dark. Those patches are changed into electro-chemical

impulses which go directly to the brain. It is the task of the brain to translate the impulses into images. There is no animal that sees with its eyes. All seeing is done with the brain. The same is true of hearing. The ears merely pick up vibrations and send them as impulses to the brain. It is the brain that interprets the impulses into sound. We do not hear with our ears. So it is with all of our sensory devices. They scan the OUTSIDE environment and transmit the data to the brain. The brain unscrambles the impulses and shapes them into audio-visual images. Since the MIND is a prisoner of the brain, it must depend on the brain for all of this information.

● See how it works? Just as the commander of a submarine gathers outside data by the way of the boat's audio-electronic devices, so does the image of God receive all of his external information by way of the body devices. As a spirit being, he has no eyes, ears, or hands. He can only experience such things as the brain, which comes with his animal house, makes them available to him. The mind is able to read the information off the conscious screen the moment it is received. But unless the senses pick it up in the first place, and the brain projects it on the screen, there is NOTHING for the mind to read. We are absolutely LIMITED to the brain which comes with our body.

> **NOTE.** Observe that I said the mind is LIMITED to the brain. I did not say it was CONTAINED by the brain. There is a difference. The mind is greater than the brain. There is an unconscious activity that transcends the work of the brain, but we are sealed off from it and limited to the awareness of the animal. Sometimes, though, because of high brain fever or some injury, the seal is not 100% complete. When that is the case, "LEAKS" occur and outside material seeps into awareness. People who have such leaks can receive information from demons or gain impressions from other minds. We call such people psychics or mentalists and it is popular to think of them as gifted.

86

But Peter Hurkos, one of the most notable, says it is a curse. He claims he is continually annoyed by impressions from the "other side." They interfere with his sleep. His credits include helping the Los Angeles police solve the Tate and La Bianca murders. This explains for example, why an Edgar Cayce could know the location of a medicine bottle lost for 30 years.

LET'S VIEW THIS FROM ANOTHER ANGLE

You've got a toothache. It's painful. You rush to your dentist. But he's not a run-of-the-mill dentist. He uses hypnotism. He talks to you. By way of words, he presents IDEAS. You listen. You believe what he says. You are NOT asleep when he says you will feel no pain. Then he goes to work on your teeth. What do you know—NO PAIN! And he didn't use a bit of Novocain. Your conscious mind functions fully.

How does he do it? **With ideas.** Ah, but ideas have to do with the MIND, not the brain. Words mean nothing to a brain. It simply stores them. The brain wouldn't have the faintest idea how to use words. Ordered speech has to do with people only. Your brain is like a computer. Computers do only what they are programmed to do. They do not think. But we learn something from this experience with the dentist. The mind is the BOSS of the brain. Really?

Your mind received an IDEA from the dentist. The brain says there is pain from the tooth. But after accepting the IDEA of the hypnotist, you don't feel it. That can only mean that the MIND has **overruled** the data coming to the brain. The mind then is the MASTER of the brain. When a dentist is successful in convincing your mind that you will feel no pain, he could pull every tooth in your head and you wouldn't feel a thing. No matter what message the nerves send to the brain, the

87

IDEA of **no pain dominates** your mind. The message from the brain is ignored. Isn't that amazing? This is no fairy tale. Hypnosis is used in dentistry today.

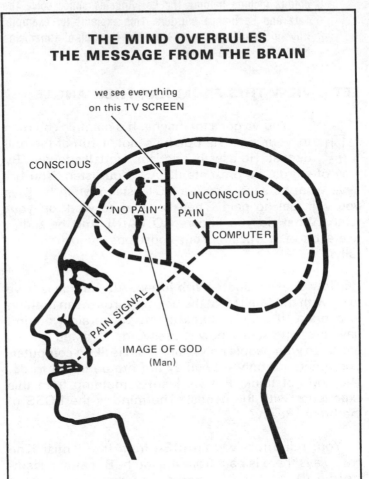

THE MIND OVERRULES
THE MESSAGE FROM THE BRAIN

we see everything
on this TV SCREEN

CONSCIOUS

UNCONSCIOUS

"NO PAIN" PAIN

COMPUTER

PAIN SIGNAL

IMAGE OF GOD
(Man)

See how the pain signal travels from the tooth to the computer. The computer then sends it to the conscious screen. This is how the image of God experiences pain. But this time the man REFUSES the signal, overruling it with the countering idea—"NO PAIN." The computer accepts the NO PAIN idea from the conscious mind and the pain signal is cancelled. From this we see that under certain conditions the MIND **can overrule the brain.**

What does this teach us?

Everything a man experiences takes place in the CONSCIOUS PORTION of the brain. All awareness occurs here. That's what consciousness means—awareness. Thus, even pain is felt here. Yet we have just seen that pain can be overruled. How? **By believing what a hypnotist says.** You may not think that is significant, but it is. The brain controls the body. When we observe that the mind controls the brain, it means the MIND can affect the body. In a way, though, that's not news. You already know that worry (a mental process) can cause ulcers (a physical result).

So—if the mind can cancel pain, it can also CAUSE pain. That's something to discover. You can see how vital that is when we're talking about sickness. What we've just seen indicates that the SYMPTOMS OF SICKNESS can be caused by the MIND.

● The point? The MIND and the BRAIN are two separate entities. The mind belongs to the PERSON (image of God). The brain belongs to the BODY (a living creature).

MAN'S MOST AMAZING FACULTY

Man is a creator. That's not surprising. After all, he's the image of THE Creator. Ah, but to create there must be a faculty not found in ANY animal—the ability to **see** something BEFORE it exists. The ability to picture something which does not have existence is called IMAGINATION. Imagination is the most spiritual faculty of man. By means of imagination we can give reality to the unseen. We can picture things before they come into existence.

NOTE. Imagination and awareness are not the same. Animals have awareness. They are conscious of what is going

89

on around them. But they do not have the ability to picture anything. Why? Animals can't think. They have awareness because they have a brain. But imagination does NOT belong to the brain, it belongs to the MIND. Consequently imagination transcends awareness. However, we must keep this in mind—as long as the mind is a PRISONER OF THE BRAIN, the imagination is **also limited** to the conscious portion of the brain. Once we are released from the body, and the limitations of the brain, there's no telling what we could do with our imaginations. This physical universe, with its wonders, gives us a clue as to what God did with His imagination. Ours is like His—it has to be.

Man's imagination allows him to create things in an endless stream. Anything he can conceive he can build—if given enough time. But to do it, he must first SEE it in his mind. That is, the finished object must appear on the conscious screen in his mind. Until he SEES the desired object, there is no way for him to set about building it. Men had to PLAN Hoover Dam before they could check the mighty Colorado. Someone SAW San Francisco Bay spanned before a bridge was started. And it was necessary to picture men on the moon before we could send astronauts there. Certainly no chimpanzee ever got a notion like that.

How does man imagine?

Now we come to the fascinating part. He **projects his thoughts** onto the conscious screen of the brain. Remember, man is the thinker. But notice, his thoughts are projected onto the **SAME SCREEN** used by the computer to display OUTSIDE information. We've already noted how man does not SEE with his eyes, he sees by way of this screen. Now we're saying that the man inside uses this **same screen** for his THINKING. Thus, not only does the animal use this screen to picture OUTSIDE data, God's image uses it for INSIDE data.

Imagination, then, is the ability to project one's THOUGHTS on the brain screen. But see that the SOURCE of what is displayed is the MAN HIMSELF. This is different from awareness. Awareness has to do with surroundings. Imagination is inside information. The drawing below shows how BOTH the man and the animal use the SAME screen:

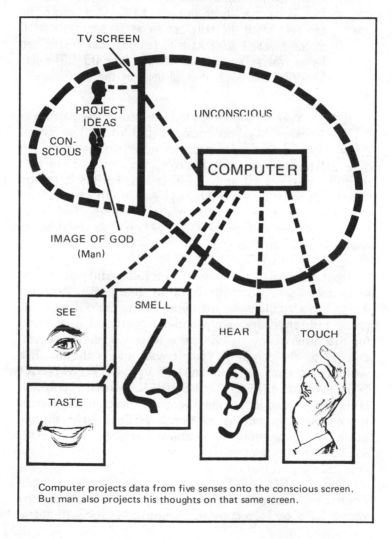

Computer projects data from five senses onto the conscious screen. But man also projects his thoughts on that same screen.

DRAWING: See how the image of God (figure inside brain) projects his THOUGHTS onto the screen. Then see how the animal computer projects the sensory data onto the same screen. The man and the computer both use the same screen. When the man uses it, it is called IMAGINA-TION. When the animal uses it, it is called AWARENESS. When man THINKS, he does so in terms of all the senses. That is, he can dream in color, he can hear music. He can even smell the salty sea air as he pictures himself at the beach. I don't have to tell you that dreams can be as real as any experience, yet they DO NOT come from OUTSIDE DATA. It is all done by the man himself.

You are walking along a trail in the Northern Rockies. As you round a big rock, you come face to face with an enormous grizzly bear. He is as startled as you are. He rears up on his hind feet ready to attack. Fear stabs your being. Fantastic things happen in your body—instantly! Adrenalin shoots into your blood stream. Your stomach tightens. The body gears itself for a fight or flight. Then you awaken. It was just a dream.

Just a dream? Then why is your heart still pounding? Why can't you go right back to sleep. It's because Adrenalin actually went into your system. Your stomach really tightened and your body did indeed gear itself for the emergency. It will be a little while before you can go to sleep again. Yes, it was just a dream. But what does that tell us? WHAT WE PUT ON THAT SCREEN CAN AFFECT OUR BODIES. A dream, you say, is nothing more than ideas passing through our mind? If that's so, then why is your body so upset? No, there's more to it than that. Your animal THOUGHT IT HAD MET A BEAR!

There is NO DIFFERENCE, you see, as far as your computer is concerned, whether the picture on the screen was projected by you (internally), or whether it was picked up by your eyes as a threat outside the body. Why not? It appeared on the SAME SCREEN. The threat was just as real because it was flashed on the COMMON SCREEN. The computer in the brain cannot distinguish between a picture **you** put on the screen and one which results from something picked up by the eyes. Your animal body cannot tell the difference between an OUTSIDE threat and one you IMAGINE. Let's picture that bear scene:

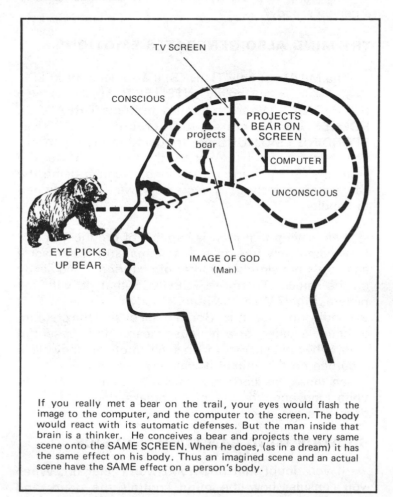

If you really met a bear on the trail, your eyes would flash the image to the computer, and the computer to the screen. The body would react with its automatic defenses. But the man inside that brain is a thinker. He conceives a bear and projects the very same scene onto the SAME SCREEN. When he does, (as in a dream) it has the same effect on his body. Thus an imagined scene and an actual scene have the SAME effect on a person's body.

That's a whopping truth. It tells us that what we think or allow to occur in our imaginations can affect our bodies. It tells us that our animal house reacts to scenes in our minds as though they were taking place in real life. Our imaginations do affect our bodies because the image of God and his animal house use the SAME SCREEN.

Beginning to see why worry does such damage to a person's body?

THE MIND ALSO GENERATES EMOTIONS

The MIND not only THINKS, it also generates FEELINGS. Man is not solely INTELLECTUAL. He is also EMOTIONAL. When the mind projects DREADFUL SCENES on the conscious screen, the CORRESPONDING EMOTIONS are triggered in the organism. The more powerful the scene, the more powerful the emotions. Since man is a thinking, creative being, he can generate feelings the creature was not designed to handle.

I am saying that man is capable of producing emotions completely foreign to his animal suit. Take worry again. It's not simply a matter of picturing a bad scene on the screen. There are FEELINGS that go with the picture. Right? Well, the human body was never meant to handle those feelings. God did not design the creature to house a hater, or a jealous, mean, bitter, resentful man. When people indulge in such emotions, they place a burden on the animal it was never intended to bear. When those emotions are powerful enough, and continue long enough, the brute breaks down. When it does, you get sick.

SO, YOUR MIND CAN MAKE YOU SICK

If you doubt that now, you won't later on. When you consider how the mind controls the brain, and because of imagination, is capable of creating THOUGHTS and EMOTIONS your brain can't handle—something has to give. The only thing that **can** give is your body. And it does, as we see—next.

● REVIEW AND REMEMBER

1. God is spirit, therefore invisible. Since man is the image of God, he too is spirit, and invisible.

2. Having distinguished between the body and the person using it, we further distinguish between the BRAIN and the MIND using it. The brain belongs to the body, the mind to God's image (the person). They are completely separate.

3. Since animals have only a brain, they cannot think as we know thinking. It is the MIND that thinks. A brain cannot think by itself, someone has to USE it. The brain is like a computer. An operator can make it useful. Mind belongs only to the image of God. Since God is a THINKER, so is man. Thinking has to do with the MIND alone.

4. Though animals possess only a brain, they nonetheless have AWARENESS. Awareness is a MENTAL process, not a physical one. Since it is mental rather than physical, a spirit being can USE it. God has ingeniously taken the awareness of the human animal (Homo sapiens) and LIMITED the thinking of His image to that of a creature. Thus each of us is "joined" to a particular animal by a MENTAL PROCESS. There is NO physical union between us and the body.

5. Limited to the mental capacity of the brain that comes with his body, man is a PRISONER of the animal brain. Even though designed to operate at the MIND-LEVEL, he is temporarily restricted to the mental capacity of the creature. This is God's way of isolating us from the spirit world during the time of our earthy probation.

6. Therefore, man is NOT literally united with a body, he USES it. A spirit-being can no more merge with a physical body than thoughts can mix with sand. Because he is a thinker, man dominates the animal. This explains why the demons who departed from the maniac of Gadara could enter the swine and bring about their destruction. As thinkers, they could meet the pigs at the point of awareness and take control of their bodies.

7. Since animals have brains and awareness, they also have a CONSCIOUS SCREEN. This screen is located in the forebrain. The five senses gather OUTSIDE information. It is processed through the brain/computer and projected onto the mental screen. This is how animals see and hear, etc. As soon as the information is displayed on the screen, the animal reacts to it by INSTINCT.

8. Man also uses this same conscious screen. He has no way of contacting the physical world except as the information comes through the animal's senses and is projected on the screen. Since man is a rational being, rather than an instinctual creature, he reacts to the displayed data WITH REASON. His reaction is a judgment. That is, man evaluates the information on the screen and then DECIDES what to do about it. The creature, of course, can't do that. He reacts by instinct only.

9. Man uses the conscious screen in still another way. He THINKS on it. That is, he can project his THOUGHT-IMAGES onto the screen. The process is called IMAGINATION. Please note that it is the SAME SCREEN the animal uses. Thus we have TWO SOURCES for data appearing on the screen: (1) outside information picked up by the senses, and (2) inside information projected by the THINKER using the creature.

10. Animals seemingly do clever things, but it is only because God has pre-programmed their tiny computers. They cannot invent anything. They are not able to project

THOUGHT-IMAGES onto the screen. Therefore, they cannot see things which as yet do not exist. Their seeing is limited to that picked up by their eyes and relayed to the screen. They cannot create an item on the screen and then proceed to build it, as does God's image. The spider may weave an ingenious web, but that's all he can do. That's the one program God has entered into his computer. The same is true of the bee, the ant, and the beaver, etc.

11. Because the mind and the brain use the SAME SCREEN, the animal is unable to distinguish between an OUTSIDE experience (event) and an INSIDE one (imagination). Consequently a person can dream of falling and the animal reacts with terror. The person awakens from his dream with the creature's heart pounding and body covered with perspiration. Yet the experience took place on the imagination screen ONLY. The animal had no way of knowing it wasn't actually happening. This proves man can affect (even control) the animal by what he pictures on the conscious screen.

12. To show that we and our animal suit function with a COMMON AWARENESS, we give the creature an anesthetic. When the animal loses consciousness, so does the image of God. This couldn't happen unless both were using the SAME consciousness. When the animal is anesthetized, the image of God goes into oblivion. Time stops. The person does NOT regain consciousness until the animal comes out from under the anesthetic. This could not be true unless BOTH were using the same awareness.

13. Hypnotism works with the MIND alone. It is a spiritual process. The therapist works with WORDS ONLY. Words are spiritual, not physical. No one can touch an IDEA. Hypnotism proves that the MIND rules the brain. If a subject believes he has no pain, even though his body is injured, the NO PAIN idea dominates the conscious mind. He PICTURES himself with no pain. That picture on the conscious screen OVERRULES any pain signals sent

by the nervous system and the computer. The person experiences NO PAIN.

14. The reverse is also true. If a person projects a PAIN PICTURE on the screen, even though NO pain signals are coming from the body, the creature will EXPERIENCE PAIN. The animal goes by what appears on the screen. Thus man, with his ability to create that which does not as yet exist, can PICTURE himself as sick even though the creature is not ill at all. Because the animal responds to the picture, it will display the SYMPTOMS of sickness. Therefore, people can make themselves sick by what they visualize on the conscious screen.

15. Animals are emotional creatures. They are designed to handle such feelings as fear and anger. But the human MIND, because it is creative, is able to come up with emotions the animal was not meant to absorb. With his creativeness, man can conceive powerful scenes on the conscious screen. These in turn generate emotions the animal can't handle. When these emotions are too powerful or come too often, they can damage the creature. This is a prime source of sickness as we will see in the next chapter.

Chapter Five

HOW YOUR MIND AFFECTS YOUR BODY

Years ago I learned to fly in a government flight training program. We had an instructor with a passion for stunt flying. He had strict orders from the owner of the contract flying school not to perform violent maneuvers in the student aircraft. They weren't built for acrobatics. The owner warned him it was dangerous. But the instructor did them anyway.

The day came when he tried his stunts once too often. He pulled a wing off the ship. He bailed out but he hit the ground before his chute could open. He paid the price for overstressing the plane. Had he stayed within the specified limits, he would have been perfectly safe. But his passion for stunting overruled his good sense. There was just too much pilot in that airplane. Something was bound to give way in time.

● The same is true of the human body. It was meant to function as an animal, designed to take only certain stresses. Some stresses are normal for the Homo sapiens. Yet if it is overstressed too violently or for too long, damage will occur. From what we know of the human organism, it can take a lot of abuse before it finally gives way. On the other hand, if we stay within the design limits, it can last a long time.

THE SITUATION WAS IDEAL IN THE BEGINNING

The day God put Adam in an animal suit (joined him to a Homo sapiens) it was an ideal combination.

The suit fit God's image perfectly. He wore it like a glove. He felt at home in it. For a time Adam was in obedient fellowship with God, and there was no real wear and tear on the creature. Had that gentle treatment continued, there's no telling how long it might have lasted.

Then came the day when Adam and Eve deliberately sinned against the revealed will of God. That changed everything. The Homo sapiens now had SINNERS living in it. The splendid creature, so ideal for living within space and time, now had a FALLEN master. Adam was capable of thoughts and feelings which were not at all like a child of God. The creature would now be subject to stresses for which it was **not** designed. In fact, it was in for a beating.

> **NOTE.** At first Adam's life was orderly and gentle. As long as he was submissive to the Father's will, he did not overstress the body in any way. But when Adam fell he acquired a satanic nature. Now the body had an owner capable of abusing it. The situation was similar to that of the stunt pilot flying the student aircraft. The body, while perfect for a godlike individual, had a master who could act like the devil. He was bound to bring stresses the creature was not designed to take. Structural failure was certain to come in time. As it was, that particular creature survived 930 years.

● We have just named the cause of all illness and disease—STRESS.

STRESS

In his book, "How to Live 365 Days a Year," Dr. John Schindler says, "Three out of every four hospital beds are occupied by people suffering from emotionally induced illness." I'm sure you've read accounts in Reader's Digest and other magazines, reporting upwards to 80% of all visits to doctors have no organic cause. Most damage done to the human body is clearly the result of EMOTIONAL stress.

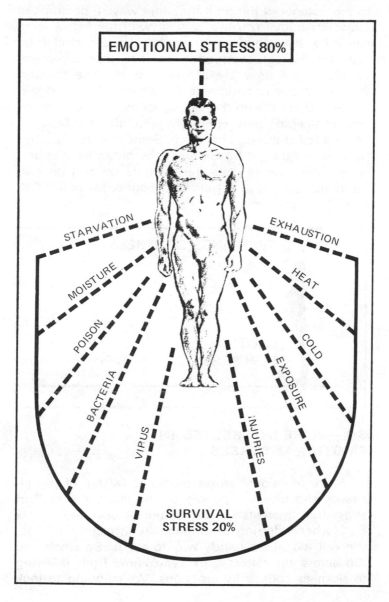

For the purpose of this book, I'm going to divide stress into two categories. There is the one just mentioned, emotional stress. The other is SURVIVAL stress. In this category I lump all the other ways a person can stress his body. You are familiar with the list. A man can exhaust his body by overwork. He can chill it by exposure. He can overfeed it, get it too hot or too wet for too long a time. He can let it deteriorate through lack of exercise or deprive it of needed nutrition. Again he can poison it with the wrong foods or take an overdose of sleeping pills. He might jump off a tall building or put a bullet through his brain. Some stresses he can't help. He might get hit by a car, be bitten by a cobra, or encounter nerve gas. The list goes on and on, but no matter how long it gets, it accounts for only 20% of all body problems.

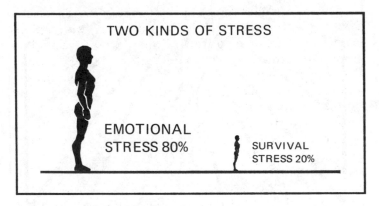

TWO KINDS OF STRESS

EMOTIONAL STRESS 80%

SURVIVAL STRESS 20%

SO—WE'RE INTERESTED IN EMOTIONAL STRESS

Since emotional stress produces MOST of the illnesses and diseases people suffer, that's the kind of stress that interests us. Dr. Schindler uses the initials E.I.I. when referring to emotionally induced illnesses. We will too. It's a handy way to say it. So when you run across the letters E.I.I., you know I am referring to sickness caused by emotions. We're going to look at this stress created by our emotions.

Consider the biblical proposition:

"As a man thinketh in his heart, so is he" (Prov. 23:7).

Did you know that truth applies to our bodies as well as our behavior? Most people know that if a man keeps an idea in his mind long enough, he'll end up doing it. But what many do not know is that what a man thinks affects his body. If he thinks SICK, he becomes sick. People can actually THINK themselves into the hospital. And if Dr. Schindler is correct, three out of every four hospital beds contain people whose THOUGHTS put them there.

The fallen mind can create scenes on the conscious screen which in turn generate emotions the Homo sapiens was never meant to absorb. That's where damaging emotions come from—right off the conscious screen. The human imagination is able to picture viciousness and vengeance, jealousy and judgment. Thoughts and feelings such as those are foreign to the animal. The creature doesn't know what to do with them. Since it was never meant to deal with them, it is NOT DESIGNED to DISPOSE of them.

> **NOTE.** If the body had some sort of an emotional exhaust pipe, these emotions would be harmless. They could then be discharged from the body before they did any harm. But since the creature was never meant to experience them in the first place, little provision was made. Consequently their destructive force is vented against the body itself. For those who might wonder if confession is not such an exhaust pipe, see discussion #7 in the appendix, "Healing in the church." Confession is wonderful for relieving the soul of **spiritual** sicknesses. When these are removed, physical healing can follow. Confession then, is an indirect process.

What is it exactly that produces emotional stress? It's the fact that man is a THINKER—and thinks in PICTURES. Unfortunately he can create BAD scenes on that screen as well as good ones. It's what the thinker puts on that screen that overstresses the body. In other words, it is the MIND that overstresses the body. Since man has a FALLEN mind, he is able to come up with some foul stuff. When it comes to vicious and violent scenes, there's no limit to his resourcefulness.

JESUS' COMMENT ON MIND POLLUTION

When the Pharisees challenged the Lord, charging that His disciples ate with unwashed hands, He rebuked them. Turning to the crowd, He said, "There is nothing outside a man which going into him can defile him, but the things which proceed out of a man are what defile him." His disciples didn't understand these words. So they asked Him what they meant. His answer bears on what we've been saying:

> "Do you not see," He said, "that whatever goes into a man from the outside cannot defile him because it does not go into the HEART (mind), but into the stomach and is eliminated? That which proceeds OUT of the man is what defiles him. For from within, OUT OF THE HEART, proceed evil thoughts and fornications, thefts, murders and adultries, deeds of coveting and wickedness, as well as deceit, sensuality, envy, slander, pride, and foolishness. All these evil things proceed from WITHIN and defile the man" (Mk. 7:18-23).

Look at the list of evils the Lord names as coming from the MIND of man! I'm sure Paul had this list in mind when he wrote that first chapter of Romans where he describes the reprobate mind (Rom. 1:28-32). But should anyone think Paul is merely describing the heathen, he will find practically the same list in Galatians where he describes the OLD NATURE of the **Christian** (Gal. 5:19-21).

104

Every one of those evils can generate powerful, destructive emotions. Our fallen nature is a filthy swamp, filled with every kind of foulness. It is a polluted thing. Out of it can come thoughts and ideas we would never tell anyone, yet we permit them on the conscious screen. If we take our Lord's word literally, and we should, we find that the mind of man is a polluted organism.

EVIL COMES FROM INSIDE

When you "join" a polluted man to an animal body—one NOT designed to take the stresses he is capable of generating—the creature is sure to suffer. But note this—the creature would NOT get sick if man didn't overstress him. There is no way for an animal to make itself sick. God did not put a sickness instinct into His creatures. There is no law of sickness written in the creation. It has come as the CONSEQUENCE of man's sin.

Did you know that NO cell or organ of your body can decide to get sick ON ITS OWN? Not even your brain can make you sick—by itself. It is programmed for health. God designed your brain to keep your body in perfect health. The instant it was conceived in your mother's womb, it was programmed for health. For sickness to occur, someone has to OVERRULE that health program and impose a stress on the creature it cannot handle.

THE BRAIN—supreme headquarters of the animal

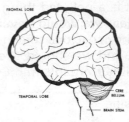

FRONTAL LOBE

TEMPORAL LOBE

CERE BELLUM

BRAIN STEM

Consider that three pound mass of jelly inside your skull. It has ten billion nerve cells. It directs every function of your animal suit. Through 100,000 miles of connecting nerves, the brain is in touch with every part of your body. There is not a cell anyplace among the muscles, bones, organs, and ducts that is not under the direct control of the brain. It is the supreme headquarters of your physical body. No, the brain doesn't control you. We've already seen how the MIND controls the brain. But as far as the body is concerned, it gets its orders from the brain. You can't do anything with your body, without the cooperation of your brain.

The system of nerves descending from the back of your brain into the spinal cord, looks like the mesh of wires one might find coming out of the back of a telephone switchboard. By means of these nerves, the brain is in touch with every speck of flesh in your body. It's a fantastic intercom that keeps the brain informed of what is going on in every part of your body. For example, a portion of your skin, the size of a postage stamp, has about four yards of nerves. Information about that bit of skin races along the nerves to the brain at the rate of 300 miles per hour.

You accidentally prick your finger. You feel pain instantly. Why? You've irritated a nerve end. The stimulation was flashed along that nerve to the brain. **By way of the brain you felt pain.** Until the brain received the message, **you felt nothing.** You don't have any contact with your flesh, except via the brain. There are millions of these nerve endings dotting every bit of your skin. There's one for heat sensing, another for cold, still others for pressure and

106

pain. It is by means of these that the brain keeps touch with your body.

The brain also SENDS messages along the nervous system. If you wanted to rise from where you are sitting right now, you would merely WILL to get up. That's all you have to do. The brain takes it from there. There are muscles of the body that obey commands originating with you. We call these the VOLUNTARY muscles. Yet, they DO NOT get the commands directly from you. The commands come from the brain. However, as far as you are concerned, the muscles SEEM to obey your wishes. The truth is, the BRAIN responds to your command and sends the order to the muscles for you. As a spirit-being, you have no DIRECT contact with any muscle or organ of the body. Everything you do is processed by the brain.

Then there are other muscles which DO NOT work this way. That is, the brain WON'T order them into action merely because you WILL it. These are the IN-VOLUNTARY muscles. The body is filled with these. We are NOT able to influence them **consciously.** They are regulated EXCLUSIVELY by the brain. These are muscles such as you would find in the heart, kidneys, liver, and stomach, etc. There is no way for you to exercise any CONSCIOUS control over them. You can WILL all you like, but nothing will happen. The brain does not order these muscles to act merely because you wish them to.

WHY THE BODY SUFFERS

Science has known for a long time that emotions which are NOT dissipated through some kind of PHYSI-CAL activity, are deployed throughout the body by way

107

of the autonomic nervous system. The autonomic nervous system is one of two branches of the central nervous system. The other branch, the cerebrospinal, communicates your orders via the brain. When you want to run, for example, the commands for your legs to move are sent through the cerebrospinal nervous system. Those muscles which are NOT subject to your will, receive their orders from the brain by way of the autonomic system. See it like this:

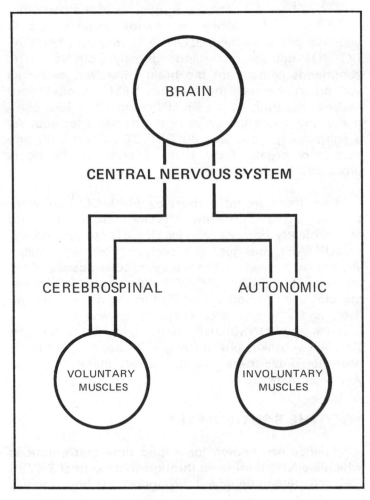

Have you ever told your kidneys to function? Of course not. They are not subject to your will. Neither have you consciously ordered your intestines into action. These organs are **automatically** regulated by the brain via the autonomic nervous system. If you wanted a glass of water, for example, your conscious mind would give the command. Your hand would reach for the glass. You would put it to your lips and swallow, but what happens after that is beyond your personal control. From there on the ANS (autonomic nervous system) directs the process from the unconscious area of the brain.

ALL ORGANS ARE VULNERABLE

Wherever the autonomic nervous system carries messages from the brain, it is possible for symptoms to appear. You can see from the chart (on next page) how every organ is linked to the brain. That means every single organ in the body could become the target of emotional abuse. The range extends from the eyes to the reproductive organs. Everything from bad eyesight to sexual problems can result from the destructive thoughts people picture in their minds. Wherever there is a muscle to squeeze, the ANS can produce pain.

 Here's a man. He's angry. That's one emotion which can't be hidden. His face turns red. His jaw becomes rigid. He instinctively clenches his fists. There's trembling in his voice and limbs. These are merely the OUTWARD expressions of his feelings. INSIDE his body a lot more is going on. His pulse increases. The outlet of his stomach contracts so tightly nothing can leave it. The arteries around his heart squeeze down hard enough to produce pain. And his blood pressure can go high enough to burst the smaller vessels in his brain.

AUTONOMIC NERVOUS SYSTEM

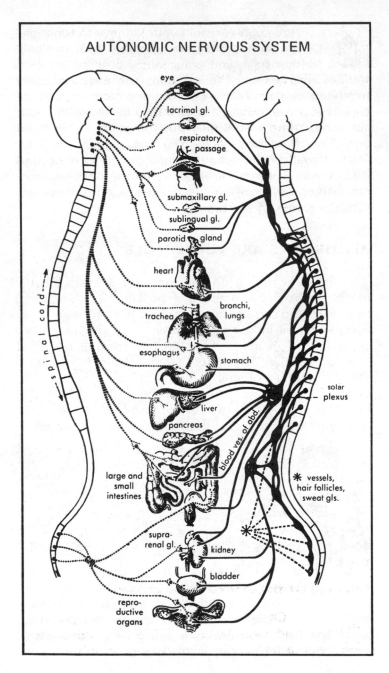

An ordinary household encyclopedia will show you the extensive domain of the ANS. Just look at all the organs connected with this system. It connects with all the SMOOTH muscles of the body, the heart and gland muscles included. When powerful emotions surge inside a person, this system is called upon to handle them. You can imagine what orders must go to some of the muscles of the organs when RAGE or JEALOUSY churn in the mind. Tremendous feelings are created. The BRAIN has to do something with them. That's right, the ANS gets the job of dumping them somewhere WITHIN the body.

> **NOTE.** Because we can't see what is happening to our organs and muscles, we are inclined to regard emotions as merely a mental matter. Not so. Every feeling that surges or trickles through our being causes a PHYSICAL reaction somewhere in the body. Take headaches, for example. It would be easy to dismiss them as mental upsets. But most of them come as the ANS contracts the blood vessels in the brain. Those vessels are common targets for deep, undetected emotions. The pounding those vessels frequently take can produce both ordinary and migraine headaches. Headaches are only one of the ways the animal brain deals with emotions.

The body can stand emotional gusts. Dramatic blasts of emotion come and go in the course of everyday living. But those which cause damage are the subtle ones. We all have problems that throb just below the surface. And when they generate unpleasant and awful feelings, those emotions are like water dripping on a stone. In time their monotonous pounding produces an illness.

The case of the distressed bookkeeper

 A Christian came to me with his problem. He had recently taken a job as a bookkeeper with a trailer sales company. It wasn't long before he was aware that the owner was keeping a double set of books. He knew it was wrong to cheat on taxes, but the job paid very well. So he developed an excuse for himself. He reasoned that it was the owner who was dishonest, not he. He felt he could continue working for him without being party to his dishonesty. Yet, he wasn't comfortable about it. It bothered him whenever he wondered what the Lord thought of it. Then there was always the possibility of being involved in an audit. So there was a steady undercurrent of distressing feelings.

In time he developed an ulcer, or so he thought. Intense pain in the stomach region sent him to the doctor. No ulcer was found, yet the pain persisted. That's what brought him to me. He was wondering if perhaps he was the victim of some kind of demonic attack. When he told me about his employer and the job situation, I suspected supressed guilt feelings. Guilt feelings are powerful. They run deep.

During our interview I explained how the body was NOT designed to handle emotions such as guilt. I was sure that he was suffering from guilts as the result of his job. Therefore, his unconscious mind was deploying those powerful feelings along the ANS and his stomach was the target. When I assured him that something far worse than an ulcer could develop if he stayed in the job, he decided to quit. Within a few hours after his decision, the pains were completely gone.

> **NOTE.** It has been estimated that more than half the people complaining to doctors of ulcer-like pains, do not have ulcers at all. The pains they feel are caused by the tightening of the stomach muscle due to emotion. They have a powerful emotion that's been created by the mind and the BRAIN has to do something with it. The stomach has been selected as the whipping boy and the emotion is vented against that organ by way of the ANS. It's a

bad solution to the problem, but what else can the brain do? The emotion has to be discharged some place in the body, and the stomach, as far as the brain is concerned, is as good as anyplace else. The pain caused by a genuine ulcer feels exactly like the pain triggered by the ANS.

● While the stomach is a frequent target for emotions, the colon suffers even more. Dr. Schindler says that the colon, more than any other organ, is a "mirror of the mind." We don't know why as yet, but the animal mechanism uses the colon as a waste basket for a lot of our unpleasant feelings. A muscle spasm in the colon produces a pain which is almost identical to that of a gallstone attack. More than 50% of those who seem to suffer gallbladder attacks are actually suffering emotional spasms in the colon. Doctors have known this for years.

> **NOTE.** Once the brain (unconscious portion) selects an organ of the body as the whipping boy for a particular emotional problem, the choice is entered into the body's computer system. The computer is in the hindbrain. After that, every time those same feelings occur and have to be disposed of, the stress will be directed against the SAME ORGAN. No one can choose which organ is to be the target for his emotions. It is unconsciously done by the animal mechanism. We are not allowed in the computer room. Consequently every organ, muscle and gland in the body could end up as a punching bag for a specific emotional problem. However, certain areas are favorite targets.

EMOTIONAL DAMAGE CAN BE DEMONSTRATED IN ANIMALS

A few years back two psychologists from Cornell University devised a clever experiment to show that destructive emotions could produce disease in animals. They used sheep in their experiment. A fine wire was tied around the leg of a sheep and so arranged that it didn't interfere with its freedom to graze. The wire was attached to a device which could deliver a small electric shock whenever the doctors pressed a button.

For a week electric shocks were sent through the wire. They were so slight the sheep's leg muscles merely twitched a bit. There was no regular pattern, the shocks were administered only now and then. These didn't bother the sheep. Whether they were regular or irregular made no difference. The conclusion was, that stress of this type had no effect on the animal. (Note that this is a survival type stress, not an emotional stress.)

Then another step was added to the experiment. Ten seconds before each shock was given, the doctors rang a bell. The sheep soon came to associate the bell with the shock it felt in its leg. It got so that whenever the sheep heard the bell, it quit eating and began to wait for the shock. It knew what was coming. Now an emotion was introduced—APPREHENSION. This we know to be a destructive emotion. When the experimenters began to repeat the bell/shock treatments at steady intervals, the sheep began to fall apart. The steady pounding of apprehension got to it. With this harmful emotion continuously slamming into the sheep's mental system, it wasn't long before signs of illness began to appear.

It was so with every sheep tested.

At first a sheep would stop eating. Then it drifted from the flock to be alone. After that it gave up walking. When it tried to stand on its feet, it couldn't. Finally it began to have trouble breathing. The doctors were careful to end each experiment before the sheep died. It was clear they could have killed them with this one emotion—apprehension. Thus they proved conclusively that a steady bombardment of harmful emotions can

114

produce disease in animals. The human body is an animal.

> **NOTE.** When we worry, when we are anxious about things, when we allow bitterness and discontentment to persist in our minds, we invite sickness into the body. The stress doesn't have to be a mighty surge, just a steady pounding. It will do the damage because the body is not equipped to absorb the pressure of emotions which cannot be vented through physical outlets. When a man languishes in lust, for example, and there is no way for the creature to discharge the emotion, he can hurt himself. He may not think any damage is occurring, but the brain has to do something with the emotions generated by his thoughts. The man who harbors resentment and reviews bitter scenes on the conscious screen does the same thing. Whether he realizes it or not, his body is taking a pounding.

● Does anyone have to tell you that there are good emotions? We know the bad ones can produce illness and discomfort. We are painfully aware of what FEAR can do, as well as guilt and despair. But there are good emotions which produce beneficial results in the body. The creature in which we live responds favorably to affection, expressions of love and appreciation. Joy and peace actually help the nervous system function at the optimum level. This in turn produces a sensation of well being throughout the body. **Reader's Digest** entitles one of its sections, "Laughter—the best medicine."

BIG JOB FOR A LITTLE BRAIN

Earlier I spoke of the three pound mass of jelly that uses 10 billion nerve cells to direct every part of your body. Your brain has complete charge of the circulation of your blood, digestion, assimilation and elimination processes. It regulates ALL of the vital forces of your body. Should an illness strike, it knows how to marshall the forces of your body and direct them against the invader. There's enough power on hand in your body to wipe out any disease. If only you had some way to direct your brain, you could deal with any sickness in a flash.

There's not an illness known to man that can stand up to the awesome power God has built into the human body. If you could figure out a way to trigger these powers, you could deliver a knock out punch to any disease that dared to invade your body.

Think of an ocean going vessel. Deep in the hold are the huge engines which propel it through the seas. Those engines, for all their might, cannot think for themselves. They rely on orders from the captain. In that they are like the great forces controlled by your brain. Just as those engines respond impersonally to directions from the bridge of the ship, so do the vast powers of the brain respond impersonally to the "bridge of the brain"—your conscious mind. What would you say if I were to tell you that this powerful mechanism can be triggered by FAITH? It can, as we'll see next.

● REVIEW AND REMEMBER

1. Before Adam sinned in the garden of Eden, he was in perfect harmony with the creature serving as his earth-

116

suit. He did not subject it to any undue stress. He was in fellowship with God and his thoughts were those of a godly man. This kept him free of unhealthy emotions. Had that situation continued, there's no telling how long the creature he was using might have lasted.

2. After Adam sinned, his animal suit was dominated by a FALLEN master. By his sin, Adam constructed within himself a corrupt nature. He was now capable of thinking things that would create emotions his body was not designed to handle.

3. Scholars agree that ALL sickness and disease is due to STRESS. We have divided stress into two categories: emotional and survival. It can be shown that emotional stress accounts for up to 80% of all illness. Dr. Hans Selye, of Canada, the world's leading authority on stress, says that emotional stress is the principal cause of all illness: that more people die from diseases associated with it than from any other cause.

4. When we persist in pleasant emotions such as love and hope, joy and peace, contentment and humor, we induce good health. But when we persist in destructive emotions such as anger, bitterness, jealousy, vengeance, hopelessness and despair, we can do great damage to the body. Why? The creature was not designed to handle them. It has no way of disposing of them OUTSIDE the body.

5. The image of God creates harmful emotions by means of the distressing and vicious scenes he puts on the conscious screen. These scenes cause reactions within the creature which are utterly foreign to the animal. Since the image of God is a prisoner of the brain, the brain has the task of getting rid of them.

6. Since the BRAIN (computer) has the task of disposing of distressing and destructive emotions, they are likely

to be dumped anyplace inside the body. Some organs, such as the stomach and the colon are favorite targets. With the brain connected to all parts of the body via the nervous system, almost any vital spot between the soles of the feet and the top of the head can become a target zone.

7. The body can withstand emotional gusts. It can take a lot of them. But when harmful emotions persist over a long period of time, there is no way to avoid a breakdown of some sort. Disease has to follow a steady hammering of destructive emotions. A person, for example, who frets over a problem day after day, is certain to experience some kind of illness.

8. Christians who are ridden with fear, can die from it. It can be shown in test animals that destructive emotions such as fear and apprehension can actually destroy the body. To kill a person by voodoo, all that is needed is to get the dreaded idea into the victim's mind. The emotion of fear will follow. As he feeds that emotion with terrifying thoughts, the power mounts to the place where damage occurs very fast. Those who indulge themselves in resentment, worry, suspicion, and anger, are slowly dying. Thus is confirmed the solemn prescription of the Word, "As a man thinketh in his heart (MIND), so is he."

NOTE. Someone has said that there are 365 "fear nots" in the Bible. It certainly is clear now why God does not want His people subject to fear. Fear can kill. Also we understand the apostle Paul's insistence on a disciplined mind. Bring "every thought unto the obedience of Christ," he says (II Cor. 10:5). Then he gives a list of positive things which he says should fill the thought life of the believer, i.e., "things which are lovely, pure and worthy of praise, etc." (Phil. 4:8). The Holy Spirit warns Christians of the danger of entertaining evil and destructive thoughts. The danger is not only to their souls, but their bodies as well. On the other hand, do you suppose it is possible

for Christians to use certain thoughts to trigger the great powers of the mind for healing? The exciting answer awaits in the next chapter.

Chapter Six

THE KEY TO YOUR COMPUTER

Here at PC we have a computer system. It keeps track of our work for the Lord. It is fascinating to watch an operator sit at the console and push the buttons. In a flash, information appears on the screen. Once the operator has done her work, she leans back and relaxes. Her job is done. From there on the machine takes over. The only effort required is getting the problem into the computer. Then it goes to work to find the answer silently and fast.

Did you know it is like that with the computer in our heads? It is located in the back part of the brain. The conscious mind, using the forebrain, is the operator. Since the image of God is at home in the CONSCIOUS, he has this fantastic machine at his disposal. That means YOU are the operator. You may not be aware of it, but you have an amazing piece of equipment in the back of your head. I wonder if you have ever considered the bewildering potential God has provided for your use.

NOTE. We get an idea of the capability of the unconscious computer when we consider that it processes billions of pieces of information coming from the senses, particularly the eyes. Did you know that all of the focusing and adjusting to various shades of light and distance are done by this computer? Your eyes don't do it. The computer does. Did you know that the 600 muscles in your body are regulated by it, as well as the 1,500,000 sweat glands spread over the surface skin? It keeps track of each of the 7,700,000 cells in the lungs. It counts the 2,500,000,000 beats of the heart as it lifts over 500,000 tons of blood over a period of 70 years. It directs over 100 trillion native red corpuscles with never a miss. No serious approach to healing can ignore this amazing machine which exercises such COMPLETE control over every vital function of the body. All glory to the Great Physician Who designed it!

Start thinking of your hindbrain as a mighty computer. Even though it is a living machine, it functions much like the latest electronic devices. In fact, those working in computer technology believe our modern computers are simply projections of the greatest of all computers, the human brain. However, it is just a device. And like any machine, it needs an operator. Even though it can solve problems and provide ways to reach goals, it cannot think for itself. It merely carries out the programs fed into it. There is no way for a computer to exploit its own capabilities.

NO DIRECT ACCESS TO THE COMPUTER

If you were to visit PC, I'd show you our computer. I'd invite you to sit at the keyboard. I'd point out some buttons and first thing you know, you'd have information appearing on the video screen in front of you. You'd sample the ease of using a computer first hand. But then, after I explained that we have a similar machine in the back of our heads, I'd have to tell you we CANNOT USE IT IN THE SAME WAY. God does not allow us to ask questions and input programs into our unconscious computer DIRECTLY. In fact He has denied ALL direct access to the computer in our heads. And how does He do it? By putting it in the HINDBRAIN and limiting its operation to the unconscious.

> **NOTE.** Isn't that ingenious? Whenever God wants us to avoid DIRECT CONTACT with anything, He simply places it beyond our awareness. Take demons, for example. He doesn't want us to be in touch with them. Neither does He want us in touch with those who have departed from this life (Deut. 18:10-12). Yet these individuals are no less real than we. So how does God isolate us? He puts them BEYOND our awareness. Remember, awareness is a **conscious** function only. The same is true of God, Himself. He does NOT want us in direct contact with Himself. If we could see and touch Him, it would no longer be necessary to walk BY FAITH. Direct contact with the Lord, before the time, would put an end to the faith program. The point: all these things are REAL, but beyond our awareness. The same is true of our computer.

Now why would God deliberately put this amazing machine beyond awareness? He doesn't want us fooling with it. Can you imagine what would happen to our animal house if we could tamper with the controls that regulate the vital functions? Who knows where our heart beat would end up, or at what temperatures we'd set

the thermostat? Scientists would produce real monsters
if they could get their hands on the computer.

> **NOTE.** If we had direct access to the control panel of
> the unconscious computer, one of the first things we'd
> probably do is alter the PAIN process. We don't like pain.
> But how necessary it is. Without the warnings of pain,
> we'd tear our hands using them as wrenches, or burn them
> up handling items too hot for flesh. They'd be useless
> in a very short time. Beyond that, we'd never know when
> we had exhausted the strength of the animal. Naturally,
> we'd try to get the maximum effort out of the creature,
> so we'd keep pouring on the Adrenalin. People have been
> known to lift cars and perform feats of strength that were
> seemingly supernatural when FEAR triggered the right
> hormone signals. The Great Physician knows we have
> neither the wisdom nor the restraint to be in charge of
> the body's regulatory system. So He put the control panel
> out of reach.

Go to an office building. Locate the thermostat regulating the air conditioning. You'll probably find a plastic guard around it. That guard
is put there by the management to keep the employees
from fooling with the control. Some like it hot, others
like it cold. The system would be in a constant state
of change if employees could alter it at will. So it is
with our computer control. God has placed a GUARD
about it. He does it by putting it beyond our awareness.
That way we can't mess with it. If we could, we'd be
fooling with the circulation, the digestion, and the respiratory system. God has preset those the way He wants
them. They belong to the animal.

> **NOTE.** I can't blame anyone for thinking how nice it would
> be to have access to the computer at times. The moment
> we got sick we could press the "GET WELL" button and
> SNAP, we'd be well. Or if we hit our thumb with a hammer,
> we could press the "NO PAIN" button. CLICK, the pain

would be gone. A person with cancer could press the "HEAL" button and he'd be free of the disease in seconds. We know the power is there. We've discussed that. Besides, the Lord Jesus (Who DOES have access to the computer) used that same power to heal people with lifetime illnesses IN SECONDS. That's what's so tantalizing. The power is there and the computer knows how to use it. If only we could get into that computer room, we'd have it made. We have an atomic powerhouse inside us, but God says, "You can't go in there."

QUESTION IS THEN, HOW DO WE USE IT?

In his book, **Psycho-Cybernetics,** Dr. Maxwell Maltz says the conscious mind is the ''CONTROL KNOB'' of the unconscious. And he has to be right. Why? Our only contact with the living computer is by way of the THOUGHT-STREAM flowing into it. Please get that, this is important. The only way we reach or influence the computer is by WHAT WE THINK.

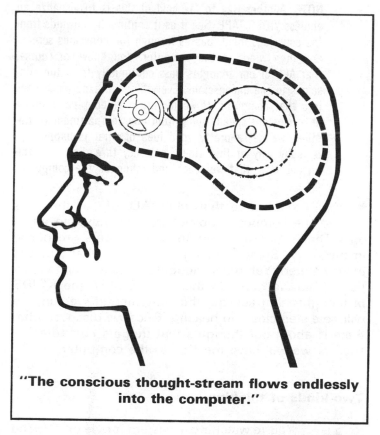

"The conscious thought-stream flows endlessly into the computer."

The image of God thinks IN PICTURES. Of course they are living pictures, for they are not only accompanied by sound, but feelings as well. Those pictures

FLOW in an endless stream into the UNCONSCIOUS. They go into the computer's memory banks. Our thoughts appear on the conscious screen and from there they pass into the VAST SEA of the unconscious. It's all there, all recorded. These scenes flowing into the unconscious are our ONLY contact with the computer. If we're going to contact that computer at all, it has to be by way of our THOUGHTS.

> **NOTE.** Another way to lay hold of this is to visualize an endless VIDEO TAPE. See it as it continually unwinds from the conscious mind, passes through the conscious screen, and then winds in the computer. You know, of course, that ALL of our thoughts pass continually from the conscious to the unconscious. Everything we experience goes into that computer. If we picture a video tape, running at a constant speed, going from one compartment to the other, we get a pretty good idea of what is happening. It is by way of this video material, threading into the unconscious, that we reach and influence the computer.

● We next observe that while ALL of our thoughts go into the computer, not all of them have an effect on it. That is, not ALL of our thinking triggers a response in the body. Some thinking has no effect at all. It is merely stored. Yet, other thoughts bring a definite reaction. What we must do then, is ISOLATE the KINDS of thoughts that activate the computer. If we can, we will be a step closer to healing. Once we discover what there is about our thoughts that triggers computer response, we will have the KEY to the computer.

Two kinds of thinking

You're watching a western movie on TV. The plot is dull. It's a routine story, not stirring in any way. What will your computer do about the material coming via your eyes and conscious mind?

NOTHING. It simply goes into storage. Since there is nothing about it to stir the emotions, the computer accepts the information as storage material only. To get a response out of the computer, there has to be something SPECIAL about the information entering the unconscious. That's a vital observation.

Now let's suppose you are watching a mystery thriller. There is great suspense built into the story. The lights are out in the room. The victim sits alone in his wheelchair. There comes the sound of footsteps on the stairs. You know it's the murderer. The situation is tense, terrifying. The story is so captivating you become involved. No longer are you merely sitting in front of a TV set. You're in the story. You're the victim. You are caught up in the drama. It's happening to you. So completely have you identified with the scene, you break out with goose bumps. The terror of the scene is upon you.

Pow! The alarm rings in your mind. As far as you are concerned—and as far as your computer is concerned—**you are in danger!** The computer gets the message. Something has to be done about the threat. Adrenalin goes into your blood stream. Your heart begins to pound. Your breathing becomes heavier. You don't tell your body to do any of these things, yet they happen. You have not said a word to your stomach, yet it has stopped all of its digestive work to gear itself for the emergency. Your body is prepared for flight or a fight. The computer has prepared your body for action.

● Now WHY this reaction from the second movie, but no reaction from the first? Ah, we're about to discover the KEY to the computer.

THE THREE SPECIAL ELEMENTS

There were three special elements in that second

movie which we do not find in the first one. Here they are:

1. You IMAGINED yourself in the situation.
2. You actually BELIEVED it was happening to you.
3. Your EMOTIONS were stirred.

In other words:

YOU SAW IT—YOU BELIEVED IT—YOU FELT IT.

That's the formula for activating the computer.

The THOUGHT STREAM going into your computer contained these three ingredients. Because they were on the tape, they signaled the computer to act. Thus the secret of USING the computer has to do with the KINDS OF THOUGHTS we allow in our minds. This tells us how important thoughts really are. If we project scenes on the conscious screen, **believe them,** and have feelings about them—the computer will do something about them. We now have the KEY for getting healing programs into the computer.

WATCH IT WORK

 Let's suppose Asian flu is going around. Here's a man who believes he's vulnerable to every virus. He seems to catch everything going around. Listen to him, would you:

"Man, I get everything. I'll no doubt get the flu again this year. I can just see myself having to take off work, lying around with a thermometer in my mouth. Right when we need the money, too. I go through this every year. It's something I have to live with."

128

Well, what do you know? He gets the flu! How come? He programmed himself for it. Anyone who truly believes he is going to catch the flu—will. Notice the triggering elements. They're all there. (1) He could SEE himself as sick. That picture was on the screen of his imagination. He saw himself in bed, suffering the symptoms of a flu victim. (2) More importantly, he BELIEVED he would be infected. This gave reality to the picture on the screen. (3) He had FEELINGS about it. He was worried about the loss of pay even before his body was attacked. He supplied everything needed to get the computer to act. It was bound to carry out the scene on the screen.

> **NOTE.** When the "bug" hit this man's body, his computer arranged for him to get the flu. Normally it would resist the virus and destroy it. That's its job. But the normal program, which operates according to the law of health, was OVERRULED by the man himself. He sent a NEW PROGRAM to the computer. Remember: the conscious mind is the BOSS. It's the control knob. Without realizing it, he actually ORDERED his computer to make him sick. He could be the healthiest man in town, with the power to resist any disease, and STILL GET THE FLU if he **really believed** himself a helpless victim. Since the computer has FULL POWER over the vital functions of the body, it can make a man sick as well as heal him. When ordered to let the flu virus invade the body, it did as it was told. This is not faith healing, it's FAITH SICKNESS.

THE COMPUTER RESPONDS TO FAITH—NOT FACTS

A group from your church has gone to a wooded park for an outing. The picnic lunch has been finished and the men and boys are playing baseball. One of the fellows slams the ball into a clump of trees. You go chasing after it. Unknown to you, a movie company is on location not far from

129

where your group is playing ball. One of the stuntmen is dressed as a gorilla. There's a break in the shooting and he wants to get a candy bar. Without removing his costume, he heads across the woods to the hot dog stand where your group is having a good time.

Now here you are kicking about in the bushes looking for the ball. Suddenly you look up. A gorilla! Wow! Your heart leaps to your throat! Your body gives off all sorts of alarm signals at the sight of this live gorilla! Of course it's NOT a real gorilla. But you don't know that. All you can think of is that you have encountered—**a gorilla!** Your eyes flash the gorilla to the conscious screen. You BELIEVE it is a gorilla. That's all that is necessary. Talk about emotion—Wow! Everything that happens in your body is based on the idea that the gorilla is real.

It makes NO DIFFERENCE that what you are seeing is merely a man in a costume. The real TRUTH doesn't matter. It's what you BELIEVE that counts. Since you BELIEVE the gorilla is real, your computer accepts it as FACT. That proves the computer operates entirely by what we believe. It works according to the law of BELIEF.

> **NOTE.** We have discovered a valid law. The law is this: whatever we consciously believe to be true, our unconscious mind (computer) accepts as FACT. It is BELIEVING what we see on the conscious screen that triggers the computer.

I have an item from the Family Weekly magazine of May 16, 1971. It tells of a man who weighed 220 pounds. His normal weight was 165. He tried dieting, but couldn't stay with it. Then he went to a doctor who gave him some pills GUARANTEED to make him loose weight. He didn't have to worry about any kind of a diet. It sounded great. He had found what he was looking for.

Each week he went back to the doctor for more pills. The doctor would routinely go to his storage cabinet and return with another week's supply. Finally his weight was close to the desired 165 pounds. But on the last occasion, the doctor didn't make the trip to the storage cabinet. He merely opened his desk drawer and took out some pills. It was an unfortunate mistake. His patient was immediately suspicious.

"Doctor," he asked, "are these by any chance placebos?" The physician couldn't hold back his smile.

The secret was out. He tried to cover up by saying, "Go on, take 'em. You only have another week to go and then you'll be where you want to be."

> **NOTE.** A placebo is a sugar pill given to a patient to make him THINK he is being medically treated for a problem. Doctors know the power of the mind over the body and use it. They say, "Take these and you'll feel better in the morning." This supplies the patient's imagination with a picture of complete recovery—and gives him a reason for BELIEVING he will get well. When a patient truly believes he is being treated and is told he will be well, this gives his conscious mind what it needs. In view of the law we've just learned, it's easy to see what happens. His conscious mind BELIEVES he is going to get well, therefore, his COMPUTER accepts the image of perfect recovery and orders the body forces to make him well. It is not the placebo that heals, but the person's own computer . . . triggered by his conscious belief.

Well the man took the pills, but of course they no longer worked. Once he knew what they were, his conscious mind neither SAW nor BELIEVED the slender image he had envisioned before. At once his weight began to climb. It wasn't long before he was over 200 pounds again.

WATCHING THE COMPUTER DO ITS STUFF

Now that we have discovered the formula for triggering the computer, we need to see it work in an actual healing situation. That's what we're going to do in our next chapter. By way of our imaginations, we're going to visit a healing meeting. If we went there without the knowledge of the three elements, and how the computer is triggered by the conscious mind, it would all be quite mysterious. But we're going with the advantage of knowing something of what is happening. We can't explain all that goes on in healing meetings, but we can explain part of it.

Everything God does is lawful. Therefore all healings come by a lawful process. We have discovered a most significant law, the law of belief. A healing meeting provides an opportunity to see this law at work in a context where the THREE ELEMENTS are so evident you can't miss them. It can be fun to attend a healing meeting when you have something in particular to watch for. That's next.

● **REVIEW AND REMEMBER**

1. The conscious mind answers to the forebrain of the animal. This allows us to think with the animal's brain. Our conscious mind actually USES the conscious part of the physical brain. Our unconscious mind answers to the unconscious part of the animal's brain, or the hindbrain. The body's computer system is in the hindbrain. It is out of reach of the conscious mind.

2. Integrated with the hindbrain, the body's computer system regulates the vital organs and such functions as digestion, assimilation, circulation, and the building of new cells. It is in charge of the animal's health. Therefore the healing mechanism of the body is beyond our conscious reach. God placed this automatic control system beyond our awareness to insure the survival of the creature.

3. Though God's image is denied DIRECT access to the body's computer, it is clear that the conscious mind CAN TRIGGER unconscious functions. Physicians have known for a long time that destructive emotions (caused by distressing thoughts) have a definite effect on the body's health. Yet such thoughts are conscious. This means that certain conscious thoughts CAN and do interfere, if not overrule, the automatic healing process.

133

4. There is only one way in which the conscious mind is in contact with the computer, and that is by way of the THOUGHT-STREAM flowing into the unconscious. Something about a person's thoughts triggers the computer into action. Since ALL thoughts pass from the conscious into the unconscious, it is obvious that only CERTAIN KINDS of thoughts affect the computer. When we identify those, we have the KEY to the computer.

5. Likening the THOUGHT-STREAM to a video tape, we concluded there must be certain elements on that tape which activate the computer. By observation (the two kinds of movies) we isolated the three elements: (1) scene on the conscious screen becomes a goal for the computer, (2) the image of God must consciously believe what he sees on that screen, (3) he must also have feelings about it. Thus a formula emerges: SEE IT—BELIEVE IT—FEEL IT.

Now we need to see our formula in action. That's next.

Chapter Seven

THE HEALING LAWS AT WORK!

Here's a young woman who cannot speak. Her tongue is paralyzed. She has received all kinds of medical treatment, yet the paralysis will not yield. After a time it became evident that she desperately wanted to speak, but couldn't. It was decided to try **suggestive therapy.**

Her doctor told her he had a new instrument that would loosen her tongue. "This device," he said, "has been effective in one hundred percent of all cases where it has been used." He assured her she would be speaking within a few minutes. Then, without letting her see it, he produced an ORDINARY THERMOMETER and inserted it into her mouth. He touched var ous spots here and there on her tongue and then removed it. "Now you can talk," he said. Within seconds she was saying a few words. Two weeks later she was speaking fluently.

This girl had been witness to a murder. She had seen her father kill a man and hide the body. The shock of seeing the murder, plus fear of betraying his secret, provided tremendous emotion. The IDEA that she must never reveal a word of it slammed into her unconscious with tremendous force. Her tongue became instantly paralyzed. That was her computer's way of sealing her lips. Now she couldn't give her dad's secret away. It was the huge emotion accompanying the SILENCE idea that caused her computer to act with such speed.

The girl's father had since died. But his death did not remove the crippling idea from her unconscious. Her computer was programmed for a silent tongue. Even when she wanted to speak, she couldn't. What then would loosen her tongue? Ah—another idea. **A new, powerful idea.** When the doctor said he had a new instrument guaranteed to heal her, she **BELIEVED** him. She could **SEE** herself speaking again. The prospect **EXCITED** her greatly. The touch of that cold thermometer sent the new idea into her computer.

> **NOTE.** In the last chapter we learned that thoughts flow like a video tape from the conscious into the unconscious. When the right kind of thoughts are on that tape, the computer is triggered into action. I gave you the three elements that had to be on the tape. Here they are again: SEE IT—BELIEVE IT—FEEL IT. All three of those elements were present in the healing of the girl. Now that healing was not instantaneous. There wasn't a lot of emotion present. Had there been, she could have been healed instantly. Soon, though, we'll find ourselves at a healing meeting where we can see these elements at work in a very emotional setting.

● I know you're anxious to get to that meeting and then on to the plan for your own healing. To you it will seem as though I have deliberately slowed down the pace of the book right when your interest is at the highest point. But trust me to know the best approach. It is essential that I lay a good foundation for your understanding. Everything you will read from here on is vital. I now want to present the healing laws the Lord has given to me. Once you see them, IN ORDER, you will better understand how they work in the healing meeting.

TEN LAWS OF FAITH HEALING

> **CAUTION:** Please do not think these are ALL the healing laws which can be triggered by faith. I do NOT KNOW all of them. God has been pleased to show me SOME of them. There are healings which occur through faith that cannot be explained by these laws. They involve other laws as yet unknown to me. But these are sufficient to give us a confident approach to the healing of our own

bodies. I have that confidence, for God has healed my body by means of these laws, as well as those I have served. Later I will tell you of my disorder that was healed.

LAW #1 "AS A MAN THINKETH IN HIS HEART, SO IS HE" (Prov. 23:7)

Yes, that is the primary law and it comes from the Word of God. Aware of this great law, researchers and experimenters have uncovered a number of subsidiary laws governing the relationship between the conscious and unconscious. There are ten of these discovered laws which have to do with faith healing. These are the ones that interest us.

LAW #2 The conscious mind is the GUARDIAN of the unconscious.

The conscious mind is the gateway to the unconscious. Not only do thoughts FLOW from the conscious into the unconscious, the conscious also has the power to decide what KIND OF THOUGHTS make up the thought-stream. The conscious mind has discriminatory powers, that is, it decides what it will or will not believe. Since it can be shown that the unconscious (computer) reacts to ideas flowing into it, the conscious mind becomes the CONTROL KNOB of the unconscious computer.

LAW #3 Whatever the conscious BELIEVES, the unconscious accepts as FACT.

It is the function of the unconscious to accept material as it comes from the conscious. The unconscious makes no judgments as to whether anything is good or bad, true or false. The unconscious does not question decisions made by the conscious. If, for example, a man really believes he cannot walk, the unconscious will not challenge that idea, even though the man is perfectly

137

capable of walking anytime he wishes. It is the conscious alone that makes such decisions.

LAW #4 **What the unconscious accepts as FACT, it seeks to express in the body of its owner.**

The unconscious reacts impersonally to information received from the conscious. It will carry out a DAMAGING idea as readily as a beneficial one. If a man really believes he is a dog, his unconscious will have him down on all fours, barking like a dog. If a person truly believes he is the victim of a certain illness, the unconscious will see that the symptoms of that illness are manifested in his body. Whatever is truly BELIEVED by the conscious mind, becomes the goal of the unconscious computer.

LAW #5 **The unconscious cannot distinguish between a "live" experience occurring outside the body and one projected onto the conscious screen by the man inside the body.**

The unconscious reads the pictures off the conscious screen without regard to where the scenes originate. If the EYES pick up a danger outside the body, the threatening scene will be flashed on the screen. The computer will react to that scene and prepare the body for an emergency. However, if the THINKER (God's image) should project that SAME SCENE (imagination) onto the screen and **believe it,** the computer will react the same. It has no way of knowing where that scene comes from, or whether it is false or real.

LAW #6 **The more deeply the unconscious is impacted or IMPRESSED with a fact, the FASTER it will try to carry it out.**

Ideas from the conscious impact the unconscious

according to the amount of EMOTION behind them. Emotion is like the amount of gunpowder behind a bullet. The greater the impact, the more urgently the computer reacts to the scene on the screen. This is why healings occur faster in an evangelist's meeting than one resulting from pastoral counseling. A child, for example, could go instantly deaf upon hearing her father shout obscenities at her mother for the first time. This would be her computer's way of solving the problem. I once believed a car was trying to run me down. The emotion of FEAR drove the idea of ESCAPE into my computer with such force that it marshalled my body forces and empowered me to leap a six foot fence.

LAW #7 **The unconscious always acts in accordance with CURRENT beliefs of the conscious mind.**

This law is demonstrated by the hypnotist who tells his hypnotized subject that he is no longer in a refrigerator, but now in a steam room. The person in the trance will stop shivering at once and begin to perspire. The new idea dominates the computer instantly. Therefore, if a person has an illness due to an OLD belief, it does NOT have to be ferreted out by a psychiatrist. He will get well when the old idea is replaced by a new one.

LAW #8 **The unconscious responds to the Christian's IMAGINATION, not to his WILL.**

A Christian may WILL to be healed, but such efforts are futile. He can WILL all he likes, but nothing will happen because the computer responds to pictures ONLY. It is when the conscious BELIEVES THE PICTURE on the screen, that the computer is given a new goal. The WILL of an individual is NOT a part of the material flowing into the unconscious. It is a part of the decision-making apparatus, not of one's thoughts. Therefore, the will does NOT go into the unconscious. When the will and the imagination are in conflict, the imagination always wins. This is why will-power is often futile in losing weight or breaking a habit. A man close to the edge of a cliff may WILL not to fall, but if he SEES HIMSELF falling, his own computer could give him a shove. This is called the "Law of Reversed Effort."

LAW #9 The law of belief does NOT refer to faith in the Lord, but the ability to believe what is pictured on the conscious screen.

When a sick person visualizes himself as fully healed—and BELIEVES what he sees—he is using the law of belief. The Law of belief operates in advance of the fact. Therefore the sick person must believe himself whole even while his body is still sick. Faith can do this. Faith can go where reason cannot follow. It can function in spite of evidence to the contrary. When a man exercises faith in advance of the fact, his computer orders his body to conform to the image appearing on the conscious screen. It is faith in God's laws that gives a man the ability to picture himself as healed even while his body is sick. The more confidence he has in Jesus, the more trust he can put in the Lord's healing laws.

LAW #10 No suggestion can be impressed on the unconscious of an individual AGAINST HIS WILL.

Even when a person is hypnotized it is not possible to program his computer without his cooperation. Before he enters the trance state, he must willingly place himself in the hypnotist's hands. By themselves, you see, suggestions have no power. They are effective only when BELIEVED by the subject. There is a sense in which the hypnotized person has already surrendered the critical and challenging powers of his conscious mind to the therapist. This is why he does NOT challenge the suggestion, even when told he is a dog. The only other way to minimize the critical powers of an individual is with the use of drugs. An exception to this law occurs when people are in great pain or a state of shock. This is why unnecessary conversation is forbidden in the operating room of a hospital.

● The Lord delights in hiding good things that we might have the joy of discovering them. Even as He is pleased to have us make discoveries in the field of science, so is He happy to have us come upon these mental laws and use them for His glory. With ten of these laws in hand, and, a working knowledge of our amazing computer, we're ready to see them at work in an exciting context—the healing meeting.

SO LET'S GO

We've just arrived at a healing meeting. We'll sit near the front. You are going to be in the healing line later on. You have a spinal disorder. It's painful. It's a chore to stand up straight. Tonight you've come expecting God to work in your body. Therefore, we will sit where we can join those going up on the platform to stand before the evangelist.

The evening gets off to a fine start. The song leader rouses the audience with stirring songs. There's a good mood in the place. An air of expectancy begins to swell. It increases as those previously healed give their testimonies. Things are keyed up as much as possible before the evangelist comes on. That's part of the process. Then the evangelist is introduced. He speaks. His message deals with the power of God. He assures his audience with calculated words. "I feel the presence of God here tonight," he shouts, "Don't you!" The crowd roars back the expected . . . "Amen!"

NOTE. In no way do I mean to devalue the healing evangelist or his meetings. It is not my place to pass judgment on God's servants. There are some sincere people in this work who seek to honor the Lord Jesus as much as I do. And, as you would expect, there are those who exploit the ignorance and gullibility of God's people. It is not within the scope of this book to evaluate the effectiveness of such meetings. Our sole reason for picturing such a meeting is to see our laws at work in an emotion-laden atmosphere.

With dramatic fervor, the evangelist stirs the crowd into believing that God is ready to move in healing power. And, of course, He is. It is BELIEVING it that is so vital to the healing meeting. When he feels the Word of God has done its work, the preacher closes his message and invites the healing line to form. Throughout the auditorium, people begin to pray. The excitement is high. The atmosphere is charged, electrified. People are on the edge of their seats at the thought of seeing miracles. The expectancy is so thick, you could cut it with a knife. Good.

TIME FOR HEALING

"All right," says the evangelist, "you may come now. The Lord is waiting to heal." The healing line starts to move. Your heart pounds as your turn approaches. You look up. There are about 10 people ahead of you. Each has his turn before the evangelist. He lays his hands on them and prays. You are close enough to hear their exclamations. "Praise God, I can hear now," says one. "Look, I can move my hand," says another. Praise rises to the Lord as different ones shout, "I can walk! I can hear!" You see it happen to them, why not you? Your faith mounts with each step. Finally it's your turn.

You feel the stare of a thousand eyes beyond the lights. It's a drama-packed moment. You look into the face of God's servant. It's wet with perspiration. He speaks first. "Well, dear friend, I see you have a problem with your back. Are you ready for God to heal you?" He knows you are, but he wants you to put your expectancy into words. It helps to crystallize it. "Do you think God has the power to heal you?" You assure him you do. Then comes the big question, "Are you ready to trust God to heal you tonight?" How you answer determines whether or not you walk off the platform with a straight back.

"As best I know how, I trust Him to heal me."

That's good enough for the evangelist. You feel his hands on your head. The touch is electrifying. Your heart is racing now. You barely hear the words as he prays. Then comes the critical moment. His grip on your head tightens for a second. His hands jerk a bit as he shouts, "In the name of Jesus—BE HEALED!" A sensation similar to an electric shock flashes through your body. There is a "SNAP." It was loud enough to hear. The evangelist heard it. "Straighten up, my brother. You are healed!"

Indeed you can straighten up. You can hardly believe it. There is no pain. You **are** healed!

Tears come easily as you walk off the platform in an erect position. It feels so good to be whole again. You are grateful to the Lord Jesus at this moment. There isn't anything you'd withhold from Him right now. However, that will pass quickly enough. The lasting power of gratitude is quite short. But for now, all you can think of is honoring Him with praise, and rightly so.

WHAT REALLY HAPPENED?

You were healed, genuinely healed. Was it because

God reached out to you in some special way? In your case you were healed (in the name of the Lord) by your OWN FAITH. Had the Lord Jesus been on the platform, instead of the evangelist, He would have said, "Go thy way, YOUR FAITH has made you whole" (Mk. 10:52). And you would have been perfectly sound that instant. Your own faith triggered the healing program God put in your computer.

> **NOTE.** I don't mean to imply this is the only way the Lord heals. That would be ridiculous. The New Testament records any number of COMMAND HEALINGS He performed solely with the WORD OF AUTHORITY. Outstanding is the raising of Lazarus. That was not faith healing, neither was it computer healing. Lazarus' body was dead. His brain had been decaying for four days when Jesus summoned it back to life with the **word of authority.** What's more He can delegate this authority to His servants. Peter, for example, was empowered to call the dead Dorcas back to life (Acts 9:36-43). Keep in mind the focus of this book is FAITH healing, so don't be bothered by the fact that I do not mention command healings. If you desire more information, turn to item #6 in the appendix where command and faith healings are treated in depth. My objective in this book is to share what I have learned about FAITH HEALING, not to explain all that happens in a healing meeting.

Did the evangelist's words have anything to do with your healing? Yes. He brought your faith to a climax. His words caused your faith to rise to the place where it was sufficient to trigger the computer into action. And that's not all. When he spoke, the IDEA (image) of being healed flooded your mind. Everything else was swept from your thinking as you SAW yourself being healed. The dominant thought in your head was, "I'm going to be healed!" Finally your faith rose to the place where you really believed it. Once you consciously believed you were going to be healed, your computer accepted

144

the picture on the screen **as an order.** The command to heal went into the unconscious AS FACT and the forces of your body were mobilized for the task.

But why did it occur so fast? What caused the spine to be healed with a "snap?" I think you could tell me what caused it. We've already seen two of the three basic signals that must be on the tape. What was the third? You're right—EMOTION! Preceding the moment of your healing was the tremendous buildup of the evening. It started with hope bubbling in your heart before you left your house for the meeting. The sights and sounds of the auditorium reinforced that hope as you sat in your seat. Then came the singing, the excited shouts, the testimonies, and the joyous hallelujahs. The evangelist compounded it when he declared the Lord was ready to heal.

> **NOTE.** See how all three elements needed to activate the computer were present? The healing IDEA was in your mind. It was there even before you left your house. By the time you stood before the evangelist, you SAW yourself healed. That picture was on the conscious screen. Then your FAITH was gradually brought to the place where you really **believed** you were going to be healed. That's what triggers the process. Then there was the third element, the huge emotional build up preceding the dramatic moment on stage. It was your intense EMOTION that sent the healing order slamming into the computer, putting things on an emergency basis. The greater the emotion, the faster the healing. You therefore invoked the healing formula. You SAW IT, you BELIEVED IT, and you FELT IT.

YOUR COMPUTER GOT THE COMMAND

Think back to your racing heart as you made your way across the platform. Were you emotional then? And how! Your being was supercharged with feeling. When

145

the evangelist gripped your head and said—"Be healed!"—that IDEA went crashing into your unconscious. In fact, it impacted the computer so hard, it became the DOMINANT TASK of your brain to heal your back. The snap you heard was real. Your spine was INSTANTLY put in place by the mighty forces of your own body. You doubt if such power is present in the human body? It is. There are far more powers in the human body than the average person realizes. We covered that in chapter five.

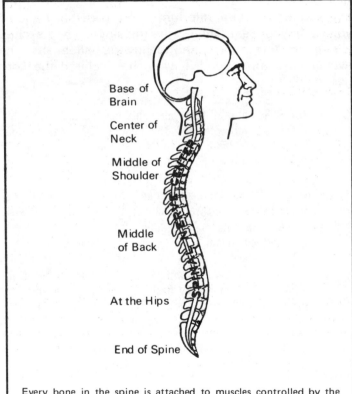

Base of
Brain

Center of
Neck

Middle of
Shoulder

Middle
of Back

At the Hips

End of Spine

Every bone in the spine is attached to muscles controlled by the autonomic nervous system. It is a simple matter for the computer to order those muscles to shift the bones into their proper place and order the body's repair system to repair any damaged parts.

In the course of researching the various methods of healing, one of our directors here at PC took a course in self-hypnosis. Now don't think we're kookie because we did that. We wanted to investigate every means at hand. In the class was a girl who was able to put herself into a light trance very easily. She had back trouble. She was able to give commands that went past the conscious discriminators into the computer. On numerous occasions our investigator actually watched this girl give the order and heard her back "snap" as the vertebra went into place. Technically we might not want to call that a healing, but it proves the computer can bring the necessary power to bear on the spine when ordered to do so. Enough, in fact, to move the vertebrae with a "snap."

THE GREATER THE EMOTION

Here's a bow and arrow. We're going to use them to picture the significance of emotion in healing. I hand you the bow. Then you fit the arrow in place. I point to the target. Then you draw the bow and let fly. It zings to the target—"impact!" The bow represents your conscious mind. The arrow is the IDEA that you are going to be healed. The pull on the string represents the amount of emotion present. The further back you draw it, the more emotion there is behind the idea. The target is your unconscious computer. The more pressure there is behind the idea, the greater its impact on the computer. The harder it impacts the computer, the faster the computer acts to carry out the idea.

We have described another law of healing: the more deeply the unconscious computer is IMPRESSED with an order, the faster it will try to carry it out. Since the computer is in charge of ALL the healing forces of the

147

body, it can heal in a flash if the urgency is there. Apparently the speed with which any healing takes place has to do with the force behind the order. Therefore, the more emotion we bring to the healing idea, the quicker the computer will do its job.

Emotion may also be pictured by a wrecking ball slamming into a wall. The greater the swing, the more force behind the ball. The ball is the idea. The wall is the computer. And the force behind the ball represents emotion. When a man believes an idea, he starts up the wrecking crane. When he has strong feelings in connection with the idea, he gives the ball a giant swing. The stronger his emotions, the greater the swing and harder it impacts the computer.

NOTE. The speed with which a person is healed depends on two things: (1) the amount of FAITH he can bring to the healing idea, (2) the amount of EMOTION accompanying the healing idea. In some circles, healing is sought by simply working up a great deal of emotion. It should be no surprise when I tell you such healings don't last. The other factors are missing. But then there are cases of dramatic healings with little emotion present. How come? The people have great faith. The prime ingredient, then, is faith—not emotion. It is FAITH that actually triggers the computer to act on the scene on the screen. But when a person's faith is not sufficient to bring an early response from the computer, emotion can stir the slumbering elements of his soul to awaken the needed faith.

● Any doctor who knows how to stir anticipation (belief) and excitement (emotion) in his patient, can dramatically affect his recovery. The physician who can get his patient to BELIEVE he is going to get well, and get a little EXCITED ABOUT it, will see astonishing results. Does it trouble you that I say ANY doctor? Remember, God's healing laws are NOT limited to Christians. The healing truths are for everyone. As with the laws of electricity and physics, the healing laws are here for man to discover and use.

THE LORD IS NOT LEFT OUT

It is the Lord Jesus Who makes healing exciting for the Christian. A new dimension is added to our fellowship with Christ when we find He is as interested in keeping our bodies well as we are. It was always the Lord's intention that His people should look to Him for healing. But what is important is seeing that FAITH IN JESUS makes possible strong faith in His HEALING LAWS. The more we trust the Lord, the more faith we can bring to the picture on the screen and thus trigger the computer.

NOTE. Longing for healing is NOT FAITH. Dreaming of being healed is not faith either. That is wishful thinking. Wishful thinking will NOT trigger the computer. To dream of a healthy body is one thing, to believe God will give

149

it to you is another. Dreams not backed by faith simply go into the unconscious as STORED material. They make no impression on the computer inasmuch as the essential signal (faith) is missing.

SPIRITUAL HEALING NEEDED TOO

Here's a girl eager to be healed. She too has come to the meeting wanting God to heal her. She has bronchial asthma. But she also has something else—bitter feelings toward her father. He abused her when she was young and she had never forgiven him. Even so her faith in the Lord is unflinching. She is ready to trust God to glorify Himself in her body.

When the evangelist gives the invitation for healing, she is one of the first in line. She confidently mounts the stairs to await her turn. When the preacher asks if she believes God is ready to heal her tonight, she shouts her assurance . . . "Yes! Yes! Yes!" There's no doubt but what she has the faith and expectancy for healing. Seconds later she is prayed for. She takes a deep breath and exclaims, "Praise the Lord, He has healed me!" The audience joins in her ecstatic praise of God. She has truly been healed—completely.

Three months go by. Signs of her asthma return. What's wrong? Did the evangelist make a mistake? Did the healing laws somehow fail? Was her faith inadequate? It was none of those things. The reason her sickness returned was because she didn't deal with the CAUSE of illness. Her trip to the platform did not get rid of her resentment toward her father. That's what caused her sickness in the first place. Consequently the healing began to fade and signs of her old illness returned.

NOTE. Observe that this girl had all the elements needed to trigger the healing process. Her faith climaxed as she stood before the evangelist. The HEALING IDEA went into the unconscious computer with sufficient force to produce instant healing. The healing was genuine. However, the healing did not cancel the terrible feelings lurking in her soul. She still had not forgiven her father. That bitterness continued to do its dirty work even though the computer took care of her asthma. It simply obeyed the DOMINANT IDEA because it had so much force behind it. Subtlely, however, the old evil idea continued to linger. As the healing began to be taken for granted, her resentment resumed the dominant place in her thought-life. Since the computer responds to CURRENT ideas and beliefs, her health yielded and the old symptoms returned.

● Healings do not automatically REMOVE the causes of illness. Evangelists are aware of this. That's why some of them challenge their prospects to get right with God BEFORE they join the healing line. It doesn't help an evangelist's reputation to have a man throw away his crutches only to pick them up again six months later. Sometimes people can be prodded to bring out unconfessed sins (removing the guilts) or forgive someone before they join the healing line. When that is the case, the healing is lasting.

NOTE. The healing meeting, because it is an emotion packed setting, allows us to see the laws do their work in a hurry. That's why I chose the healing meeting over a clinical setting. Also, many readers will have attended one or more of these meetings and can easily check for the Holy Spirit's witness as to the validity of the laws. However, I must point out that we cannot explain ALL healings on the basis of these laws. There are other laws which can be invoked by faith besides these, some of which undoubtedly have to do with supernatural healings. I can't deal with those simply because I do not know them. But for those that I do know, the healing meeting is an ideal place to see them at work.

This book offers a plan for SELF-HEALING. That is, you will be using God's laws for the healing of your own body. The book does NOT offer a plan for the healing of others, except as you show them how to use their own computers. Even though we call it self-healing, it is the Lord who heals. We use the Laws, but it is the Lord Jesus Who sees that they do their work in our bodies. Now we're ready to work with Him in using the laws. That's next.

● **REVIEW AND REMEMBER**

1. There are three types of healing: automatic, faith and command. Doctors rely on automatic healing. They repair the body and wait for the natural process to finish the job. Automatic healing is also the type people rely on when they get a cold. They give themselves plenty of liquids and rest and wait for the body to heal itself. Faith healing is the type featured in this book. In a way, it is a SPEED UP of the natural process. By faith, the computer is ordered to marshall the body forces and deal with the illness. This book does not deal with command healings.

2. Faith healing occurs when the computer is given the healed image as a new goal. The THINKER projects the healed image onto the conscious screen and believes what he sees. The more emotion present, the faster the healing will take place.

3. A dramatic use of faith healing occurs in the healing meeting. The nature of these meetings provides the THREE ELEMENTS needed to trigger the computer into action:

a. When the victim sees others healed before his eyes, he is able to VISUALIZE himself as healed. His imagination is aided by the sight of others made whole.

b. Exciting testimonies and spirited preaching cause him to rise in faith to the place where he BELIEVES he is going to be healed. He then believes what he sees on the conscious screen.

c. The emotionally charged atmosphere of the healing meeting stirs his feelings. EMOTIONAL PRESSURE builds behind the healing idea. That idea slams into his unconscious on the evangelist's command. It impacts the computer with such force that the healing is carried out on an emergency basis.

4. The healing meeting does not deal with the CAUSE of an illness except as sick ones get right with God before their healing takes place. When the cause is NOT removed before healing, the illness can be expected to return. This is because the destructive thoughts, which generated the sickness in the first place, again dominate in the victim's mind.

5. While FAITH is the principle element needed to trigger the computer, we distinguish between faith in the Lord AND faith in His healing program. This is NOT a minor distinction. It is one which causes confusion if not understood. There are many who deeply believe in the Lord who are NOT healed by their faith. At the same time, there are people who do NOT believe in the Lord, who are healed by faith in His laws. See it like this:

a. Faith in the Person of Jesus brings salvation.

b. Faith in His healing laws brings healing.

6. God has provided a remedy for sin—**the cross.** He has also provided a remedy for sickness and disease—the **healing laws.** The healing laws are meant to be applied AFTER a man has dealt with the sin in his life. Until the sin causing the illness is cared for, it is useless to seek healing. This is why the cults have difficult times with their healings. They don't have any real way to deal

with sin. God deals with it by giving us a new nature. The unsaved don't have it.

a. Even though this book is on healing, sickness and suffering play a vital role in the plan of God. He USES them to discipline and refine His people. It would ruin the human experiment if God banned suffering. Let something go wrong in the Christian's body, and God has his full attention. The sickness should result in a spiritual checkup.

b. God does not want people sick. Yet He would rather have them PHYSICALLY SICK than SPIRITUALLY SICK. Why? One is temporary, the other eternal. Physical health lasts but 70-80 years, whereas spiritual health is an eternal matter. Spiritual health must therefore have the priority over physical health. This is why God uses sickness to get Christians to check on their spiritual condition.

c. Once physical suffering has accomplished its purpose, God does NOT want a person to remain ill. He WANTS His people well. That's why He established the healing laws. God is delighted to have His people use the healing laws to recover from a disease as soon as the spiritual problem (destructive thought-life) causing their illness has been cared for.

It's time for you to apply what you have learned. You have the healing laws. Now get ready to watch the Lord back those laws as you put them to work in your own body. That's next.

This book was written for Christians, those who have RECEIVED Christ as their personal Savior. However it is possible that non-christians will read these lines thinking to use the healing technique about to be presented in the next chapter. While it is true that anyone can use these laws for healing, there is a caution to be observed:

THE HEALING MAY NOT LAST.

Why? The non-Christian cannot cooperate with those laws in the same way the Christian can. The human nature inherited from his parents will keep him from it. Since he has but that one nature, it is natural for the non-Christian to be jealous, vengeful, bitter, critical and anxious without limit. It is guaranteed that he will indulge in some destructive emotion and lose his healing—in time.

The only way to avoid the destructive power of that human nature is to become a partaker of the divine nature. A person does that by opening his heart to Jesus and receiving Him as Savior. When Christ comes into a person's life, he receives the power to live above evil—if he wants to. There is no damaging emotion which can block the healing of a Christian, if he truly sets his heart on a godly life. Receiving the Lord is as simple as opening the door of your home.

Get alone some place where you can pray. Jesus will hear you. Speak out to Him like this:

"Dear Lord, it makes sense that spiritual health is the basis of physical health. Therefore I ask You to come into my heart and heal me spiritually. If You are willing to save me from my sins, I here and now open the door and invite You into my life. I now put my trust in You as my personal Savior. Amen."

If you can do that, and mean it, Jesus will come in—INSTANTLY! You'll feel the peace He gives. That in itself can start much healing. After that, you can enjoy His presence and power and use the healing techniques with confidence. You'll find those old destructive emotions passing away as you seek to become more like the One Who shares your life with you. That's what guarantees your healing will last. But without Christ, there is no such guarantee. Why don't you stop right here and take care of this matter. Then as you read the next chapter which presents the actual technique, you'll have the confidence you need to make the plan work in your life.

UNTIL A PERSON RECEIVES CHRIST IT IS EASIER TO BELIEVE IN SICKNESS THAN IT IS TO BELIEVE IN GOD'S HEALING LAWS.

Chapter Eight

USING THE LAWS YOURSELF

(The Healing Plan)

You have the formula:

SEE IT—BELIEVE IT—FEEL IT.

Now it's time to put it to work. The technique for triggering the computer consists of an exercise done three times a day: morning, noon, and night. 15 minutes are devoted to the exercise each time. Here is the exercise:

I. GET YOURSELF COMPLETELY RELAXED

The technique works best if you can get yourself into a sleepy, drowsy state. The reason for doing the exercise while relaxed, is because the critical, challenging powers of the conscious mind are less active then. That is, you are not as apt to get a lot of static from your conscious mind when you set yourself to believe the scenes on the screen. When we want to believe something contrary to fact, our conscious mind is ready to protest. The protests are diminished in the relaxed state.

> **NOTE.** The opposite of relaxation is tension. People do not realize how tense they can become in the course of a day. Some have a hard time "unwinding" when they go to bed at night. They start off fine in the morning, but accumulate considerable tension before the day is over. We forget that we live in animal bodies. Just as other animals must stay alert and cautious during the day to survive, so do our animals. The creature we use for our earth-suit is INSTINCTIVELY TENSE during the wakeful hours. It is a built-in characteristic. Watch a bird

nervously turn its head this way and that before it bobs for a drink of water. That's instinct. Our bodies are beasts of the field. The survival instinct functions in them too. Consequently tension mounts as a matter of course in the daily business of staying alive.

Here's a student taking an exam. He's uptight. He stares at the questions he must answer. But the answers don't come. Why? Tension is defeating when a person wants to use his imagination. The student finds his mind goes blank. That's because his imagination is NUMBED by tension. So step one in our exercise has to do with bringing our physical body under control. When we relax, we turn our attention from things outside us, to things INSIDE.

Doctors tell us that relaxation is nature's tranquilizer. When we relax, we ease off our natural defensiveness. Our external defense system shuts down. The watchful, conscious powers subside. Then the imagination can go to work. It's like that when we daydream.

So make yourself comfortable. The best time is just after you retire. It's easier then and more natural to enter into a drowsy state. Your body is ready for it. That helps. It feels good to close your eyes and let your head sink into a soft pillow. Let your arms go limp at your side. Take a deep breath. Hold it for a second. Then slowly exhale. Do this a few times.

NOTE. Once you are in a drowsy state, conscious interference is reduced to a minimum. That's what you want. Your imagination cannot do its job as long as the conscious mind is trying to protect you from threat. It will be critical of every scene you put on the screen unless you are relaxed and sleepy. Why? What you are projecting on the screen does not jibe with external evidence. You are picturing something contrary to fact. But as you become sleepier, the conscious stops inspecting every idea in your mind.

Finally you will be able to get a good picture on the screen. Your imagination will be free. As fewer criticisms come from your conscious mind, you will be able to visualize yourself as healed with a clear, sharp picture.

Plop in an easy chair. If you've been working, it will feel good to relax. Let yourself become drowsy. No forcing is needed. Very soon your imagination will start to work. Then you can use it.

II. TALK TO THE LORD

As soon as your body relaxes, go into the "secret place." You know where I mean, that little room in your imagination where you meet Jesus. Maybe you've never thought much about it, but such a room exists (Psa. 91:1). I want you to become conscious of it from now on. It is going to be the WORKROOM of faith.

NOTE. I have built a little room in my mind all fixed up to suit myself. It's imaginery, of course, but that's no reason for taking it for granted. I've used items from my home, plus things I've seen here and there and dolled it up to provide a cozy "secret place." You can fix your room to suit yourself. Mine is done in a New England motif with a brick fireplace, brass lamps and maple furnishings. It has autumn colors. Over the fireplace is a painting of the Lord my daughter has done for me. When I go into this room and shut the door, all of my anxieties and pressures are left outside. It's a place of absolute peace. I move across the room and sink into my favorite chair. I close my eyes. At once the room and all of its furnishings fade away and I am aware of nothing but the presence of Jesus. The person of the Lord fills my mind. Soon I am speaking to Him.

Take a little time. Furnish your "secret place" to suit yourself. You might as well, you're going to spend hours in it. Every Christian should spend time with Jesus. So why not have a permanent place to enjoy each other? It's a great thing to feel AT HOME in the presence of the Lord. The fact that the meeting occurs in your imagination doesn't make it any less real. Everything we do in this life takes place in our minds first. That's where things are REALLY done. Our lives are LIVED in our minds, not some physical abode. There is nothing artificial about this kind of fellowship with Jesus. He is the most solid fact of our lives.

● Do you have a prayer list? I mean, is it your custom to go through a short prayer list before you fall asleep? I do. I usually have a few things I want to say to the Lord before I drop off. There are times when I am so sleepy, I only manage to say, "Good night, Lord." Then I am gone. But I'm not that tired very often. I usually spend a few minutes thanking the Lord for what He's done for me that day. That helps me to relax. After I've given my thanks, I'm quite relaxed, ready to talk about my healing.

NOTE. If you are one who falls asleep too quickly, then save your prayer list for last. Talk to the Lord about your healing first. Let the need to give thanks or make requests help you remain awake. You can train yourself to stay awake until you have finished that prayer list. Again, don't feel this is in any way UNREAL. It is not. When God asks us to worship Him in SPIRIT and in truth, this is precisely what He means. This is the TRUE sanctuary. It is spirit. You must worship God in TRUTH here, for your thought-life is bare before Him. The imagination is the sanctuary of the soul, the only true meeting place for us and God as long as we live in these bodies. A church building is NOT the house of God. You are. (I Cor. 6:19).

● A good way to start talking to Jesus about healing is with an affirmation. Make it something like this:

"Lord Jesus, I thank you for your healing presence in my life, and for acquainting me with the healing program. I know you want me well. You have established laws for my healing and health. I praise you Lord Jesus that those laws are at work in me this very instant. Even as I talk to you, I sense your power rebuilding my body according to the law of health in my computer. By faith, O Lord, I am using my imagination to see myself as healed. As far as I can determine, BELIEVING what I see on that screen is the best way to exercise faith in the healing program."

Another affirmation could go like this:

"Lord Jesus, I thank you that right now your power is flowing through my body healing every tissue and organ of my body. According to your laws the creative power of my blood stream is so great that I get a new body every eleven months. There is no way for an organ to remain diseased in the face of all this power if it is your will for me to be healed. And I am satisfied that you want me well. Therefore, I trust You Lord to teach

161

me how to work with the computer to overrule the destructive program that has obviously gotten into it."

The exact words are not important, but affirming what we believe about the Lord's working in us is. Being aware of the Lord's **presence, power,** and **program** is no light thing. The best way to fix that truth in our minds is to affirm it to Him again and again. The practice is a basis for both fellowship and praise. After all, the affirmation is itself an expression of faith in Him.

You can't fool Jesus. He knows our thoughts and the intentions of our hearts. When we affirm that we believe in His healing program, we put our faith on the line. No one should make such an affirmation unless he is ready to trust the Lord. It amounts to a commitment. Our faith grows each time we affirm our confidence in His program.

III. DESCRIBE THE HEALING SCENES

Aware that affirmations are simply expressions of confidence in the Lord's healing program, make your affirmation to the Lord. After that, get ready to flash some scenes on the conscious screen and describe them to Him. Remember—the computer works from pictures. They tell the computer what to do. Even as you SEE the scenes, keep talking to Jesus. Describe them to Him. That's how you work WITH the Lord.

The steady dripping of water wears away the stone. That same principle can be used for healing. The persistent visualization of a healed body (repetition) can accomplish the desired result when no emotion is present.

163

Here are four scenes that can be effective:

Scene one: First of all try to picture the organ itself in perfect condition. If you don't know what it looks like, go to a library and look it up in a medical book. Fix in your mind a rough sketch of what the organ looks like in the original state and have it ready to flash on the screen for your first scene.

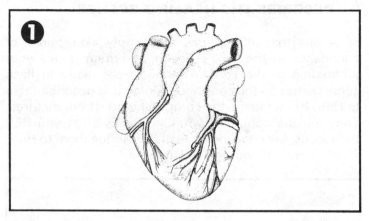

Scene two: See yourself using that organ or limb after it has been restored to perfect health. If you are crippled with arthritis, for example, see yourself doing all sorts of things you have been denied because of the affliction.

Scene three: Make a trip to the doctor. Picture the surprise on his face when he discovers the healing. Be sure to go through all the details of undressing and dressing if that is called for.

Scene four: See yourself before a Christian audience telling your brethren how the Lord has been gracious to teach you His healing laws. Tell how you used them for the restoration of your body. Picture the praise going to Jesus as different ones rejoice in your testimony.

NOTE. Even though we are using laws for the healing of our bodies, the Lord Jesus is the Healer. It is He Who heals. The Laws are no better than the Person behind them. They work because He is faithful to see that they do. Like the evangelist who preaches God's Word, we are Jesus' AGENTS to administer His laws to our own body. He must get the credit. We do almost nothing in the process. The one important thing we do is BELIEVE. It is the Lord Who does the work. Even though unsaved people refuse to credit Him, we must not. Our healing must bring all the honor to Christ we can possibly give Him, **even in our own minds!**

LET ME DEMONSTRATE

First I'll start with an affirmation I am using in connection with my eyes. The optometrist says I have irregular vision. There is nothing wrong with the eyes themselves. This disorder has to do with the large muscles which move the eyeballs. Since those muscles are controlled by the computer, I am satisfied they can be corrected by the computer. It is now a matter of reprogramming the computer for perfect vision.

> **NOTE.** Apparently my unconscious selected my eyes as the target for some destructive emotions. I do not know what those emotions are. However I am making headway in disciplining my thought-life and eliminating some suspicious emotions. I have started to work with the Lord for programming the computer and I am happy with the progress WE are making so far. The computer is getting the message.

Here's the affirmation:-

"Lord Jesus, thank You for this body. Since I have dedicated it to You, it is as much Yours as it is mine. Thank You for the healing power built into it. You put it there. Thank You for the healing program built into the computer.

166

The computer made my eyes in the first place, so it knows how to fix them. I have asked You to heal my eyes and I now affirm that You ARE. I praise You for the privilege of working together to reprogram the computer for perfect eyesight. Thank You Jesus."

Without interruption I go right into the four scenes:

Scene one: "And now dear Lord I can see the muscles of my eyes. How wonderfully you have made them. I see them working in perfect unison. There is not a speck of disharmony, nothing but perfect coordination. The focus and vision are perfect."

Scene two: "I am reaching for the telephone book. It falls open to columns of names. My eyes go down the column. Wonderful! I find I can read each one with no effort. Every name and address stands out in bold relief. It feels good to be able to read like this again. Thank you, Lord."

Scene three: "I see myself in the doctor's office. I'm sitting in the lounge looking through a magazine. Here comes the nurse. It's my turn. The doctor eases me into the examination chair. I won't say anything. I'll let him discover the miracle for himself. I feel the cold machine against my forehead. The dial clicks as he tries the different settings. He moves the machine away. His hand is holding his chin. He stands there perplexed. I'm excited inside. I know what's happened."

"I think we'd better check that again," he says, "there's something strange here." He does. Then he says, "I don't know what to say. Either we have a miracle on our hands, or else my machine has gone crazy. Your eyes check out perfectly." Now it's my turn. "Doctor, would

167

you like to know WHY my eyes are perfect now? It is because the Lord Jesus has healed them. He has shown me how to work with His laws. What you see today is His faithfulness to me!"

Scene four: "And now dear Lord, I see myself on the platform of our church. I am behind the pulpit looking upon a sea of faces waiting to hear what I have to say. 'Brethren, some months ago I stood here before you wearing glasses. Without them, you all looked fuzzy to me. But today I am not wearing any and you are all in focus. The Lord Jesus has healed my eyes completely. He has taught me some natural laws that are available to us all. I used them and now I am healed. Praise the Lord!' "

"The audience liked my testimony, Lord, for now I see myself surrounded by excited people all wanting to know more about the way You heal us through Your laws. It's a thrill for me to tell them."

● As I go through those scenes, I describe to the Lord the action as it occurs on the conscious screen. As far as my unconscious is concerned, it is a genuine experience. Those things are really happening—in my imagination. Remember, the unconscious cannot distinguish between a "live" experience and one that is imagined. All I have to do is BELIEVE what I see. If I do, the computer will accept it as FACT and act accordingly.

NOTE. The above dialogue is brief to save space. I spend much more time on each scene than appears here. For example, I would describe to the Lord the nurse's desk and what was on it. And I would go into great detail as to what was in the doctor's examination room. Why? The more detail we put into the scenes, the more believable they are. The scenes, of course, are based on actual visits.

> The mind is more inclined to accept new ideas when mingled with that which is familiar and already accepted as true.

I like doing the exercise when I go to bed. But not all Christians can do the scenes then. They fall asleep too quickly. They work hard and their bodies are tired. They drop off as soon as their heads hit the pillow. When should they do it? Obviously they will have to do it earlier in the evening—perhaps in an easy chair. They will probably get drowsy fast, even then. But they are more apt to have a ''limbo span,'' for doing the scenes, than had they gone to bed.

● In the morning when I awaken, I assume I have spent the night in the Lord's presence. As I find myself waking up, I greet the Lord. First I thank Him for the night's rest. Then, before I am thoroughly awake, I make my affirmation and go through the four scenes with Him. After that, we get up and go to work together.

BE SYSTEMATIC

You've seen how I do it. Now you know what to do. Be systematic. Plan on doing the exercise in the secret place three times a day:

● In the morning before you get out of bed.
● At your noon break.
● In the evening as you retire.

> HINT. A housewife should find the noon exercise most effective. Do you have a nice big easy chair? Stretch out in that chair and make yourself comfortable. Relax your body. Then let your mind go to the secret place. Not only will you have the joy of doing the exercises with the Lord, you will feel refreshed. Now the husband might have difficulty finding a place to relax at work. If your

169

car is not parked too far away, the back seat would be fine. 15 minutes is all the time you need. Maybe you can find a spot atop some crates if you work in a warehouse, or in the employees lounge if you are in an office building. Noises could bother you at first. But as you learn to SHUT THE DOOR when you enter the secret place, you'll find the outside environment fading and Jesus' presence increasingly real. In time, you will be able to do the exercises anyplace.

You can see how difficult it is to bring much EMOTION to the exercise. Yes, it is exciting at first, and enjoyable. But if we had to depend on the emotions generated in our imaginations, the computer would never go into action. So what do we use instead of emotion? Repetition. This is why we must be systematic. It takes self-discipline to stay with it. Yet if you really want that healing, you'll do what you have to. So get the morning-noon-and-night habit.

CAUTION. Don't start the program unless you are ready to be faithful to it. There is a risk. Sometimes people start and then get careless and slack off the exercises. Then they become discouraged. Discouragement is a powerful emotion. It can turn around and reinforce the illness, so that you get worse instead of better. We are working with fixed laws. Like any of God's laws, the healing laws are impersonal. If we work with them, they bless us. If we trifle with them, they can hurt us. So if you want healing, you must respect God's laws. The only way to avoid trifling is to take the healing program seriously and be faithful with the exercises.

If you are faithful in the exercises, you should see some encouraging signs in your body within three months. For some it could be less, a lot less. Especially those who are already used to trusting Jesus for big things. Please take it to heart when I tell you that . . .

DISCIPLINE IS THE KEY TO SUCCESS.

NOTE. It is possible that your illness may become worse before your technique is perfected. If worsening symptoms bother you, by all means see your doctor. There is no conflict between this approach and good medical practice. If your doctor warns that immediate surgery is needed, let him operate. If there is no emergency, then see if you have the faith to be healed by using the laws. If your doctor says your case is hopeless, then your only hope is the faith method. If you can bring yourself to the place where you are once healed by faith, you'll never be the same again. It definitely is "higher ground."

If you will faithfully do the exercises morning, noon, and night, your computer will get the message and go to work. How long before healing finally comes depends on two things: (1) how quickly you can bring yourself to BELIEVE the scenes on the screen, (2) how faithfully you DISCIPLINE yourself to do the exercises. Should you find some way to bring emotion to the scenes, healing will come faster. For the most part, you will have to depend on repetition. That means self-discipline. We have to keep constant pressure on the computer.

PERSISTENCE PAYS. While I have said healing can come in three months, don't depend on that as a hard and fast rule. No two of us are alike. We all discipline ourselves differently. Faith can rise slowly in one person, fast in another. For some, it might take as long as two or three years before the healing is complete. I am thinking of a man who worked with this technique for three months and saw only the tiniest improvement. He had crippling arthritis. It was three years before he could say, "The Lord healed me!" So don't give up. Stay with it, even if it takes years. Your healing will come. You have nothing to lose but your illness.

MY OWN HEALING

 It's time to tell you how God used this technique to heal my body.

I hand you my major medical insurance policy. Look at the date. It was issued in 1961. There's an exclusion attached which reads, "This policy does not cover any prostate gland impairment on the applicant." Yes, that was my problem—chronic prostatitis and enlargement of the gland. As most men know, this is a common ailment within our male population.

For years it bothered me only slightly. Then in the last couple of years it caused a lot of difficulty. I won't mention the details, they're fairly well known. You are aware that something is seriously wrong when it is extremely painful to go to the bathroom. My doctor was reluctant to operate. He wanted to hold off as long as possible. I'm glad he did. It gave me time to go to the Lord about it. As I mentioned in the introduction, this was how He led me to investigate faith healing.

First of all I went to God's Word, then to a mountain of written material. The laws listed in the last chapter emerged. Using them three times a day was most natural for me, so I made that a basis of fellowship with the Lord. I'd go into the secret place and together we'd work on the problem. At first I had difficulty believing the scenes on the screen, but I described them to Him anyway. In time I gained the solid conviction those laws just had to work. I pictured the prostate in perfect condition and thanked God for the healing. The more I did this, the more convinced I was that the healing was as good as done.

Within the first two weeks I had signs of a change. It was very slight. Some weeks later the improvement was really noticeable and I began to get excited. When three months had passed—THE PAIN WAS GONE! By the end of the 5th month the urinary stream was better than it had been in 15 years! When I saw my doctor for the next checkup, six months later, he was happy to tell me my prostate was in perfect condition—and

172

almost normal in size. There was no inflammation of any kind. Praise the Lord!

● You will understand my excitement over this healing when I tell you there is NO KNOWN treatment for it. Medical science as yet doesn't know what causes it. They're trying all sorts of things, but nothing has been successful so far. As of now, the best medical advice is frequent checkups so that any sign of cancer can be detected as early as possible and surgery performed.

I am sold on the effectiveness of God's healing laws and His faithfulness to back them. I am convinced there is healing for any believer who will TRUST God to heal his body through them. I am further convinced that the technique presented in this chapter puts those laws to work in a way that brings the most glory and honor to our precious Lord Jesus.

God's laws are fully dependable.

The experience of being healed is a lot like the discovery of the planet Neptune. Until 1846 the planet Uranus was regarded as the outermost planet. But there were certain movements about Uranus that led astronomers to suspect another planet, hitherto undiscovered, was having an effect on it. They set to work with their theories and mathmatics and came up with a place on their charts where they agreed this planet, if indeed there was one, had to be. Their calculations convinced them it was there, but when they scanned the heavens with their telescopes, the planet was not to be found.

Finally, after midnight on the morning of September 14, 1846, a student astronomer turned his telescope to the designated place and waited. Before long the great planet Neptune swam into view. The theories on which the astronomers had based their faith all proved to be true. The planet was exactly where they said it would be even before they saw it. It was their faith in the laws of the universe, and the dependability of those laws, that led to the discovery of this great planet.

● The story of the discovery of this heavenly body is akin to the healing of the Christian's body through these laws. The astronomers put their faith in the laws of the universe. That faith was rewarded when the planet Neptune appeared. Similarly, you can fix your faith in God's healing laws. Get that picture on the screen of your mind—BELIEVE IT—and wait. In time the healing will come to pass as surely as that great planet came into view. The laws of God are dependable. We can trust in them. When we do, we honor our Lord Who established them and He will not let us suffer disappointment. But you say it's hard to trust in laws—hard to BELIEVE in advance. Well, there's help for that, as we shall see—next.

● REVIEW AND REMEMBER

1. The formula for programming the unconscious computer is SEE IT—BELIEVE IT—FEEL IT (repetition). A person who disciplines himself in this program morning, noon, and night, could see results within three months. The speed with which healing occurs depends on how quickly a person can bring himself to believe the scenes on the conscious screen. That's why faithfulness with the exercises is so important.

2. Our program for self-healing does not enjoy the thunderous emotion of a healing meeting. However, repetition can accomplish the same thing. Repetition keeps constant pressure on the computer. The unconscious is finally impressed to the place where it must act. Action is guaranteed because we are working with FIXED LAWS. They must do the job when the conditions are met.

3. The four steps for installing the self-healing program are:

a. **RELAXING** to get the conscious mind in a drowsy, unguarded state.

b. **RETIRING** in one's imagination to the secret place to be in the presence of the Lord.

c. **SPEAKING** to the Lord concerning His presence, power, and program, affirming that healing is going on in your body that very moment.

d. **DESCRIBING** to the Lord scenes in your imagination which evidence your faith in His healing laws:

1. Seeing the organ (or whatever part is afflicted) as completely healed and in a perfect state—and thanking Him for it.

2. Seeing yourself doing those things which you would normally do if you did not have the affliction. That is, carrying on as though the illness did not exist.

3. Seeing yourself in the doctor's office, rejoicing in his reaction when he discovers your healing.

4. Seeing yourself standing before a Christian audience testifying to the healing received from the Lord. In your imagination you are clearly telling the people how you served as God's agent to your own body. That is, you administered His laws as He showed you how to use them for healing. Picture the glory coming to the Lord Jesus as you declare Him the only true Healer.

4. Train yourself to do the exercises daily. Remember: self-discipline is the key to success. As you become systematic in carrying out the steps each day, your faith will rise steadily. The more faithful you are, the quicker your

faith will reach the required level for triggering the computer.

5. Keep your mind off the illness. If your symptoms worsen, Satan will have an easy time getting you to dwell on your affliction—if you let him. He will inspire dreadful scenes in your imagination. Order him away. Those frightening scenes can stir destructive emotions which will cause the computer to reinforce your illness. This will perpetuate your affliction or worsen it. Because God's laws are impersonal, Satan can use them to hurt you.

6. Consider how the planet Neptune was discovered by faith. The astronomers knew, on the basis of God's laws, that it had to be there even though they couldn't see it. It was an act of faith for them to fix their telescopes on the spot where they believed it had to be. Their faith was rewarded when it finally came into view. Similarly, we put our trust in God's healing laws and fix our faith in the scene on the screen. What we see there simply has to come to pass in time. If we will trust in God's laws as definitely as did the astronomers, it will come to pass. But that's where we need help. So coming next is—**faith for healing.**

Chapter Nine

FAITH FOR HEALING

Let's say you and I have gone to visit some friends in an old Arizona mining town. We're gathered in the living room of our friend's antiquated home. You are sitting across from me. You're not paying too much attention to what I'm doing, but you hear me very well when I say . . .

"Don't move. There's a coiled rattlesnake under your chair!"

What happens next? It all depends on whether you think I am serious or it's a joke. If you BELIEVE me, all kinds of things will happen in your body. Your computer will pick up the IMAGE of a coiled rattler ready to plunge its fangs into your leg. The Adrenalin will really flow as your body gears itself for the emergency.

But if you DON'T BELIEVE me, nothing will happen. Your body will experience no reaction and you'll laugh it off as a joke. See—what happens in your body depends entirely on **what you believe.** And remember: my remark about the snake was just an IDEA. You didn't actually see it. I think we can agree that **what we believe** has a fantastic effect on our bodies. This is the KEY to healing.

● While you have learned everything you need to know about the healing laws and how to use them, the hardest part of this plan is bringing yourself to the place where you actually BELIEVE the scene on the screen. But you MUST, if healing is to occur. Therefore I have included this chapter to help you rise to the needed faith.

THREE THINGS TO KNOW
ABOUT FAITH

1. **Faith is a human quality.**

God designed man with the capacity to believe what he cannot see. While there are different DEGREES of faith, there are **not** different KINDS. You hear of blind faith, but that is the SAME faith operating apart from any reasons to justify it other than God's Word. Then there is faith based on **evidence** such as answers to prayer. Even so, it is ALL HUMAN. God does NOT open our heads and pour faith into us. Faith is human response to divine revelation.

Directed toward Jesus, human faith brings salvation. It's human faith based on the Word of God. That same faith placed in His healing laws, brings healing. There is not a nickel's worth of difference between the trust a man exhibits when he drops a letter in the mail box and that which he places in Christ for salvation. It's what we DO with our faith that counts. Faith is faith. Therefore it is up to us to DEVELOP our faith. God has made us capable of it. That's a gift. But it is our task to bring our faith to the place where it will activate the laws of God.

2. **Faith always operates in advance.**

It is easy to place your confidence in something you can see or something that has already happened, but that is NOT faith. Confidence can only be called faith when the desired result is not yet in sight. The man who drops his letter in a mailbox must TRUST the postal service to get it to its destination. That is an act of faith because the thing he hopes for has yet to be achieved. The Bible defines faith as the "substance of things hoped for, the evidence of things not seen" (Heb. 11:1). When a man ACTS in faith, his action is the substance of his faith. When he cannot express it in a physical act (as in the case of healing), his inner convictions become the evidence.

The Christian who is ready to exercise faith in God's healing laws must first SEE himself as healed, even though the sickness is still in his body. When he projects the healed image onto the conscious screen and BELIEVES WHAT HE SEES, he is exercising faith. Why? He has this confidence IN ADVANCE of the fact. Until he can believe what he sees on that screen, he is **not** exercising faith.

3. **Faith for healing is expressed in the imagination.**

When the Christian projects the healed image on the conscious screen and does NOT believe what he sees, he is indulging in wishful thinking. That certainly is not faith. The computer will not accept the image as a command or new goal. But if he truly BELIEVES what he sees on that screen, the computer will act on the picture. Believing that the picture **is true** is the needed act of faith. His believing becomes the "substance" of his faith in the healing laws. There is no way to express faith in God's healing laws apart from seeing yourself as healed. The only place that can be done is in the imagination.

FAITH TRIGGERS DIVINE LAWS

Remember when Jesus' disciples were on the sea of Galilee working against a fierce storm? They saw Jesus approaching—**walking on the water.** At first they were afraid, but He calmed their fears. "It is I," He said, "be not afraid." Then Peter spoke up, "Lord, if it really is You, command me to come to You on the water." Then it was that Jesus said, "Come."

Peter climbed out of the boat. That took faith. He

179

actually walked on the water as he made his way to Jesus. But then he shifted his eyes to the waves and his faith was replaced with fear. You see, you cannot trust and fear at the same time. It must be one or the other. So he began to sink. He cried out to the Lord Who took his hand and saved him. ''O ye of little FAITH,'' said Jesus, ''why did you doubt?'' (Matt. 14:31). We wouldn't have known that doubt moved in, had not Jesus said so.

> **NOTE.** Peter walked on the water. And he did it by faith. Don't miss that. True, he asked the Lord to bid him come. But what happened depended on Peter's faith, NOT the Lord's command. Can we be sure? Indeed. Had it depended on Jesus, Peter would not have sunk. As it was, his faith waned. Only then did he begin to sink. As long as his confidence was in Jesus' word, the command of the Lord was effective. But the moment he considered his danger, his faith evaporated and Jesus' command was nullified.

What laws were invoked by Peter's faith? I haven't the slightest idea. Obviously they were laws as yet unknown to us. But whatever they were, Peter's faith made it possible for him to do what seemed impossible. So it is with the healing laws. We do know them. And they too function in the face of the impossible. If a man can believe that he is healed—even though what he believes is contrary to the facts—he will invoke laws which will heal his body. This is the exciting thing about faith. This is what makes healing such an adventure in Christ.

THE BASIS FOR FAITH IN HEALING

The Bible offers a sound basis for faith in this approach to healing. In fact, it is very easy to develop a case for faith healing from the Scriptures. But others have done that so well, it is not necessary for me to go over established territory. I do, however, want to make three scriptural observations which will fortify your faith in the techniques I've set forth in this book.

1. **The case of Abraham**

Abraham was asked to believe something that was CONTRARY to nature.

When Abraham was around ninety years old, and his body could no longer produce any male seed, God promised him a son. Sarah, his wife, who was ten years younger than he, had already gone through the change of life and was incapable of bearing children. Yet God held out this promise to Abraham. All the old patriarch had to do was believe God. In spite of the circumstances which said such a thing was IMPOSSIBLE, Abraham BELIEVED GOD. Isaac was born some 14 years later. (Gen. 15:6; 17:1; 21:5).

As the "father of all who believe," Abraham becomes our example for believing in the Word of God, even when outward FACTS say it is foolish to do so. To believe in that healed image on the conscious screen, while your body is still sick, is certainly contrary to nature. But that shouldn't bother us when we have such an outstanding example as Abraham. Believing God's laws is no more ridiculous than believing in His promises. The One Who stands behind the laws is the same One Who stands behind the promises.

Besides, Abraham's body was healed in the process. He not only had Isaac, the promised heir. He went on to have more sons and daughters by Keturah, whom he took to wife after Sarah died (Gen. 25:1-6).

2. **The counsel of the apostle Paul.**

Paul asks Christians to VISUALIZE truths in their minds, knowing they will come to pass in their lives if they do.

Faith can go where reason cannot follow. Never was this more true than in the exhortation of the apostle Paul in the 6th chapter of Romans. Here he orders Christians to RECKON themselves "DEAD to sin" (Rom. 6:11). For a person to visualize himself as DEAD TO SIN is absolutely contrary to the fact. Christians are NOT dead to sin. Far from it. They are alive to sin. They sin all the time. The man who says he doesn't sin has deceived himself (I John 1:8). The truth is, our old nature (old man) is only LEGALLY DEAD. He is legally crucified with Christ, not literally. Any believer who is honest with himself has to admit that he sins. This would not be possible if the old nature were **literally** dead.

The Spirit-filled apostle knew a man's actions are determined by the way he PICTURES himself. If he sees himself a sinner and REALLY BELIEVES it, he will sin more and more. On the other hand, if he PICTURES HIMSELF as dead to sin, he will sin less and less. What he sees in his mind and believes about himself gradually becomes true in his life. Let a man SEE HIMSELF as holy as Jesus . . . AND BELIEVE IT . . . and he will be transformed into the likeness of Christ in a matter of time. Imagine the faith that would take!

The SEE IT—BELIEVE IT method isn't new. It wasn't invented by C. S. Lovett. It was laid down in God's Word long ago. The entire faith program is based on it. Isn't it helpful to see the same formula applied to other areas in God's Word? Sure it is. It gives real confidence in our approach to healing when you see how it coincides with the Scriptures.

3. The logic of the patriarch Job.

Job's faith came to its climax as he REASONED his way through the truths available to him.

It was by logic that the old patriarch Job brought

his faith to its zenith. He debated with himself and his friends. His faith worked its way through various reasonings until he could utter that grand statement . . . "I know my Redeemer liveth and that He shall stand at the latter day upon the earth" (Job 19:25). That faith was afterwards rewarded with a visible appearance of God as a whirlwind, and he was able to stand and commune with Him as a friend (Job 38:1).

In this same way, following the example of Job, we must think through the facts of the healing program and come to a solid conclusion concerning God's laws. If we are consistent in our thinking, there is only one conclusion we can reach; Jesus wants us well and has provided the healing laws for that very purpose.

There is no special honor for God in blind faith. In fact there's a risk. Who knows what blind faith will do in a crisis? It is better to be convinced about spiritual things. The apostle Paul says "amen" to that. His word on it is, "Let every man be **persuaded** in his own mind" (Rom. 14:5). It is REASONED FAITH that Paul advocates. The approach of this book is based on reasoned faith. We are working with logic and laws. Put the two together and a believer can't help but be convinced of the soundness and reality of the healing program. God says, "Come now, and let us reason together . . . " (Isa. 1:18). In that case it had to do with the miracle of transforming dirty sinners into snow-white saints. God thought that miracle was a reasonable matter.

As I said above, faith is NOT a substance God hands us. It RISES in us as we become convinced of the certainty of His program. **But the convincing is up to us.** God persuades no one. He wants every man FULLY PERSUADED in his own mind. Yes, He supplies all the evidence we need, but we must take it from there. I have supplied the facts. I've listed the laws. Now you must weigh those facts as they have come

183

to you and satisfy yourself that God means for you to be well and has provided laws for that purpose. Think it all through carefully and you will come to only one conclusion—"those laws were given for me to use."

• Put the three Scriptural observations together:

The example of Abraham teaches us that God expects us to believe things which are CONTRARY to fact. Paul teaches us that such things can be VISUALIZED on the screen of our minds. If we really believe them, they will come to pass in our experience. The example of Job teaches us that we can put logic and the laws together to REASON our way to the necessary faith. Therefore this method of healing is biblically sound. That helps, doesn't it?

All right, let's go through a series of steps one might travel in elevating his faith by reasoning. Naturally I must list them briefly. You can see how each one would provide a lot of material for a full blown discussion with yourself.

REASONING WITH YOURSELF BUILDS FAITH

1. The Lord has established the healing principle in my body.

> How can I deny this? I see automatic healing every time a cut heals or a bruise gets well. It truly works according to law, for I get well every time I get sick. This indicates that the Lord has designed me for health, not sickness.

2. The Lord must have laws for maintaining the health of my body.

> Everything God does is lawful. Obviously the health of my body could not be insured without laws for maintaining it. Some laws can be observed, particularly those governing

the effect of the conscious mind on the unconscious. The fact that these are discoverable, means God has provided them for our use. On the surface it is difficult to believe that thoughts can actually damage one's body. Yet it is common knowledge that worry produces ulcers, tension brings on headaches, and distressing news brings tears to the eyes. It is clearly a law that a person's mind can affect his body.

3. If one's mind can make him sick, shouldn't it also be able to make him well?

If destructive ideas such as worry and anxiety can produce an illness, according to law, then wholesome and corrective ideas should produce the opposite. Laws work in two directions. If you cooperate with them, they favor you, if you violate them, they hurt you. Consequently, if bad thoughts can induce illness, then healthy thinking should induce healing. This has to be true if IDEAS in the mind are reflected in the body.

4. Seemingly the body has ample resources (power) for healing.

I'm thinking of the amazing blood stream with its ability to create millions of new cells every second. Under normal conditions I get a new body every eleven months, but under certain conditions, organs have been repaired almost instantly. In healing meetings the body forces appear to do the job in seconds. This would indicate that the Lord does NOT have to use external power for healing. There must be an abundance of it on hand in the body itself. I can believe that speeding up the natural healing process is neither impossible nor unduly taxes the forces in the body.

5. Hypnosis demonstrates the ability of the mind to affect the body.

Hypnosis works solely with IDEAS (suggestions). The trance

185

is induced to bypass the critical powers of the conscious mind. Then ideas are fed to the entranced subject which can reach and manipulate nearly every organ of the body. Controlled experiments in university labs prove that such involuntary functions as taste, smell, breathing, digestion, circulation, nerves (pain) can be affected by oral command given a patient. All these PHYSICAL functions are altered by IDEAS introduced into the patient's mind. This proves that the body is ruled by thoughts.

6. Hypnosis proves that the mind can accept ideas contrary to fact.

Tell a hypnotized subject that he is in a refrigerator and he develops a chill, when in fact his body is at room temperature. Tell him he is in a steam room and he will start to sweat. It seemingly makes no difference to the unconscious that the suggestion is CONTRARY TO FACT. The body apparently reacts to whatever idea is ACCEPTED by the conscious mind regardless of what the real circumstances are. Hypnotized subjects BELIEVE what they are told. Unless they do, the command will not be manifested in their bodies. Hypnotism confirms the law of belief.

7. It is BELIEVING the idea that is important, not the science of hypnotism.

Hypnotism is merely a way to prove a point. The point being: the unconscious accepts as fact whatever the conscious believes is true. This means that the unconscious operates according to the law of belief, regardless of whether a person is hypnotized or not.

The same law can be demonstrated in the alert state. I am thinking of the teacher who THOUGHT the snake in her drawer was real. It wasn't, but she BELIEVED it was. Her body reacted as it did because of what she consciously believed. She was not in a hypnotic state. Take the person who BELIEVES there's a prowler in the house. Even though no such prowler exists, the body becomes keyed up for flight or a fight. Tremendous powers are summoned to action because of an idea contrary to fact. All that is necessary to get such a reaction is for the conscious mind to believe it.

8. The Lord's program calls for the healing of my body.

My computer is programmed with the KNOW-HOW for healing any illness or disease brought on by destructive thoughts. To get sick in the first place, I had to overrule the automatic healing process with a harmful thought-pattern. If I get rid of the destructive thoughts, automatic healing may heal me. If not, then I know I will have to reprogram the computer for healing—by faith.

9. Now it's up to me. Will I or won't I see myself healed IN ADVANCE of the fact—and BELIEVE it.

The program is sound, I'm convinced of that. There's plenty of evidence to support the laws. It all boils down to whether or not I'm ready to put my trust in them to the place where I can SEE myself as healed and BELIEVE what I see. As I go through the logic of the program, I don't see why my faith can't come to this point. Since the Lord is present to help me, how can I refuse the challenge? I know it means trusting Him more than ever before, but that's what I want to do. How wonderful He is! Who ever thought of using his own body as a laboratory for developing his faith! I'm ready to accept Jesus' offer.

● After a person has systematically reasoned his way through these steps, or similar ones, it seems wrong—no it seems like an act of unbelief—not to accept the adventure. Every bit of the reasoning can be demonstrated one way or another. There's no guess-work. The laws work. They are rigid. If a person meets the conditions, he will be healed. That's all there is to it.

187

The entire Christian program is based on believing without seeing. Trusting IN ADVANCE is normal for believers. "He that cometh to God must FIRST believe that He is." It's that way in all of our dealings with the Lord. He says, "When you pray, BELIEVE THAT YOU HAVE RECEIVED IT, and it will be granted you" (Mk. 11:24).

Any person who has reasoned his way through the program should be able to pray like this:

> **"Lord Jesus, thank You for giving me the opportunity to prove the healing laws in my body. It's thrilling to know that You have established them for our health. I know I will have to exercise more faith than ever before, but I want to grow in faith to please You. Please help me Master, to believe what I see on the screen, and thank You for using my body as a laboratory for faith. It will be thrilling to watch my faith rise and trigger the healing laws. Who knows what You and I will be able to do together after that. Thank You for the privilege, Lord Jesus!"**

By God's grace I can write this book in such a way that you become convinced the healing laws are yours to use. But I cannot give you the faith to trust in them. I've given you as much help along that line as I can. What I can do, is challenge you to try. On the basis of God's laws, I promise that if you can SEE yourself as healed and BELIEVE it—even while your body is sick—YOU WILL GET WELL. God's laws can't fail. Is not this very blessing contained in His promise . . .

"All things are possible to him that believeth!" (Mk. 9:23).

RECEIVE YOUR HEALING AS A GIFT

"Brother Lovett, your approach doesn't work for me. It isn't because I haven't tried. The Lord knows I have. I desperately want to be healed. I've worked hard to get the healing signal to my computer just as you show. I've even forced myself to pray. But nothing is happening. What's wrong? Is there something else I should be doing?"

I could get letters like that. Let's head them off.

When you find yourself making an all out EFFORT to be healed—STOP! I realize what I have given you could sound like a complicated plan requiring a great deal of work and concentration. Really it isn't that way at all. I want you to think of your healing as you did your salvation—AS A GIFT.

● Did you work to be saved? No. If you did, then you are not saved. Salvation is a free gift, there is no way to earn it (Eph. 2:8, 9). Similarly there is no way to work for healing. It is done without effort. In fact there is nothing you CAN DO to be healed. It comes entirely by faith—and faith is the opposite of effort. Faith has to do with RESTING, not working (Heb. 4:10). The secret of this approach is RELAXING in the Lord and letting Him bring you the GIFT of healing via His laws.

SO RELAX

When people are desperate for health, they become obsessed with the thought, "I don't want to be sick." See where that puts the emphasis? On the idea of being SICK. Without meaning to, they concentrate on the illness rather than the "picture" of health. What does that do? It triggers the law of **Reversed Effort.** Simply stated, this law says, the thing you try the hardest not to do, you end up doing. Energy invested in this effort, serves only to make people sicker.

Healing comes by faith. Therefore it cannot come by works. Faith appropriates what God has for us. All a person has to do is lean back and picture himself

189

as healed—BELIEVE WHAT HE SEES—and it's done. That's all there is to it. There's not one bit of effort involved. The apostle Paul uses the same formula, though his words are different:

> **"Be anxious for nothing, but in everything, by prayer and supplication, with thanksgiving, let your requests be made known unto God"** (Phil. 4:6).

The formula is there. Paul says, make your request, give thanks IN ADVANCE, then cease to worry. If healing is indeed a gift, then all a person has to do is accept it by faith. If works of any kind were required, it would not be a gift, but a reward. Even though it comes by way of God's Laws, with ourselves as His agents, it is still a gift.

SATAN MAKES IT SEEM LIKE WORK

> "You aren't stupid enough to think you can get well this way, are you? Just look at your symptoms. You feel pain. That's real. The damage is there. The doctors know about it. It's ridiculous to think you can get healing by running a mental movie on the screen of your mind. That's just wishful thinking. How can an intelligent person like you believe he's healed, when his illness is there for everyone to see?"

See the power behind that idea? There's logic in Satan's suggestion. And he's got the critical and challenging powers of your conscious mind on his side. He has little trouble persuading those who listen to him (and most do) that it is stupid to believe something contrary to fact. He wants you sick. Such suggestions are his way of keeping you that way. He can prevent your healing, if you let him.

> **NOTE.** The devil has a cute bag of tricks. He can make you fall asleep when you should be going over the scenes

190

with the Lord. He can distract your thinking by introducing random ideas into your mind. He can suggest that this approach is too simple. If it were that good, everyone would be using it to get well. He will say that if God meant for us to use the mind/body laws, He would have said so more clearly and doctors would be unnecessary. There's no limit to the number of suggestions he can come up with. If we don't deal with him, he has an easy time of discouraging believers, especially when the results are slow in coming.

What to do about the devil.

1. Jesus told us to WATCH and pray. Which came first? Watching. Why? The Christian is NOT immune to Satan's working, even in prayer. He usually drops his guard while talking to Jesus, thinking Satan can't get to him. But that's false. Many saints have difficult times in prayer due to the devil's distracting influence.

2. As soon as one of his suggestions arrives in your thinking, ORDER HIM AWAY. I mean speak to him directly. Tell him to ''take off'' in Jesus' name. God has given us authority over him. The Word tells us precisely, ''Resist the devil and he will flee from you'' (James 4:7).

> **NOTE.** Most Christians accept the idea of speaking to lost souls in Jesus' name, inviting them to COME to Him and be saved. But speaking to Satan in that same name, telling him to GO, might be new to some. Yet this is exactly what we must do to rid ourselves of his damaging presence. He has the power to BLOCK healing, if we buy his ideas. We must learn to dispatch him just as Jesus did in the wilderness (Matt. 4:10). This is why I mention my book, **Dealing With The Devil.** If dealing with Satan IN PERSON is new to you, you will appreciate this four-step plan for making him flee. When he departs, the mental relief is glorious.

3. In the beginning it may be necessary to deal with Satan 20 or 30 times a day. But as soon as he realizes your seriousness and determination, he will back off rather than endure those painful blasts from God's Word. (In the plan you use God's Word as a sword against him). Every time you make a scriptural thrust, the Holy Spirit stabs Satan where it hurts him most—in the ego.

Now that I've alerted you to the devil and how he can keep you from believing the scenes you project on the conscious screen, dealing with him must become part of your strategy for getting well. He is the one who makes you nervous and anxious about your sickness. It is a lot easier to believe in the HEALED image after you are free of his disturbing suggestions. When he tells you that healing is not a free gift, don't believe him. It is free. And God means for you to have it.

FEEL BETTER NOW?

Isn't it comforting to see how it all fits together?

The formula is simple: SEE IT—BELIEVE IT—FEEL IT (repetition). I've laid out the morning, noon, and evening exercises and told you how to do them. Then to aid you in believing the scene on the screen, I included this chapter on faith. When you understand that faith is a HUMAN quality, that we can INCREASE our own faith by putting logic and God's laws together in the light of His Word, the program gets real solid.

Reasoning one's way through the logic of this approach does not minimize the glory of God's part in healing. Healing is still a miracle. And the Lord remains the only Healer. The difference is, we now understand what is taking place. The mystery is lifted, that's all. Remember the illustration of the transistor radio in the introduction of this book? What a miracle such a radio would have been in Paul's day. And yet, because we know the radio laws, those little sets are commonplace to us. But does that make it any less a miracle? Not really.

So it is with the human body. Even though we now know a lot about the way it functions and a few of the laws concerning healing and health, we are still in awe at what God has provided. Oh, the wisdom that fashioned our earth-suit.

> **NOTE.** This book could force the faith of some readers to a showdown. The test will be . . . "Do I believe in my sickness more than I do in God's Word?" In other words, which offers the sturdier basis for faith? Because a man experiences crippling in his body, feels pain or other symptoms, he's tempted to think those are somehow MORE REAL than the promises of God. The fact is, God's Word is more real than the symptoms of any disease. God made our bodies. Symptoms are merely by-products of situations which are in His hands. We're all believers —and we're capable of putting our faith in our sicknesses or in God's promises. But we can't have it both ways. If the symptoms of our sickness are more real to us, then our faith will be in our disease and we'll continue to be sick. If God's Word is more real to us, then our faith will be in His laws and the healing will come. God's Word asks us to SEE ourselves as healed (Mk. 11:24). The laws presented in this book guarantee it will come to pass. So it boils down to whether our confidence is going to be in the signs of sickness or in God's Word. If we will SEE ourselves as healed—BELIEVE IT—and then act like it, the healing must come.

Our book could end right here. But my job isn't quite finished. There's more to healing and health than giving you a formula for getting well. Jesus offers us an **abundant life.** How can we really experience the abundant life unless our bodies are not only well, but vigorous

193

and bouncy? Ah, we haven't said anything about that, have we? We should.

That's what you are going to meet—next.

Chapter Ten

GIVING THE COMPUTER WHAT IT NEEDS

Here's the winner of the Indianapolis 500 auto race. He's a man who really knows how to handle a racing car. And that's no ordinary vehicle he drives. It is the finest machine money can buy—tuned to the peak of perfection. But what happens when we add some diesel fuel to the high test gas in his tank. How does our skilled driver make out then? He just barely creeps along. Try as he might, he can't get up any speed at all. How come? Without the right fuel in his machine, his rare talents are wasted. The skill and sense of timing of this great driver are helpless without the right fuel for his engine.

So it is with the computer in our heads.

It is an expert when it comes to healing and maintaining the health of our bodies. This amazing device which God has put in the back of our brain really knows how to do its job and do it well. If we get sick and can get the healing command into that computer, our bodies will get well. It will also keep the body well. But—like the skilled driver, it has to have what it needs for its job or it is handicapped. Its skill, as far as health is concerned, is the ability to take raw materials and convert them into new body tissue. Then it uses that new tissue to heal the body and put it in perfect shape.

WHAT ARE THOSE RAW MATERIALS?

The most urgent raw material the computer needs is AIR or oxygen. Cut off the air supply and our bodies die quickly. I don't have to tell you to breathe. However, modern pollution being what it is, it is getting harder to find clean air for breathing.

The next vital raw material is WATER. We can go only a few days without it. About one half to two thirds of the body is made up of water. Water is the medium of body fluids, carrying materials from one part of the body to the other. Unless a person drinks enough water each day (approx. 2 1/2 quarts) his computer will not be able to get rid of all the WASTE products generated by the body cells. The secretion and excretion of waste is absolutely essential to good health. Some doctors call water "one of nature's best medicines."

The third most vital raw material is FOOD. While the body may consist of two thirds water, the solid part is practically all food. There is no way to discuss health and healing without mentioning food. A person can get healing without the right kind of food, but he can't keep it. There are dietary laws that govern the effect of food on the body. There are foods the computer must have. If it doesn't get them, some part of the body must be robbed of nutrients for healing to occur. It is entirely possible that certain healings are thwarted by the lack of needed food elements in the body.

> **NOTE.** Proper diet is essential to the success of this approach to healing. A person may bring his faith to the place where he can use the mental laws to secure healing, but if he fails to observe the dietary laws, his healing could be only temporary. At the same time, some readers might be tempted to think they can use the dietary laws ALONE to accomplish the healing, but that is also a mistake. It is folly to ignore either the mental or dietary laws. Both are needed for the body to be restored and kept in perfect health. Proper nutrition and disciplined thinking offer the greatest hope for staying vital at any age.

STUFFED—YET STARVING

We live in a land geared to denying the computer what it needs for its job. That is, we are in a time of history and in a country that is almost dedicated to keeping us from getting the right kind of food.

Here's a housewife. She has come to the supermarket. We'll follow her around. Watch as she stops here and there to take items off the shelves and put them in her cart. In time that basket is piled high with goodies. Then she wheels to the checkout stand. As we eye that mountain of stuff we think to ourselves, "Man, that family eats well!" Ah, but does it? We'll see.

For all their appetizing looks, those pretty packages contain practically NO nutrition. Nutrition, as you know, is the business of nourishing the cells of the body.

Unknown to our housewife, most of the nourishment, which was once in all that food, has been taken out and fed to the hogs. Long before it was packaged and offered to the public, the good stuff was removed. What's left in those packages even the weevils won't eat. They'd starve if they tried to live off it. Most of the processed foods we buy today are practically value-less as far as our computer is concerned.

There are three reasons why modern eating is so lacking in nutrition:

1. **Our foods are refined to death.**

Our food was designed by God Who meant for us to eat it as close to the natural state as possible. The fruits, grains, and vegetables were to take from the soil and air the elements necessary for keeping us in good health. And this they would do if we didn't destroy them by some process before we get them into our mouths. In recent years man has decided that he would rather have his food fancy than nutritious.

It wasn't that way a century ago. Our ancestors lived close to the soil. They kept cows and drank whole milk. Their chickens scratched for food. They raised their own vegetables. Consequently they were a rather sturdy lot. But then came the rolling mills. These plants with their giant rollers could mash the very life out of grains, stripping them of everything. These mills began to produce nice white flour. All the good stuff, the wheat germ and nutrients close to the shell, was thrown away. Then heart disease began to rise. White flour, you see, is nutritious grain with all of the vital elements for health and healing removed. The sugar, rice, and cereals we buy in the stores today are stripped of vitamins and nutrients. Even though they have the fullest stomachs in the world, Americans are starving to death nutritionally.

NOTE. Congress recently investigated the $400 million dry cereal industry and found there was more nourishment in the paper boxes containing the destroyed grains than in the products offered by the manufacturers. In contrast to the American way of eating, in those lands where the people are yet primitive, eating foods natural to their environment, the families are healthy. They tend to stay that way until the white man comes. Then they take up his ways and turn on to the suicide road of eating nutritionless foods. Their health declines almost at once.

We live in a nation with more good doctors, more great medical schools, more tremendous hospitals, more famous scientists, more education, better sanitary conditions, and more money than any place on earth. But we need them. In spite of all our wealth and technical know-how, there is something wrong with almost every person in this land. Our people are sick because they feed off of ''sick food.''

Try telling Americans they shouldn't eat hamburgers, cokes, ''finger-lickin''' fried chicken, hot dogs, candy, popcorn, doughnuts, pizzas, and drink black coffee and they'll get upset. They can't believe all that ''good'' food is bad for them. They scoff when you tell them it is dangerous, but it is. It's deadly. The truth is, they are committing suicide with their teeth.

2. **We serve food on the basis of taste, rather than nutrition.**

Here's another housewife. She wants her husband to go to work with a big breakfast under his belt. So she sets before him a big plate of pancakes made with white flour. It's lathered with gobs of butter and drenched with syrup. It's topped off with some pork sausage. Then it's all washed down with black coffee. Well, her husband will leave with a full stomach all right—full of calories. He may feel stuffed, but he has received almost nothing that will nourish him. His body cells will be starved for nutrition. Around mid-morning, he'll be needing something to pick him up. Some more black coffee, probably. He'll feel faint without a coffee break.

Now if all he got out of this was a weakened body, it wouldn't be so bad. But those nude calories have to go some place. If they don't end up around his middle as fat, they'll go into his arteries as cholesterol. His body is really loaded with stuff that can hurt him. He might seem to get away with it while he is young, but after he hits fifty, he'll be sorry. His dear wife may think she's taking good care of him, but she's sending him to an early grave.

● We Americans are on a sugar kick. Did you know that the yearly consumption of refined white sugar in the United States is over 100 pounds per person? The use of this deadly product has doubled in the last century. So have the degenerative diseases, especially of the heart and brain. Mental illness is rising at an alarming rate now. Heart disease is the number one killer. And excessive sugar is a prime contributer. Not only does sugar have absolutely NO nutrition, it is dangerous in the quantities in which we Americans consume it. There is medical evidence available to show an important connection between the amount of cholesterol in one's blood stream and the quantity of sugar he consumes.

On top of that, sugar is the enemy of the nervous system. It doesn't attack the nervous system directly. It does it indirectly by upsetting the body's insulin balance. This can result in a host of symptoms ranging from feelings of tiredness to imagining people are in the room with you. Sugar is so soluble that it passes directly through the wall of the stomach without being digested. When it gets into the blood you enjoy a burst of energy for a time. But shortly the pancreas is ordered to secrete an excess of insulin to handle this sudden load of sugar. Insulin, as you know, cancels excess sugar in the blood. That is why it is given to diabetics. They have too much sugar in their blood.

We have to have blood sugar. That's where we get the energy to drive the body. But when there is an overload, the body must discharge insulin to the blood stream to counteract it. When it does, the blood sugar is dropped to a much lower level because of the quantity of insulin that has been secreted. Therefore, eating sugar DROPS your blood sugar. Sounds like a contradiction, but it isn't. Just remember: taking on a lot of sugar in any form, whether a soft drink or a candy bar can actually ROB you of blood sugar.

The first organ in the body to feel the effects of this robbery is the BRAIN. And since it is the one organ that controls the rest, it acts to protect itself. And when it does, all sorts of freakish things can happen. People with low blood sugar (Hypoglycemia) can experience nervousness, tiredness, mental depressions, forget what they are trying to say, thoughts can go completely out of their minds, emotional breakdowns, and be hard to live with. If allowed to continue, it can produce serious mental problems. I suppose it would be too extreme to say that the use of sugar ought to be against the law. No one would buy that proposition, but it is every bit as hazardous to health as smoking.

NOTE. Dr. Lawrence Lamb, former Chief of Clinical Services for the USAF School of Aerospace Medicine, says that by the age of 35 nearly ALL Americans have fatty deposits in the arteries of the heart. Autopsies performed on young Americans (average age 22) killed during the Korean War reveal that nearly 80% of them had such deposits in at least one of the large arteries of the heart. The degree of these fatty deposits, which bring on heart attacks, increases sharply with age. Americans simply do not eat with caution. One out of every two deaths in the U.S. is due to atherosclerosis. Their arteries are choked with fats.

Now let's go back to the housewife so anxious to please her husband. It is dinner time. Her man has come home from work. He's ready for a big meal. Tonight it's macaroni and cheese. He just loves it. And there are biscuits made with white flour and plenty of butter on the table. To top off this delightful meal, she gives him a sugar-loaded piece of apple pie with a scoop of ice cream on top. She knows it's fattening, but to her mind it's okay to spoil him once in a while. What she doesn't realize is that she is poisoning him.

To say that good old apple pie a-la-mode is deadly, is almost like attacking motherhood. It is an American institution. But it needs to be said. There is no way to maintain the health of the body and at the same time ingest quantities of white flour and sugar just because they taste good.

NOTE. This poor husband might still survive if his wife would simply scrub her vegetables instead of peeling away the skins. When potatoes, for example are peeled, most of the vital elements go down the garbage disposer. If, on top of that, his wife proceeds to boil what's left, the tiny bit of good stuff that does remain goes into the water and that too is poured down the drain. What she then serves her mate is pure starch. She has thrown away the best and given him the worst. Had she merely scrubbed his potato, baked it, and given it to him with the skin on, his body could have received some useful nutrients. In many vegetables and grains the nutrition is in the skin or outer shell. Preparing food on the basis of taste and looks is a mistake. A man doesn't have to starve to suffer from malnutrition. He can be stuffed and yet completely undernourished.

3. **Our soil is depleted.**

The third reason for the lack of nutrition in modern foods is due to the depletion of our soil. There is no way for fruits and vegetables to take vital elements out of the ground if there are none there to begin with. Fertile soil is full of vitamins and minerals and enzymes. These are fragile substances which modern scientists have established as absolutely essential to health and healing. The body MUST have them. But when the soil is worn out, there is no way for them to be taken back up into the plants.

For years we have been robbing our soil, putting nothing back. As a consequence, much of our food lacks the essentials for healing. It's true that commercial fertilizers have helped to bring forth bigger harvests, but chemical farming and poison sprays do not really add to the health of the soil. Some modern methods actually put DISEASE into the ground. From there it travels into the plants, then into the animals that eat them, and finally into our bodies.

> **NOTE.** If we made a trip to a forest and studied the ground, we'd learn how the Lord meant for soil to be rebuilt. Nature puts back into the land three parts of dead plant matter and one part of dead animal matter. As this leaf mold decays it produces amino acids and carbonic acid which experts say are necessary for good soil. In addition to the death and decay of the organic matter, bacteria and earthworms are needed to produce really fertile soil. That's the kind of ground needed for growing healthy foods. From it comes the vitamins, enzymes, and minerals the computer must have to heal and maintain the body.

● Have you noticed how the food supplement business has mushroomed? A number of firms are doing a land office business. And rightly so. We need help. Something has to be done to make up for the lack of nourishment in modern foods. Either a person must raise his own vegetables, which is hard to do in our urban society, or buy organic supplements. It is a blessing that the food supplement business has come along. It meets a real need in our time.

With the minerals gone from our soil, any vegetables we care to eat raw, don't really taste very good. The organic minerals which would normally give them full rich flavor are missing. Consequently our produce is flat and sometimes bitter. So what do we do? We put SALT on it. We also add pepper and spices and sauces and creams to help get it down. That's too bad. The natural flavor of good vegetables is really great. But few of us know anything about natural flavor. So we join the salt generation. But salt is also a killer. It not only destroys what natural flavor might be present in food, it kills people too.

> **NOTE.** Americans consume as much salt as they do sugar, more than 100 pounds per person each year. The use of salt has steadily increased in this country, and along with it, the incidence of high blood pressure, kidney and liver ailments, dropsy, ateriosclerosis, heart failure, and skin diseases. Did you know that no animal, including the human animal, can digest salt? That's true. Plants can take inorganic salt and convert it into organic salt suitable for human use, but inorganic sodium chloride (the same as in our salt shakers) is indigestible. The only reason people became addicted to it is because it has been used as a food preservative for thousands of years. It isn't all that good to eat. People have to acquire a taste for it. Some people get a violent reaction when given salt pills. High blood pressure is relatively unknown in those areas where little salt is used.

You go to your doctor for a checkup. He takes your blood pressure. It's too high. What is the first thing he asks? "Are you under any kind of an emotional strain?" When you say, "No, not really," he then wants you to give up salt. As best you can, you are to eliminate it from your diet. If you have been a heavy user, chances are your arteries have already begun to harden. Salt which is not passed from the body, remains in the tissues until it finally makes its way into your vital organs.

When salt gets into your arteries, it forms crusts which can make your arteries look like the inside of old water pipes. As the salt continues to accumulate, the passageways in the vessels get smaller and smaller—and harder and harder. The heart must then increase its pressure to get the blood through the restricted passages.

NOTE. When you stop using salt, foods taste flat for a time. But as your taste buds come back to life, you begin to enjoy the natural flavor of the fruits and vegetables. In time you find you don't mind going without salt. If you stay off permanently, it becomes hard to eat anything salty. You wonder how you were able to eat salty foods before. As your body begins to get rid of the accumulations of salt dispersed throughout your system, you can feel the improved health. Your kidneys function better when relieved of the burden imposed by the excess salt. Because salt makes the body store water, cattlemen put out "salt-licks" for their livestock. And don't think to substitute sea salt. It's still salt with only a slight redeeming factor.

● When you consider how little our soil has left to give to our foods; how thoroughly the manufacturer devitalizes his processed foods so that they will keep indefinitely in warehouses and market shelves; how the housewife finishes the job of peeling, boiling, or otherwise cooking her food to death—it's no wonder Americans are overfed but undernourished. When you know the whole story, it's easy to see why illness and disease overtake us. It's really a mess, isn't it?

THE BODY CRIES FOR NUTRITION

One health expert, Gaylord Hauser, says there is no reason why a person shouldn't be as healthy at 80 as he was at 30. The body, he says, when properly fed is easily capable of reaching 100 without any vital part wearing out. This isn't hard to believe when we consider that when the race was young, men lived to be over one hundred. Moses was 120 when he died. The Scripture says his eyes were good and that none of his body strength was gone (Deut. 34:7). That was only fourteen centuries before Christ.

Medical evidence agrees. There is no record anywhere of ANYONE dying because of a worn out body.

Death comes as disease strikes some vital organ without which the body can't function. Experts in the field of nutrition feel we have reached a new frontier in medicine, one which will see the organs of the body able to defend themselves against all disease as a result of being supplied the nutrition they need. They regard nutrition as the ammunition of the body. But they can only be right in part. From what we already know about a person's mind making him sick, nutrition isn't the whole story by any means.

Nutritionists also agree on the elements the body must have:

1. PROTEINS. This is the chief tissue builder, the basic substance of every cell in the body. New cells cannot be manufactured without protein. How vital that is to the computer which must order new cells in any healing. Now protein is made up of what are called amino acids. There are 22 of these in good protein. When food is eaten, the proteins are broken down (digested) into amino acids which are then rearranged to form the various special proteins. The amino acid makeup of a food protein determines its nutritive value. The body can make its own supply of 10 of the 22 amino acids, but the rest must come from food. Those derived from food are called **essential** amino acids.

All healing requires the replacing of tissue. There is no way for the body to restore kidneys, bladders, livers, and hearts without building new tissue. Everything is made of protein, even the brain. So it is absolutely necessary that we eat those foods which supply proteins in the proportion needed by the body. Foods that provide good amounts of the essential proteins are the ones which best meet the computer's needs.

NOTE. Protein is a puzzle. For all of his know-how, man is unable to manufacture it in a form useful for food.

Researchers know the chemical composition of protein, they can break it down into its 22 amino acids, but they can't turn it into food. Therefore man is dependent on natural food for protein. The richest sources are animal in origin—meat, fish, milk, eggs, cheese, and yogurt. Strict vegetarians are up against it when it comes to sources of the whole protein. Proteins from cereal grains, vegetables and fruits do not provide the complete assortment of amino acids as do animal proteins. However, proteins from nuts and soybeans and some other legumes are almost as good as those from animal sources. But it takes a lot more of them.

2. FUEL. Our bodies run on fuel. Like our automobiles, our bodies convert fuel into heat and energy. But the fuel we burn is food. But here's what's so amazing about the human body. We burn fuel in our bodies at the incredibly low temperature of 98.6 degrees. Contrast this with the high combustion temperature inside an auto engine. Outside the body, protein cannot be broken down unless you heat it to 1500 degrees in a furnace or boil it at 212 degrees for 24 hours.

All foods burn, but some are better as fuel than others. Scientists have figured out for us the amount of heat the various foods provide and have given us the values of each in terms of calories. A calorie is simply the basic measurement of the amount of heat a food will produce. Foods high in calories are fuel foods. They are also called carbohydrates.

Carbohydrates come in three forms—starches, sugars, and celluloses (fibrous materials). Starches and sugars are the main sources of ENERGY for humans. Celluloses furnish bulk in the diet. The body converts starches into glucose (blood sugar) as this is the form in which the cells use it to provide energy for the body process and support activity and growth. If we didn't have carbohydrates, then all the energy would have to come from proteins. So carbohydrates are needed that the proteins might be spared for tissue building and repair.

NOTE. When the fuel foods are burned in the body, they give off both HEAT and ENERGY. When they do NOT burn, they are converted to fat and stored in the body. People who are overweight, have obvioulsy taken on too much fuel. The danger lies in the fact that the fats do not merely collect around the middle, but also in the arteries to produce heart disease. Americans have gone on a binge of refined sugar rather than natural starches. Consequently we are the most unhealthy country in the world in terms of heart disease. If you have trouble taking weight off and keeping it off, you may want to read my book **"HELP LORD—THE DEVIL WANTS ME FAT!"**

Many Christians are overweight. They've taken on more fuel than their bodies can convert into heat and energy. So the surplus is stored as fat. Most human fat is saturated fat. Unfortunately it collects in the blood stream as well as the organs. Since blood is mostly water, these fats do not dissolve in the stream but circulate. Blood which is high in these fats (triglycerides) has a tendency to clot. Should a clot form in an artery that has already been reduced in size because of deposits of cholesterol, it could plug the artery completely. Should this happen in one of the main arteries of the heart, the result is coronary thrombosis. This is a major cause of heart attacks today and it is occurring in young people as well as old.

> **NOTE.** Christians who are overweight would do well to reduce their intake of fuel foods and get more protein into their diets. It is NOT wise to skip meals in an attempt to lose weight. It is better to eat more small meals which can be burned completely than overload the system with big meals which it cannot handle. Any unconverted food has to go to fat. All diets should include some carbohydrates for they help the body use fats efficiently. But these should be NATURAL starches for natural foods contain OTHER NUTRIENTS which aid the body in USING the fuel that is eaten. Examples of natural starches are whole grains (such as wheat, oats, corn, and brown rice), potatoes, sweet potatoes, dry beans, and peas. Fruits and vegetables contain smaller amounts of carbohydrates. In vegetables the carbohydrate is mainly in the form of starches; in fruits, it is chiefly sugars. Refined white flour and white sugar and processed cereals are no-nos.

3. VITAMINS. Did you know that the average American consumes over 150,000 pounds of food in his lifetime? That's over 70 tons! And for the most part he doesn't care what's in it, as long as it tastes good. What he's not aware of, is that his food must have a balance of vitamins and minerals—and not very many.

The amount of vitamins a person gets out of that 70 tons of food, says Carlton Fredericks, can be measured in teaspoonfuls. Think of that! These substances are so miniscule that the entire 70 tons contain less than a cupful. Yet, they are so vital, that if a person ate all that food and left them out, he'd starve to death.

Without vitamins and minerals the food we eat does not convert to energy, neither can it be used to build new cells. Instead it turns to fat and waste. Vitamins make food useful to the body. Without them the body can't use food. One can stuff himself with protein, but if there are no vitamins present, the body cannot convert the protein into new cells. Without the presence of vitamins and minerals the food we eat becomes nude food. Everything we eat has to be synthesized in the presence of vitamins.

> **NOTE.** Vitamins are fragile things. They are frail substances found chiefly in fruits, vegetables, and whole grains. Some are so delicate that they are killed if they are exposed to the air. They are sometimes referred to as "living elements," but they are not really alive. They are chemicals. These crystalline-like substances are incredibly important to life and health, yet most of them are destroyed by heat—yes, ordinary cooking heat.

● This might startle you. Scientists can reproduce nearly every human disease in animals simply by WITHHOLDING certain vitamins and minerals from their diets. That tells us how vital these little substances are. Without a balance of vitamins in the system, the tissues DO NOT receive the nutrition they need.

> **NOTE.** See how essential vitamins are to healing? Healing requires damaged cells to be replaced with new ones. New cells must come from protein. But without the presence of vitamins, protein cannot be broken down to build those new cells. Vitamins are FOOD IGNITERS. They trigger

the combustion of food. In just a few hours these vitamins can convert the protein into cell-building substances. Without them, no new cells can be made from the food we eat.

Can you sense the harm being done to our bodies through the removal of vitamins and minerals by the food processors and the careless way we fix our meals? Think what this means to the brain and nervous system. It is composed of cells just like the rest of the body. The computer is also made from food. It has to stay in good condition to keep the rest of the body healthy. If anything goes wrong with that computer, we're in trouble. The material that keeps that marvelous machine in top notch shape comes from only one source—the food we eat.

For the past 20 years, Dr. George Watson, a bio-psychologist and psychochemist at the University of Southern California, has been treating mentally and emotionally disturbed individuals with vitamin therapy. In collaboration with medical doctors, he has done amazing things with damaged people simply by altering their chemistry with massive doses of vitamins and nutritional diets. He has found that he can produce the symptoms of mental illness in people, simply by changing their vitamin balance. That's shocking. Imagine revamping a person's mental health by what you put into his stomach!

Dr. Watson has just published a book, "Nutrition and Your Mind." When it goes into wide circulation it is sure to have an effect on medical opinion. It is brand new at this writing, but I was able to get hold of a copy. Dr. Watson asserts that mental and emotional disorders are caused ALMOST EXCLUSIVELY by the physical malfunction of the body's metabolism. This, he claims, is caused by poor diet and should NOT be treated with psychotherapy, but with vitamins, minerals, and other nutrients! Now that is a remarkable statement.

ILLUSTRATION. In his book, **Nutrition and Your Mind,** Dr. Watson tells of a woman who was diagnosed a catatonic schizophrenic. She had gone through years of fruitless psychotherapy, chemotherapy, and electroshock. Finally this woman was turned over to Dr. Watson and his team as a "hopeless case." She was headed for commitment in an institution. Within THREE MONTHS she was restored to full health through injections of vitamins and minerals plus a nutritious diet. Dr. Watson reports hundreds of other cases of disturbed people who were completely restored after psychotherapy failed to help them. He sees a number of mental disturbances as linked to the body processes which are in turn governed by what we eat.

Why do I devote so much attention to nutrition? Anything that interferes with the brain can have an effect on the healing program. When the brain suffers from poor nutrition, the COMPUTER itself can be affected. When the computer operates at less than its best, we cannot expect either the automatic or faith healing processes to function normally. Therefore we must see that the computer does not lack for the nourishment it needs. Even if we have to pay a little more to get the right kind of food, it is worth it.

WHERE MEDICINE WENT WRONG

"The most basic weapons in the fight against disease are those most ignored by modern medicine—the numerous nutrients that the cells of our bodies need."

A wild, irresponsible statement? Hardly. The man who made it holds top notch credentials. He is Dr. Roger J. Williams, Ph.D., D.Sc., professor of Chemistry at the University of Texas. He made this remark and others equally strong before the nation's highest scientific body, the National Academy of Sciences. His new book, "Nutrition Against Disease," like that of Dr. George Watson of U.S.C., is bound to create a stir in the medical community. He takes the position that many of the widespread diseases of our day could be prevented by vitamins and nutritious diets. He is satisfied that those in the medical field are making a big mistake by neglecting the discoveries which have been made with respect to vitamins. Here's his comment:

"It is my considered belief that medical science has taken an extreme and unfortunate wrong turn in its neglect of nutrition, and that this wrong turn is evident in connection with the thinking about all diseases, including cancer."*

In his first chapter, "The Flaw in Medical Education," Dr. Williams decries the fact that medical students are taught very little about nutrition. The result of this "woefully weak clinical nutrition education," he says, "is that most physicians ignore nutrition in the treatment of disease." That's a strong statement, yet I believe each of us can check it out for himself. All we have to do is ask our doctors what they think of a nutritional approach to our particular problem. We can expect them to smile and tell us to watch out for quacks.

For awhile, doctors are going to feel that drugs and antibiotics offer the best way to treat disease. Yet the basic fault with all these drugs, says Dr. Williams, is that they have "no known connection with the disease itself. They do not eliminate the cause, but often complicate the physician's job." He cites aspirin as an example. No one really believes he has headaches because his system LACKS ASPIRIN. In no way does aspirin TREAT the cause of headaches. It merely covers the real trouble which needs attention.

NOTE. Dr. Williams joins with those who blame the excessive use of sugar as the reason for the high incidence

---

*"Nutrition Against Disease: Environmental Protection," copyright 1972, Pitman Publishing Corp., New York.

of heart disease in our country. He quotes the noted English nutritionist, Dr. John Yudkin, in support of his claim. Dr. Yudkin's tests prove that people taking more than 100 grams (4 ounces) of sugar per day were FIVE TIMES as likely to suffer coronary thrombosis and massive cell damage in the heart (heart attacks), as one who took only 60 grams a day. Americans, says Dr. Yudkin, consume about 140 grams of sugar a day. He says refined white sugar is deadly because all of the vitamins have been removed from the sugar cane.

Dr. Williams also denounces white flour and refined cereals. They too have been robbed of their B vitamin content as well as precious minerals which are so necessary for converting the starches and sugars into energy. Now for a real shocker. One half of ALL the food eaten in the United States is made up of white flour, processed cereal food, and white sugar. No wonder our hospitals are overcrowded.

On my desk I have a box of malted breakfast cereal. I'm looking at the label. It's easy to see what they have done with this product. The label tells the story. They took the whole grain as God made it, then removed every bit of the nutrition (vitamin and mineral content) through the refining process. Then they put back 2 or 3 parts of the B vitamin complex. How do we know? It says so right on the box—"Niacin, Thiamin and Riboflavin ADDED." What a giveaway that is. Why do they have to ADD something that was there to begin with—unless they have already TAKEN IT OUT?

In view of the delicate balance which God has established in foods, this is criminal. It is a crime against the human body. Nature likes things whole. And whole grain is one of man's basic foods. The Lord meant for our bodies to have all the elements He put in the grains. When the giant milling industry removes the entire B complex and then returns only a bit of it, an imbalance

217

is created which God never intended. To have whole grains reduced to white flour, white rice, and all the highly processed breakfast items stripped of nutrition is a shame. It may be some time before we learn just how much damage has been done to American health by this kind of food technology. But it is like man to ruin the good things God put in his hand.

WHAT SHOULD CHRISTIANS EAT?

It is not within the scope of this book for me to prescribe diets. Besides, there's no need. A number of good health books have been marketed by people expert in nutrition. I am NOT a nutritionist to anyone but myself. It is my opinion that every Christian ought to do some reading on the subject and become his own nutritionist. It is certainly within the realm of Christian stewardship for every believer to know something about the relationship between the health of his body and modern foods. We live in a dangerous age as far as nutrition is concerned. It is impossible to give the Lord a good body and ignore what we put in our mouths.

I think, however, that it is in order for me to make some general observations and mention two things on which most nutritionists agree:

1. The **foods** which contain the most protein are also the ones which supply the B complex of vitamins:

Liver and the other meat organs
Eggs
Milk, cheese
Meat, fish, poultry
Green leafy vegetables
Whole grains, nuts, seeds, legumes
Food yeast

When fruits are added for their vitamin A and C content, we have a fairly complete diet. Dr. Williams reminds us that the protein in body cells is continually wearing out and must be replaced. He thinks the most desirable food for replacing protein is **eggs.** He has no patience with those diets that forbid them.

If it were possible to locate wholesome food today, we'd find it contained everything the body needs. But getting a balanced diet out of the stuff produced in this age of synthetic and stale foods is something else. Dr. Fredericks, whom I cited earlier, says, "It is worthwhile to remember that animals fed on the average American diet not only become diseased, but in three generations lose their ability to reproduce." Today you almost have to go to a health food store to get the things you need for proper nutrition.

Dr. Henry C. Sherman of Colombia University lists five "wonder foods," as he calls them, which are fairly easy to come by. Made a part of a person's daily diet, they supply the essential proteins, all of the B vitamins, calcium, iron, and other minerals. Here's his list:

Powdered skim milk   Wheat germ
Brewer's yeast   Yogurt
Blackstrap molasses

2. **Food supplements.** We CANNOT rely solely on the foods we eat to supply the vitamins and minerals we need. To be sure we are not going without the essentials, we should supplement our diets with vitamins and minerals in pill or capsule form. A lot of research has gone into the vitamin business. There are companies that offer tablets and capsules containing everything we need in the right dosages. Most of the larger companies deal with the public by direct mail. It's a good idea to get on the mailing list of a number of the big suppliers and order when they offer their items on sale. You can save a lot that way. I do.

I'll leave it to you to brush up on the subject. It is a good idea to experiment. You cannot depend on what is called the "minimum daily requirement." Even in the same family, for example, one person may get along fine on 1000 milligrams of vitamin C, whereas another might require 3000. Usually you can take good doses for about 3 weeks and get results if you are actually deficient in a particular vitamin. But be sure that you are taking a high potency before reaching that conclusion. If you are thinking of treating a DISORDER with the megavitamin approach, it would be wise to have a doctor supervise your program.

> **NOTE.** Have you read any of the recent items in the news concerning vitamin C and the common cold? Nobel Prize winner, Dr. Linus Pauling has reported amazing results obtained from using large quantities of Vitamin C. By large quantities is meant doses measured in GRAMS, not milligrams. When it comes to Vitamin C we can forget the term MINIMUM daily requirement. We should think about MAXIMUM doses. There is mounting evidence that Vitamin C can have a tremendous effect, not only on the short term illnesses such as colds, flu and stomach upsets, but also on the wrinkling of the skin in older persons and the accumulation of cholesterol in the important arteries. Vitamin C is necessary for the formation of Collagen, an important protein in teeth, bones, muscles and skin. The older we get, the more we must have of this vitamin and in larger doses. It is NOT toxic. For most people it is harmless in very large quantities. It is water soluble, so any excess is quickly excreted from the body.

Tests in laboratories show that cells in tissue cultures **cannot** survive when supplied with synthetic nutrients alone. What does that tell us? Something is missing. It is believed that there are vitamins not yet discovered which are supplied only when **natural** sources are used. It is also believed that these missing elements exist chiefly in RAW foods which have not been subjected to heat. Therefore most food supplements are made from natural sources at very low temperatures. In the multivitamin I use, the label shows more than 24 natural ingredients such as alfalfa, parsley, watercress, cabbage, rice, bran, brewer's yeast, fish liver oil, bone meal, organic kelp, raw beef liver, kelp . . . and on and on.

NOTE. Dr. Williams insists there is an intended team work among all the vitamins. If ANY are missing, he says, a link is broken in the environmental chain. It is his opinion that body cells cannot remain healthy unless attention is given to ALL the vitamins. He says there is no such thing as a MINOR vitamin or mineral that is essential to life. Regardless how little or how much a certain vitamin is needed, he says the whole nutritional chain must be kept intact. The only way to provide complete nutrition is to get RAW fruits and vegetables into one's diet. And when supplements are used, to make sure they are from natural sources. Even when we have done our best, it is possible for us to end up with mediocre nutrition.

THESE BOOKS CAN HELP

Here are some titles that will give you an exposure to nutrition, diet, and vitamin therapy.

1. **"Nutrition, Your Key to Good Health,"** by Carlton Fredericks, Ph.D. This is a 272 page paperback. This man is very sound and maintains a full time staff for research and keeping up on the latest discoveries. He is easy to read. The publisher is London Press, in North Hollywood, California.

2. **"Stay Young Longer,"** by Linda Clark. This is a 400 page paperback. Linda is really up on nutrition and the nutritional approach to diseases. She is the author of a number of books on nutrition and health and her articles appear regularly in "Let's Live" magazine. The paper back edition is published by Pyramid.

3. **"Let's Get Well,"** by Adelle Davis. This is a 560 page book that has been out since 1965. It is something of a standard now. It has recently been produced in paperback and is now on the stands.

222

NOTE. There are numerous health books on the market. Your local health food store can help you in selecting titles that deal with any particular health problem that interests you. But in the end, you must become your own nutritionist. As you start your reading, you will come to appreciate the work that has been done in this field. Big strides have been made and exciting results have been produced. The works of Drs. Williams and Shute are real eye-openers. Along with Dr. Linus Pauling of Stanford University, these men are staunch believers in using massive doses of vitamins for treating a number of serious diseases. They have achieved phenomenal cures without the use of any drugs.

You should also subscribe to a good nutrition magazine. There are two I feel are excellent:

1. "Prevention," published monthly by Rodale Press, 33 East Minor St., Emmaus, PA 18049. You can get an education in nutrition reading this magazine. It really is geared to preventing illness. It costs less than a news magazine.

2. "Let's Live," published monthly by Oxford Industries, 444 North Larchmont Boulevard, Los Angeles, CA 90004. This magazine is very contemporary. It features public figures who have been successful in achieving vigorous and bouncy lives through eating the right things. The articles are full of good ideas on nutrition. Just one article could save a trip to the doctor and justify the price of a subscription.

I have before me a copy of "Let's Live" magazine telling the story of a rough outdoor man who had a severe heart attack which doctors said damaged his heart terribly.* They gave him little hope for recovery. His arteries were partially blocked with cholesterol. In the course of seeking help, he read

---

*"How I conquered Heart Disease," by Al Cappelletti, **Let's Live,** April '72, page 35.

Dr. Shute's book, "Vitamin E, the Key to a Healthy Heart." Interested, he went to a health food store. There he received a little advice which got him on Vitamin E, lecithin, and wheat germ oil. His health started to improve.

Then he visited his physician to see what he thought of the vitamin approach. The doctor replied, "Well, Al, it won't help you any, but you can take it if you want to." He did take it. In fact he decided to stop the blood thinning medication his doctor gave him and follow the advice of a nutritionist. He increased his vitamin E intake from 400 units a day to 1000 units three times a day. Within one week his angina pains stopped completely. Three months later he dropped back to his regular 400 units per day. He has had no trouble since. Today, three years later, this man is back to climbing mountain peaks with a pack on his back. The best that medicine had to offer was to thin his blood and give him nitroglycerine pills.

CAN DIET ALONE BRING HEALING?

Not long ago Margie and I visited the world famous San Diego Zoo. The people who run it take great care in the feeding of their animals. Signs are posted everywhere asking the visitors not to feed them. They are on strictly controlled diets. Undoubtedly their meals are more nutritious than those of the average American. It's an investment as far as the owners are concerned. By seeing that their creatures get the right food, the owners can make them last a long time. It's good business to make them last as long as they will. Given the proper nutrients, animals stay healthy and fit. They do not get sick.

Is the same true of the human animal?

Yes, as far as the body itself is concerned. But we

have seen that man is NOT a body. He merely wears one during his earthly probation. If there were NO MAN using these animals, they could be kept in perfect condition through nutrition alone. Of course then they would function solely as earth creatures. Should something go wrong inadvertantly, or by accident, the healing principle would easily care for it—as long as the body was supplied with the necessary nutrients. In other words, if we were not using the human animal as our earthly dwelling, good nutrition could provide perfect health.

But God has given us these creatures as earth-suits. And while believers have a new nature through Christ, we still have our old natures. That old nature is capable of destructive thoughts and emotions. We've already discussed what happens to our bodies when we allow evil thoughts to churn in our minds. By THOUGHTS ALONE we are able to create physical problems nutrition cannot handle. We bring on illness that cannot be resolved no matter what good food we put in our stomachs.

Then why a whole chapter on nutrition?

There are SOME DISEASES brought on by poor eating habits. We shouldn't blame emotions for arteries that are loaded with cholesterol when we stuff our stomachs with sugar and white flour products. We can stop that kind of damage simply by changing our eating habits. Think of the salt we eat. Should we ask the computer to bring down our blood pressure and soften our arteries while we continue to eat the very things that make them hard in the first place? It doesn't make sense to ask God to heal us while we indulge in things that make us sick.

Then there are those diseases brought on by DEFI-CIENCIES in our diets. Again, why expect the computer to care for a deficiency disease when it should be cared for by giving the body what it needs? See now why I had to talk about nutrition? There are laws which God has laid down for the dietary maintenance of the animal. When we work with those laws, we prosper. When we work against them, we suffer. If you didn't know such laws existed, you do now.

> **NOTE.** Among Christians with whom I have worked, I have known some who strictly followed the laws of health God laid down for the maintenance of the body. At the same time though, they ignored the mental laws which He also established. Because they refused to discipline their minds, they failed to get the healing they wanted. On the other hand, I have known Christians who concentrated on triggering the computer but ignored God's dietary laws. They too failed to get the desired results. You can see what it does to the computer to have its owner trying to trigger healing by faith, while at the same time violating the law of health. It's true, of course, that the computer can heal by taking nutrients from other organs of the body, but it is not the best way. For healing to be **permanent** and the Christian enjoy it, the body should be healthy throughout. Nutrition plays a key role when it comes to a bouncy, buoyant body.

REVIEW

There are physicians and researchers who recognize the danger of poor nutrition and are doing something about it. Dedicated investigators with impeccable credentials are reporting their finding in scholarly, well documented books. The truth is getting out. Those concerned about their health are beginning to learn what dead food is doing to their bodies. People are discovering that the only way to give their bodies what they need is to return to natural foods. God designed food the way He meant for it to be used. The closer we stay to the natural, organic source, the more nutritious food is. Since we cannot always get foods that way, supplemental foods are needed. All Christians should supplement their diets with items which provide proteins, vitamins, and minerals in abundance.

There is yet another thing we must do to assist the computer in carrying out the healing command. That's next.

Chapter Eleven

IF YOU DON'T USE IT, YOU'LL LOSE IT

"The great danger from automobiles is not from accidents, but from the fact that they take people off their feet."
—Dr. Paul Dudley White

I know a man who drinks like a fish. I'm going to call him George. That's not his real name of course. George is fifty-five. He eats well and exercises regularly, running five miles a day at a downtown athletic club. Though he looks good and seems to be in top shape, he became worried about his liver. He knew alcohol was toxic. He feared the effect his heavy drinking might be having on his liver. If anything happened to that vital organ, he'd be a goner. The function of the liver, as you know, is to protect the body from toxic substances, poisons.

So he went to his doctor for a checkup.

After the examination the doctor reported, **"Your liver is like new."**

"How can that be when I drink so much?" asked George.

"It's your blood." replied the physician. **"All that increased circulation due to your running has been flushing your liver, keeping it from damage. If you didn't run every day as you do, you'd be suffering from cirrhosis right now."**

Why do I tell that story? Only to point out the fact that our bodies are designed for exertion and steady work. They are so constituted that we must work them or suffer.

DESIGNED FOR WORK

"By the sweat of your brow shall you eat bread!"

Who said that? God (Gen. 3:19). He meant it too. He designed our bodies for work even before the fall of Adam. Man was a lot healthier when he had to hunt for his food and walk everywhere he went. But we don't do that today. We don't even walk to the neighborhood store. If we need something, we pile in the car and drive. And when we get there, we park as close to the entrance as we can. As a consequence, our bodies are in poor shape. We forget our bodies are animals. Anyone who has cared for animals knows what happens when they don't get enough exercise. They deteriorate fast. Our earth-suits need exercise to last.

You've gathered by now that this chapter has to do with exercise.

 You go to the hospital suffering an appendicitis attack. Surgery is necessary. But it isn't too long after the operation that an attendant comes into your room wanting to get you on your feet. You can't believe it. But he's serious. Doctors now get their patients up within hours after some types of major surgery. They know a few steps help the patient's blood to get moving. That hastens the healing. Not only that, his digestion and elimination will be much better too.

If you went to bed and deliberately stayed there for three or four days without getting up, you'd be amazed at the serious changes in your body. With astonishing speed your muscles would grow weak, your joints stiffen, your bowels clog, and your sense of balance leaves for a time. But even worse, your arteries and veins would tend to clog. That's why doctors want their patients in motion as soon as possible after surgery— even though it is painful for the patient. They fear the dangers of idleness.

Now a person wouldn't go to bed and let his body go to pot. I mean, he wouldn't do it deliberately. Yet, the same thing takes place slowly, over a long period of time, when we don't exercise. When we fail to work the muscles, especially the large ones, it weakens the body. In the end, it is the same as if we had gone to bed and stayed there. The lack of exercise has the SAME EFFECT as spending time in bed. The only difference is it TAKES LONGER for the damage to occur. But it is happening. We may not be aware of it, but our vitality is fading.

This wasn't a problem half a century ago. In those days people walked to work or rode bicycles. They used their muscles. Life was a lot harder. But as soon as Americans got wheels, they gave up walking. Now we've become a nation of sitters. We sit in schools, busses, and cars, and in front of TV sets. As a result, our bodies are in trouble.

COLLAPSED CAPILLARIES

Here's a word we don't hear often—capillaries. We

hear a lot about our veins and arteries, but little about our capillaries. Maybe that's because they are so small and we don't think they are important. These tiny hair-like blood vessels are about .000315 inches thick. They are hollow with the passage so tiny it barely admits a red blood cell. Many biologists feel these capillaries are the most important part of the circulation system. While the arteries carry blood FROM the heart and the veins carry it BACK, the capillaries are the vessels which actually deliver blood to the individual cells and tissues. A vast network of them connects the arteries with the veins.

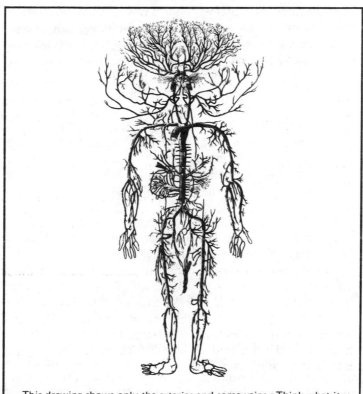

This drawing shows only the arteries and some veins. Think what it would be like if we added the 100,000 miles of capillaries.

Earlier I said that if it were possible to dissolve away all flesh and bone, leaving only the capillaries, veins and arteries, you would still have a recognizable model of the human body. You'd be able to make out all the parts and organs. There are over 100,000 miles of this fine tubing supplying food and oxygen to the cells of your body. Why do I mention this? When people do not exercise their bodies, the capillaries tend to COLLAPSE. Then the muscles begin to starve as the cells are denied necessary nutrients. When the capillaries are unable to carry off the wastes from the cells, the health of the muscles has to degenerate.

> **NOTE.** When patients lie in bed and do not walk around, they suffer from collapsed capillaries. Even though they receive the best possible diet in terms of proteins, vitamins, and minerals, it still does not help their condition. Why? There is no way for that good nutrition to pass through their collapsed capillaries. The automatic healing principle is BLOCKED when capillaries are closed by inactivity. Unless damaged areas can be reached with nutritious blood, new cells cannot be formed from the proteins and the wastes removed. The computer orders the food delivered to the distressed area, but it cannot pass through collapsed vessels. Then the muscles begin to deteriorate. Yet, if the patients could get up and walk a little, some of the capillaries would be forced open and their health would begin to improve almost immediately.

● Christians who do not exercise their bodies have thousands of collapsed capillaries. Sedentary ones have unbelievable numbers of them completely out of action. The result is that millions of the body cells are denied food and oxygen, to say nothing of the waste materials allowed to accumulate. With so many cells undernourished, these people become sluggish. Their vital organs become subject to disease. They may eat balanced meals, but they still suffer poor health.

OBSERVE. Look around you. Do you see Christians anywhere near the PEAK of health? Rarely. Most have allowed their vitality to slip away. They haven't noticed it, perhaps, but it was steadily taking place. How many do you know who have the vigor, the bounce, the snap that accompanies buoyant health? Who in your church exhibits the zip, the pep, the effervescence, the GLOW of perfect health? You just don't see it. Oh yes, the people are alive and move around, but you don't see the bounce that comes from radiant, good health. It just isn't there—except in the very young.

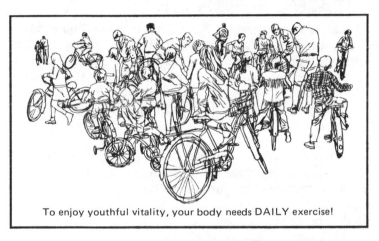

To enjoy youthful vitality, your body needs DAILY exercise!

Exercise **alone** can open closed capillaries and get them back into operation. But it must be prolonged, systematic exercise. Weekend blasts won't do. An outing or a game of tennis from time to time is not at all sufficient. It takes prolonged pressure on the capillaries to open the ones that have been closed a long time. Prolonged pressure means **prolonged exercise.** It doesn't have to be violent exercise, just steady, gentle pressure on those capillaries. Any Christian who will get himself on some sort of a program for prolonged exercise will notice the difference right away. Get those capillaries open and the bounce comes back. It isn't long before a person begins to feel really great!

Now collapsed capillaries is just one reason for our discussion on exercise. There's another which is perhaps even more urgent.

YOU CAN BE CLOSE TO DEATH
AND NOT KNOW IT

Here's a man complaining of dizziness. He has it from time to time. He thinks he'd better see his doctor. He makes an appointment. The doctor runs a number of tests with blood samples, checks his blood pressure and then asks if he's been worrying about anything lately. The patient can't think of anything. Then the doctor gives him an EKG to see what it can tell him about the condition of his heart. Things seem to be okay. So the physician sits down with him and tells him that nothing serious showed up in the exam.

Then the patient goes out of the office feeling better. But as he walks down the street he collapses and is pronounced dead on arrival at the hospital. Imagine having a heart attack right after visiting the doctor. How is this possible?

● People who do not exercise invite a silent killer into their bodies. It's name—atherosclerosis. You may not be used to that name, but doctors use it plenty. It keeps them busy with about 2 million heart attacks a year. Atherosclerosis is a disease of the arteries which is more dangerous than a disease of the heart itself. Atherosclerosis is a form of hardening of the arteries, but the hardness is caused by a buildup of fat on the innermost lining of the artery. The arteries can become almost choked as cholesterol and other fats collect on the walls of the arteries. The flow of blood can be restricted to a tiny stream and the person not aware of it. It won't show up on an EKG either.

234

NOTE. Atherosclerosis resembles the accumulation of minerals in the water pipes of your house. If you live in a hard water area, the flow of water in your house is seriously restricted. You may not notice it, but you are not getting the same water pressure you used to when your house was new. The same thing happens to our arteries. The excess fat in our system enters the blood stream as "biological rust" which accumulates on the sides of the arteries gradually making them narrower and rougher. Arteries should be kept smooth and satiny because of the fantastic amount of blood the heart has to pump throughout the body. But as the waxy deposits continue to build, the passages get smaller and smaller. The danger comes when blood clots form and lodge in one of the restricted passages. That cuts off the blood completely. Should this happen in an artery going to your brain, you have a stroke. When it happens to one of the arteries supplying blood to the heart, you have a heart attack.

Regardless how good a physician might be, he usually cannot detect atherosclerosis until it is too late. Even doctors themselves have heart attacks after their own tests show everything to be okay. Why? Most examinations cannot tell us where troubles are likely to develop. There is no way, for example, for a physician to know a clot is forming somewhere in your body. Without an expensive arteriogram, it is impossible to tell whether or not a person is free from atherosclerosis.

Even if a clot could be located, it might be in a position where it couldn't be reached without great surgical risk. Usually it is an AUTOPSY that tells us how bad our arteries WERE. But that's too late. The only way a person can protect himself against this silent killer is to exercise his body and get on a proper diet. If you discontinue white flour, refined sugar, give up salt and the processed foods, you can live to a ripe old age. But if you don't, there's better than a 50% chance that atherosclerosis will kill you before you realize the condition exists.

NOTE. Three out of every ten people who have heart attacks or strokes, never reach the hospital or are dead within two weeks. Even if a Christian had come to the place where he could trigger the healing program in his body, atherosclerosis could kill him before he could get his computer into operation. He might have all the faith in the world in the picture on the screen, but if there isn't time to activate the healing program and get the computer into action, what good is all that faith? He's dead before healing can start. It's too risky to gamble on being able to get the computer to heal with a silent killer lurking who can strike without notice. It is far wiser to think about prevention than counting on triggering the computer after the killer has struck.

● The sad thing about this disease is that it is unnecessary. For a long time it was thought that atherosclerosis was brought on WHOLLY by what we eat. Doctors thought for a time that the most important fact was the amount of cholesterol in one's blood. Today that's not the opinion. Doctors now know that fats can come into the blood from **stored** body fat. That is, it can come from around your belly and go back into your blood. They are now convinced that a vital key to the balance of fat in the blood is EXERCISE.

Dr. Jean Mayer of the Harvard School of Medicine asserts:

"I am more than ever convinced that medicine in the United States has yet to recognize the formidable health problem caused by the . . . physical inactivity of our citizens. It may well be that no currently available medical measure could be as beneficial as an increase in the amount of exercise taken by our population. The main concern is, of course, the relationship of inactivity to heart disease . . . "

When a person has cholesterol in the blood com-

236

bined with inactivity, he sets himself up for a heart attack.

You can be sure his circulation system is in top shape.

● God didn't intend for us to use our brains only. Since we are using these animals for bodies, we must WORK the creatures. To a great extent the health of the BRAIN itself depends on how much we move the muscles. If we refuse PLANNED EXERCISE or the hard labor God intended for these creatures, we have no one but ourselves to blame when illnesses befall us. That's why I have devoted this chapter to exercise. If you know it is God's will for you to WORK your body, and that HE guarantees the benefits which derive from it, you might be more inclined to do it.

237

NOTE. I am not saying that God can't heal diseased arteries or that the computer can't handle the situation once the danger level is reached. Of course it can. Healing is always available. That's not the point. Isn't it better—no, isn't it safer to cooperate with God's laws than to violate them and then holler for help after the fact? Those who love the Lord should take my word seriously. It is better to do things God's way in the first place than become diseased and seek healing afterwards. If I didn't believe that, this chapter wouldn't be in the book.

YOUR HEART NEEDS YOUR HELP

Consider your heart. Did you know that little 3 pound muscle, which measures about 4x6 inches has to pump tons of blood a day? It has to push your blood, about 8000 gallons of it, through more than 12,000 miles of arteries and veins, plus the capillaries. All the blood in your body passes through that little pump every three minutes. This amazing muscle needs all the help it can get.

Why does it need help? Because man uses his animal house as an upright creature. That is, he walks erect, straight up and down. The blood in his system has to move AGAINST GRAVITY. All of the blood has to be pushed STRAIGHT UP. Blood coming from below the heart has to be pushed up to the heart. Blood from the heart has to be pushed up to the brain. All of the blood going to your brain is resisted by gravity. Think of that! Blood going to the most vital organ of the body has to fight the law of gravity all the way.

Now if we walked on all fours, the task would be a lot easier. The head and the heart and the vital organs would all be on the same level. But the Homo sapiens walks erect. To help the blood move through the body, the creature is equipped with auxiliary boosters—the MUSCLES of the legs and abdomen. When a person walks, when his legs are in motion, it can relieve the heart of as much as 30 PERCENT of its load.

> **NOTE.** When the legs are in motion, the muscles of the feet, calves, thighs, abdomen rhythmically contract and release. As they do, they squeeze the veins forcing the blood along. This keeps the blood moving and helps it get back to the heart. Without this extra push, the blood below the heart would pool in the abdomen and feet. Then the heart would have to come up with bigger surges to get that blood into circulation.

IT WORKS GREAT FOR ME

About two and a half years ago, I went to my doctor for a routine checkup. He found my blood pressure too high. He wasn't worried about it, but he didn't want it to stay that way. He also noticed some flab around my middle. "When are you going to do something about that?" he asked, reaching over and giving my roll of fat a friendly squeeze. "You preachers don't get enough exercise. You ought to get out and jog. That blood pressure would come right down if you did. And that roll of fat would disappear too."

That did it.

Now I didn't start jogging the next day; my doctor warned me against it. For a few weeks he had me walking about the neighborhood. I tried to get in an hour a day. Then I began to jog a little. After some weeks of that, I started riding my bicycle to a nearby high school where I could do laps about the quarter-mile track. A month later I was doing the mile in 10 minutes.

> **NOTE.** I jog three miles every morning, except Sunday. I don't go very fast, somewhere around a 10 minute mile. That's just a little faster than walking. Speed is not important, circulation is. And circulation is best helped

by prolonged jogging. The idea is to get your heartbeat high enough to open your capillaries and keep them open for 20 minutes. Once I learned that God expected me to do this, jogging became a matter of Christian obedience. Now He has shown me a way to make jogging fun—doing it with Jesus. In my book, **JOGGING WITH JESUS**, I share all of the know-how anyone needs for getting started.

I have fun praying for other joggers as they read the back of my T-shirt which reads, "powered by Christ." It opens the door for witnessing situations.

My doctor promised that jogging would add as much as ten more years to my life. That pleased me greatly. It is my desire to serve the Lord Jesus as long as I can. We all want to give Him our best. But how can we serve Him apart from these bodies? We can't. And the apostle Paul is thinking of that when he says, "Present your bodies unto the Lord as a living sacrifice . . . " (Rom. 12:1). Getting them into shape and keeping them that way has to be a part of Christian obedience.

It takes me about 30 minutes to go the three miles. It's a great way to fellowship with the Lord. As we chug along together, I praise Him for His own precious blood that makes me whiter than snow. Then I also thank Him for the physical blood surging through my body, making the organs like new. I'm on the track by 7 a.m. It's clear then, and there's no smog. Usually there's no one around to hear me go through my prayer list. I even shout praises to the Lord now and then. Yes, this is one Baptist preacher who really gets "turned on" for Christ.

NOTE. In my imagination I visualize my heart pounding 175 beats per minute, sending the blood through the capillaries and washing and nourishing every cell in my body. I think about the computer in the back of my head. On the screen I picture the capillaries being forced open and visualize the perfect health of my animal. I think of the 10 million new red cells being created every second and the tremendous power available to heal any area of my body. It wasn't too long ago that physiologists believed a man past forty should slow down and take it easy. Doctors now believe the opposite. Most of them, including our nation's leading heart specialists, now insist that vigorous exercise is not only permissible for older people, but also necessary. I am now 62 and gaining more vitality every day since I started jogging nine and a half years ago.

241

HOW TO GET STARTED

Walk. That's the way to begin. Plan on giving yourself plenty of time before you reach the strenuous levels.
If you gave yourself two years before you were jogging
two miles, it wouldn't be unreasonable. I am NOT telling
you to go right out and start running. Some of you
might drop dead if you tried it. What we need is to
get the blood moving, and walking will do it.

Yet I am telling EVERYONE to do it. Anyone who
can stand on his feet should walk, even if he is sick.
The only one who is excused is the person whose sickness requires bed rest. Those with a history of heart
trouble should ask their physician for advice on how
to begin. You can be sure he will prescribe some kind
of walking. Idleness is deadly. Sitting around and doing
nothing is a terrible way to treat a fine animal like the
human body.

Start with a 15 minute walk. After a week or two

of that, see if you can go for half an hour without fatigue. In a few more weeks try for an hour. If you can walk for an hour and a half without feeling too tired, you are ready to start jogging. If you are over forty, then start your jogging program by jogging a quarter of a mile and then walking a quarter of a mile. Let it build gradually. Don't strain—train. Since you are going to be doing this for the rest of your life, ease yourself into condition. In time you'll be able to jog for a half an hour without stopping. If it takes you a year or two to get there, so what. There's no hurry.

NOTE. Even though a person has neglected his body for years, PLANNED EXERCISE such as I have outlined, can not only STOP the advance of atherosclerosis, it can REVERSE it. **The disease is reversible.** Of course jogging alone won't do it, the diet has to be changed. Sugar, salt, white flour products, and coffee must be eliminated. More than anyone else, the Christian should eat the right food and exercise his animal. He owes it to the Lord to keep his creature in good health. Older Christians must walk. When we examine the histories of people who have lived in good health for a long time, we find they all have one thing in common—walking. A great many studies have been compiled on those who have lived vigorously to 90 and 100. All reveal they were great walkers.

NOTE. Dr. Thomas K. Cureton, Director of the Physical Fitness Lab of the University of Illinois, has pioneered the work of helping older men come to full vitality through exercise. He has taken men in their fifties, sixties and seventies; men who were decrepit and feeble, and put them on walking programs. After he got them to the place where they were walking five miles a day, he started them jogging. First they went a half mile a day, then a full mile. In time they were jogging five miles a day. At the end of two and a half years, he had these men where they were not only feeling terrific, but their medical tests showed splendid improvement of their hearts and other vital organs. Older Christians who follow this advice and eat nutritious food with plenty of vitamins, can expect their bodies to stay healthy and useful to Jesus long after they have buried many friends of the same age. Wouldn't it be nice to be alive when Jesus comes?

● Dieters especially should be interested in this kind of exercise. I know that exercise alone does not burn many calories. But here's what is **not** commonly known. Exercise forces the body to produce enzymes at a faster rate and this speeds up the fat-burning process. But let's not forget that a person who is exercising faithfully can STILL GET SICK if he fails to discipline his thought-life.

THE MIND REMAINS THE BOSS

While diet and exercise are vital to good health, we must keep their importance in perspective. They are tools for the computer. But the computer, on the other hand, is a tool of the MIND. Therefore, it is the mind that controls the body. It decides what foods will go into the stomach. After all, it is the PERSON who decides what he will eat and whether or not he will exercise. It is the MIND that determines what thoughts will appear on the screen.

The drawing opposite shows the relationship of the MAN to the computer and his body. Observe how the image of God uses the computer, and the computer in turn makes use of the nutrition and exercise. Also, it shows why a person can eat the right food and exercise his body and still be sick. If destructive thoughts are allowed on the screen, the computer becomes programmed for sickness regardless of nutrition and exercise.

NOTE. Consider the wisdom of God! What genius it took to wed the invisible image of God with a creature of the field. The union is so intimate that every THOUGHT and every EMOTION is reflected in the creature's body. It is

244

a spiritual relationship so close that when the man is upset, the chemical balance of the creature is altered. Now that is close. The body fits the man like a glove. Yet the body, via the computer is the SERVANT of the mind. That is why sick thoughts produce a sick body. If his thoughts are harmful and destructive, his body must handle them. If his thought-life is wholesome, his body reflects his mental health.

THE MIND USES THE COMPUTER, AND THE COMPUTER USES NUTRITION AND EXERCISE

COMPUTER

NUTRITION EXERCISE

The image of God projects a perfectly healed body on the TV screen of his mind. He believes what he sees and the computer accepts it as a command to heal. Then the computer, in turn, uses the nutrition and exercise in the process of restoring his body to perfect condition.

● REVIEW AND REMEMBER

1. The disciplined mind.

The mind is the BOSS of the computer. Therefore it is absolutely necessary for the Christian to discipline his thought-life. He must develop that sereneness which comes when one trusts the Lord for the answer to EVERY problem (Phil. 4:6). He can do it if he learns how to detect Satan's working in his thought processes. Once a Christian is able to DEAL with the devil BEFORE vicious and harmful thoughts churn in his mind, he can keep himself godly and tranquil. If he can do that, then his computer will be free to see that the law of health reigns throughout his body.

2. A nutritious diet.

The Christian should live on a high protein, low carbohydrate diet, supplementing his meals with vitamins and minerals derived from natural sources. He must eliminate sugar and white flour products from his meals. Coffee and salt should be discontinued. Given the essential ingredients, his computer will manufacture the necessary enzymes and have an abundance of raw materials for replacing damaged cells. Without essential nutrition, the computer cannot keep the body in vigorous and buoyant health. Bodies loaded down with the nude food of our generation are wide open to disease—heart disease in particular.

3. Planned Exercise.

The Christian must exercise his body daily. Everyone can walk. If a believer will walk his body for an hour a day (or jog for 30 minutes) he will give the creature the workout it needs to open the capillaries feeding the cells. It is futile to pour good food into a body without providing for the exercise needed to stir up the enzyme action. Much of that food will not be useful. Exercise is the KEY to the assimilation of food.

> **NOTE.** For those able to jog, half an hour a day is just right. It is PROLONGED exercise that benefits the body. Bursts of speed are useless. A steady pushing of the body can restore the arteries and make them like new. Exercise REBUILDS the capillaries. Riding a bicycle or swimming is as beneficial as jogging, but it takes a lot more of it. Not everyone has access to a pool. But most of us are close to a public park or school where it would be proper to walk or jog. Age makes no difference. The older a Christian is, the more he needs exercise. We don't need strenuous exercises, but we do need PLANNED exercises in order to stay healthy and fit for the Master's service.

● The Christian who will go to work on these three steps can reach the peak of condition. It might take him a few years to get there but once he is in shape, he can expect to live to a ripe old age and be full of vitality. The average Christian is a long way from that. He is caught in the American way of eating and he rides every place he goes. As a result he doesn't have the BOUNCE God means for him to enjoy.

How about you, dear reader? Are you sincere about giving your best to Christ? Then you'll start getting yourself into shape. Once you do, you'll have lots of energy and find yourself wanting to do things for the Lord. Good health and spiritual vitality go together. For the zestful believer there's only one place to invest his energy—in Christ Jesus.

The next chapter tells how.

Follow the advice set forth in these chapters and you'll throw your cane away too!

Chapter Twelve

NOW THAT YOU HAVE BEEN HEALED

Remember the story of the man with the balky mule? Whenever he got ready to work his mule, he would seize a two by four and bang the animal over the head with it. On this particular occasion a passerby saw him do it. Perplexed and startled, he stopped to inquire why the man treated his mule that way.

"This is a really stubborn mule," said the owner. "Whenever I want to work him, I have to make it clear to him that we have a job to do."

"I see," said the spectator, "but why do you hit him with that board?" He wasn't ready for the owner's reply . . .

"I HAVE TO GET HIS ATTENTION FIRST."

SICKNESS—GOD'S TWO BY FOUR

Sickness is a great attention getter.

When God's people enjoy good health and comfortable circumstances, it is easy for them to drift from the things of the Lord. They tend to occupy with their families, careers, and the necessities of life. When that happens, they take their relationship with Jesus for granted. The Lord doesn't like that. When we become careless with Him, we also become careless with our personal holiness. You can guess what that does to our thought-life. Then sickness comes. He allows it because He can use it. Besides, we bring it on ourselves.

When the distress is great enough, we turn to the Lord. He then has our attention.

GOD WANTS CHANGED LIVES

Picture an inclined plane. See yourself somewhere in the middle. That plane represents your life on earth. It is an uphill pull. Christianity is NOT easy. If you want to get ahead in Christ, you must "strive to win," as the apostle Paul puts it. Salvation is free. It is received without effort on our part. But Christian maturity and life changes come only through struggle. It's an uphill fight all the way. If believers do not "press on" in Christ, they will roll backwards. There is no way to be stationary on a slope.

The influence of the world acts like the law of gravity on a Christian. He has to resist the downward pull of this life if he wants to get ahead in Christ. This is why it is dangerous to pause along the way in Christian development. It's much easier to slip backwards than move up in the Lord.

The Lord will not allow us to stand still. If a Christian refuses to move up in the Christian life, God will send pressures and jarring circumstances to shake the board. He hates the status quo. Most of us can think back and recall how our biggest strides in the Christ-life came at a time of crisis. It seems that until a crisis occurs, we are content to let things stay as they are. In fact, we have an expression which speaks to this very thing: "Don't rock the boat." By that we mean, don't make waves, leave things as they are. God hates that attitude. He wants the boat rocked. He rocks it Himself.

It seems a shame that God has to use sickness or take a loved one home to get our attention. But that's the way we are. We all like the status quo. We don't do anything until we have to. When God's hand is laid on the Christian, he will either look to Him for help or slide backwards. People don't always notice it when they slip backwards. A year later they can look at their lives and see they have nowhere near the spiritual vitality they once had. But they are not the same, you can be sure of that.

Doctors tell us that when a person's physical health declines seriously, some common symptoms appear: (1) usually there is a marked loss of appetite, (2) there is little desire to see people and converse with them, (3) there is no desire to put forth physical effort. Someone has observed that the symptoms of SPIRITUAL decline are much the same. They occur gradually, of course, but they do occur:

1. **A loss of appetite for the things of God.**
2. **A greatly reduced prayer-life.**
3. **Little or no interest in reaching others for Christ.**

Those are the symptoms of spiritual sickness.

I'm not saying the spiritually sick Christian stays away from church. The power of habit would see that he continues going. In fact, he will probably be just as churchy as ever. But the symptoms will be there too. He will have no yearning for those things that please

251

the Lord. His appetite has changed. It matters less and less what the Lord wants and more and more what he wants. Finally he ends up doing his own thing entirely.

The prayer life of this believer drops to a low level. He may ask the blessing at meal time and toss a few words in God's direction before he goes to bed, but that's it. Intimate and warm fellowship with Jesus is a thing of the past. The presence of God is no longer real to the man who rolls backwards down the plane.

The last thing in the world he cares about is getting out and speaking to people about Christ. He will drive into the gas station with one thing on his mind, his car. It won't even occur to him to hand a tract to the attendant or leave one in the restroom. The same could be said of all the other places he visits in the course of his routine. Finally he comes to feel that church is the place for Jesus and the rest of life is his own to do with as he pleases.

Isn't that sad? You've seen it happen.

IT CAN HAPPEN TO THE HEALED CHRISTIAN TOO

Once a person experiences a dramatic healing, it is up to him whether or not he STAYS HEALED. The safest course is to look on his healing as a TURNING POINT in his life. It is a precious working of God. The healed believer should determine, that from that time on, his life will be different. If he doesn't make that kind of a commitment, he will drift back to his old ways. The devil is on hand to see that he does. With Satan working so subtly, it can happen easily and naturally. In fact, unless you determine otherwise, backsliding is AUTOMATIC.

It's RISKY to be healed by faith and then do nothing with your life. The person who accepts healing via God's laws and then fails to use that healing for His glory, invites the possibility of something WORSE happening to him.

Jesus said as much.

Remember the lame man who was healed by Jesus at the pool of Bethesda? The story occurs in the fifth chapter of John's gospel. For 38 years this cripple had been coming to this particular pool, hoping to be healed by getting into the water at the right moment. But his lameness prevented him from making it on time. Then Jesus visited the pool and the man was healed. On Jesus' orders he picked up his heavy quilt and carried it into town. Later Jesus found the man in the temple and gave him this stern warning:

"Behold you have become well; sin no more lest a worse thing befall thee" (John 5:14).

NOTE. A particular sin was connected with this man's disease. We don't know what it was, but Jesus did. By means of His penetrating knowledge, He was able to discern the specific sin responsible for the man's condition. The man knew what it was, too. And he understood the warning. A continuation of that sin, which had already brought him 38 years of infirmity, would mean disaster. Since there is no indication of repentance on the part of the healed man, or forgiveness on the part of the Lord, we can assume the CAUSE remained with him. It would now be up to him to TURN from that sin in order to retain the healing he had received. This meant a changed life. That's what the Lord wanted. The man could have made such a commitment since Jesus did find him in the temple later on.

● If we accept the Lord's words to this lame man as a principle, it means that a worse illness can befall the Christian who allows himself to DRIFT to a lower level of faith. Once he has risen to the place where he can use God's laws to get well, he should maintain himself at this higher level and go on from there. It is a struggle, but this is what God expects. The believer who has the faith to use the healing laws has an opportunity, an obligation and a privilege.

1. His opportunity.

If a believer has the faith to effect a healing of his body, God expects him to live on a higher plane. Why? His healing is proof that he is capable of trusting God for greater things. The Lord has every right to expect this man to press on. Faith is a fragile thing. Once a believer is able to make an advance up the faith-ladder, he should cherish the gain he has made. He should do everything he can to exploit his progress. He now has an opportunity to climb to the next higher step. Any victory of faith should make us hungry for more. Fantastic things can be done for Jesus when we reach the higher levels of faith. The Christian who has been healed has a good chance of becoming such a man.

2. His obligation.

The healed Christian is obliged to USE his new found health for Jesus. He owes it to the Lord. The Lord has made it possible. Our Master has no interest in healing for the sake of healing. It is not His purpose to make people comfortable. He wants His people to SERVE Him, even as He served the Father. But more than Christian duty is involved. There is no way for a believer to maintain himself at a higher spiritual level WITHOUT SERVING THE LORD. Failure to do so is disobedience. God cannot bless disobedience. And without God's blessing there is no way for a Christian to keep himself at the new level. To fail to serve the Lord with one's new health is downright ingratitude. The believer who treats Him that way is no different from the lepers who were healed and didn't even bother to thank Him (Luke 17:18).

254

A picture on the nightstand by the bed and saying "goodnight" to the Lord help give Him reality.

3. His privilege.

The greatest privilege of the Christian is moment by moment fellowship with Jesus (I John 1:1-3). The Lord wants His people to accept His presence BY FAITH and move into an ever closer relationship with Him. For this to happen the Lord must become increasingly real. I'm speaking of practicing the presence of Christ. Even though we cannot see Him, He is as close to us as the animal we're wearing. In fact we share it with Him. To give reality to Jesus, we make use of the imagination. The highest purpose to which we can dedicate this wondrous faculty is to give reality to the Lord Jesus. God means for us to picture Jesus by faith and then enjoy Him. Perhaps you didn't know our capacity to realize Christ can be increased. It can. The more real the Lord becomes to us, the closer we can draw to Him. The closer we get to Him, the more our faith rises. The more our faith rises, the more we can do WITH Him. The Lord has many exciting tasks for those with the faith to work closely with Him.

● It is natural for the sick Christian to cry to the Lord. When he is reaching for the faith needed to trigger the computer, he automatically talks to Jesus a lot. More and more he finds himself making affirmations and chatting with the One Who wants him well. The intimacy deepens. The Lord becomes more real. In time he finds his faith has increased to the place where healing gets under way.

The danger period comes AFTER the Christian has been healed. It is easy for him to become careless with Christ once the pressure is gone. His frequent chats with Jesus become less and less. Satan has other things for him to do. He drifts from his higher ground. His interest shifts from Jesus to family, job, and routine matters. That's sad. The believer who does this willfully, abandons the most coveted spot in Christianity—a place near the Lord. The man who doesn't cherish the presence of Christ in this life, will find himself NO CLOSER to Christ in heaven. That's something to think about, isn't it?

> **NOTE.** If being A DISTANCE from Christ in heaven is new to you, you should read the author's book, **Jesus Is Coming...!** There you will find a startling expose of the Judgment Seat of Christ. It will cause you to become serious about making your time on earth count for eternity. You want to be close to Jesus in heaven, don't you? Sure you do. Then you should learn all you can about investing yourself in Him NOW. The Lord's own counsel to us is for us to lay up for ourselves "treasures in heaven" (Matt. 6:20). The hard fact is that if we don't lay up treasure now, we won't have any when we get there. Poverty in heaven will be no more enjoyable than it is here. Those who fail to invest this one life in the Lord will be poor throughout eternity. Do you know what the wealth of heaven is? It's people. To be close to Jesus in heaven, every believer should be involved in some work that wins and builds men in Christ.

SO KEEP YOURSELF AT THE HIGHER LEVEL

All right, you have been healed. I praise the Lord with you. You have risen in faith to the place where you can use God's laws and become whole again. This is a wonderful victory over unbelief. Don't lose the priceless gain that you have made. As far as your faith is concerned, you are at your highest level right now. Plan on a new life based on your higher level of faith. Don't throw away the opportunity that now beckons.

From here on I will present a program for maintaining the higher ground you have won by faith. I want to show you a way to make the most of your opportunity. At the same time you will have the feeling of fulfilling your obligation to Jesus. Now this is my suggestion:

BECOME A WITNESS FOR CHRIST!

Don't panic. I know the word **witness** is terrifying to some Christians. But will you notice I did NOT say I wanted you to win souls. I merely said become a witness. There's a big difference between winning souls and being a witness. They are NOT the same. Perhaps you didn't know that. Let me explain the difference. Then you will see why witnessing could be just right for you. The whole thing is not nearly so frightening once you know what it really means to witness for the Lord.

The difference.

 Come with me to a courtroom. Watch the witness take the stand. After he is sworn, he is asked to make statements from his own personal knowledge. He tells what he knows, that's all. He neither challenges nor probes. He doesn't ask anyone to do anything. That's not

257

his job. He simply presents his information and is then dismissed.

Now watch the prosecutor. He doesn't take the stand. He is a lawyer. He doesn't tell much of anything. Instead he is highly skilled in extracting information and using that knowledge to prove his point. He knows how to handle people. He manipulates them. That's how he wins cases. His moves are aimed at convincing a judge or jury.

● The soul-winner is like a prosecuting attorney. His moves are designed to extract information from a prospect. Then, in the power of the Spirit, he uses that information to bring his prospect face to face with Christ. It is a skill, a sharp skill. He works with words so cleverly that people are manipulated by him without realizing it. Yet all of his efforts are geared to getting his prospect to DO SOMETHING with Jesus. He is a persuader of men. It's no wonder Christians panic at the thought of having to win souls to the Lord.

Now consider the Christian witness. He is not like that. He does nothing more than TELL OTHERS ABOUT CHRIST. There he stops. In no way does he ask people to do anything. Once he gets Jesus' invitation into another person's hands, he's through. His job is done. It doesn't matter how easily or simply he goes about doing this. If he can somehow get the news of Christ to an unsaved person, he has completed his work as a witness.

It helps to know that.

I had just brought a soul-winning message in a fundamental church, when a tearful lady hurried forward to speak to me. She was nervous, perspiring. Her hands kept tearing at a knotted handkerchief.

"Dr. Lovett, I'm ashamed to say this, but I can't witness for the Lord. I don't know how to win souls!"

"Forget soul-winning," I said to her. "It has nothing to do with you right now. Why don't you consider becoming a witness first. You can think about winning souls later on."

At first she was puzzled. Like so many Christians she thought she couldn't witness without being a soul-winner. When I explained the difference, her face brightened. Her shoulders dropped in relief. Just those few words lifted the burden from her soul. Then I gave her some EASY helps for starting out as a witness.

The lady went away rejoicing. As long as she thought that witnessing meant she had to win souls, she was reluctant to learn or try anything. The very thought of approaching strangers and dealing with them made her spirit numb.

Just as a man cannot go from the ground to the roof of his house without a ladder, neither can a Christian go from silence to active witnessing without a plan which breaks the distance up into easy steps.

NOTE. I have already mentioned the faith-ladder. There are different degrees of faith and a person can climb to different levels during his Christian life. Now let me mention another ladder, the LADDER-METHOD of witnessing. To become an effective witness—AND ENJOY IT—a

Christian should start at the bottom of the ladder and work his way to the top—one rung at a time. He shouldn't move to the next step until his strengths have developed to the place where he can make the advance comfortably. There are thousands of ways to witness, ranging from leaving tracts in secret to telling someone what Jesus means to you. Between those two extremes are 10 steps (categories actually) a person may climb gradually as he learns to work with the Holy Spirit. When you approach witnessing in this fashion, it is FUN!

● Isn't that a relaxing truth? Now that you've seen the difference between witnessing and soul-winning, it shouldn't be so frightening when I suggest that you become a witness. In fact, aren't you pleased to think there is a non-threatening way to maintain yourself at the higher level in Christ? Now let me make it still easier for you. There is a way to get started as a witness which offers NO THREAT AT ALL.

GETTING STARTED

See the book to the left? That's **Witnessing Made Easy.** It sets forth in great detail—256 pages of them—the ladder-method of witnessing. It provides everything a person needs to get started as a witness without threat of any kind. You begin by leaving tracts secretly. No one is to see you do it. Now then, couldn't you do something as easy as that? Of course you could. And you would enjoy it. This book shows how to do it in such a way that you sample the power of the Holy Spirit on your very first attempt.

The first action, which is done in secret, is actually an experiment with the Holy Spirit. You do the assign-

261

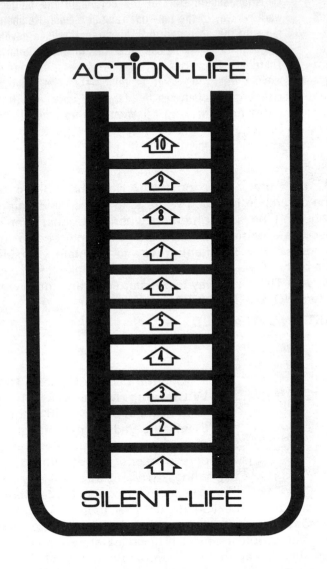

Becoming a witness is easier — one step at a time.

ment in such a way that you experience His presence and power. It is all done privately. It is the Spirit of God, you see, Who makes witnessing easy. And while you may agree with that idea IN THEORY, it is something else to SEE HIM in action. It is a comforting experience to find Him at work IN YOU as you do a witnessing exercise. When you see how He settles the flutters in your heart, you'll wonder why you didn't get started long ago.

Listen to the testimony of someone who started witnessing the EASY way. I have permission to use his letter as well as those which follow:

> "My life started to change with the third lesson. It has continued to change as I made my way up the ladder. I have found great enjoyment in working with the Holy Spirit and seeing Him work through me. I have grown from an inactive Christian to a bold witness. I have little fear and I do not allow anything to interfere with a witness situation. I now know for a fact that the Holy Spirit supports a person from the very first move he makes. I feel the Lord can now use me anywhere, not only because of the know-how I have acquired, but because I know how to listen to the voice of the Holy Spirit. I could never go back to the life of a routine Christian."

> Eugene Walters
> P.O. Box 62
> St. Marys, OH
> 45885

Isn't that something? I have hundreds of letters like that from people who have been lifted to a new level in Christ. This is the way to exercise your faith and stay close to Jesus. Don't you think you should send for a copy of **Witnessing Made Easy** and examine the ladder-method for yourself? A little hesitant? Listen to another testimony.

263

"I feel my ministry has just begun. I'll never be the same Keith H. Whiteman again. Never in my life have I experienced the marvelous power of the Holy Spirit as I do today. No longer is He a doctrine to me, He is my partner in the witnessing business. If only other brethren knew what would happen to them if they had this know-how power in witnessing. Why this whole world would be turned upside down for Jesus! I can't praise God enough for getting me started on the ladder-method of witnessing!"

Keith H. Whiteman
371 Walnut St.
Portstown,   PA
19464

See now why I say that witnessing is the way to keep yourself at a higher level of faith and use your HEALED BODY for Christ at the same time? It really is the best way I know. And I am in touch with thousands of Christians who will echo the words of those testimonies.

IT CAN DO THE SAME FOR YOU

Here comes your boy to the breakfast table. Wow! Does he look different this morning! His hair is neatly combed, his shoes are shined. Not only are his clothes fresh and bright, he's even cleaned under his finger nails. What's happened? What's come over him. You know. There's a new girlfriend at school. He has a new affection and it has taken hold of his life.

Are you aware of the transforming power of a new affection? People behave differently when seized by a new obsession. I have a friend who took up short wave radio. He built a "ham" station in his garage. He became obsessed with talking to people in different lands with his radio. He'd miss meals and stay up all night to contact someone in the Far East. His whole life got caught up in it. Finally it was all he could think about or talk about. That's what I mean by a new obsession.

That's what witnessing can do for you.

It's a new adventure to learn how to witness WITH JESUS. The thing that really hooks you is the power of the Holy Spirit. When you are able to speak to people in the Spirit's might—with His power operating as though it were your own—you get drunk on the joy of it. Experience that thrill and you'll never be satisfied with routine Christianity again.

● Imagine what this could mean to the person who has been healed by faith. It gives him an opportunity to use his new health for Christ. At the same time, he is able to maintain himself at the HIGHER LEVEL of faith reached as he was using the healing laws. The healed person who becomes infected with the Spirit's power as a witness, finds a new obsession engulfing his life. Imagine a believer swept up in an obsession that kept him on a higher level of faith! Think of the astonishing things that would happen as a result of the fire burning in Him! Such a person could trust God for supernatural things—and see them come to pass!

SO USE YOUR HEALTH FOR CHRIST

I guarantee you won't be sorry. Thrills and adventure combine to bring a new obsession to your life—**serving Jesus!** That will keep your faith at the high level. Then, as you go on from there, think what you will be able to do in His power! Wow! Your life will take on a new glow as you radiate His presence and your new health!

● Our bodies respond to the exhilaration of witnessing. When you know you are pleasing the Lord, contentment saturates your being. When you see God using you in power, deep satisfaction fills your soul. The fun and enthusiasm which accompany Spirit-filled witnessing put new bounce in your body. You become a whole new person. Just wait and see.

I want you convinced. I am doing my best to persuade you. But I will not lie to you, nor exaggerate, for then the Holy Spirit cannot bless what I say. I must speak the truth or His witness will not accompany my words. Therefore I trust Him to apply the warning. You must not drift back into your old ways once you have been healed. Why run the risk of returning your illness—or something worse? I don't want that to happen to you. The Lord has been dealing with you through your sickness. He is after a CHANGE in your life. Won't you say, "Yes, Lord Jesus, I get the message." And then get started as a witness.

Here's how one man found his life changed by witnessing. I am quoting from a letter he sent me:

> "I am having the thrill of a lifetime WITNESSING for Jesus! I never dreamed it would be this way! From what I have tasted already, I know I have to be a witness for the rest of my life. Thank you, brother Lovett, for your wonderful course and the help it has given me. My life has changed completely! I am a TRANSFORMED MAN ALL OVER! Witnessing for Jesus is the one big adventure of this life!"
>
> Roger E. Duperree, 318 Elk Run Ave.
> Punxsutawney, PA 15767

Those exclamation marks you see in that paragraph are all his, not mine. He was struggling for words adequate to the thrills that go with action in Christ. "I feel like I am at last interested in the same thing the Lord is interested in." That's the way Roger closed his letter to me.

Now listen to the testimony of Donald Ross of 4201 North 66th St., Birmingham, Alabama, 35206:

> "My life was exciting, or so I thought, until I started witnessing as per your course. I soon found my life was really nothing more than an UNLIT FIRECRACKER. Now that I have gone into action for Christ, that fuse has been lit. I praise the Lord for the thrills that come from serving in His power! What a life!"

How about it? Are you ready to present that healed body to Jesus? I hope so. Take my word for it, the easiest and most exciting way to do it is by becoming a witness.

COME ON, TAKE THAT STEP

In the back of this book you'll find a list of the titles mentioned in this book, among them **WITNESSING MADE EASY.** Before Satan has a chance to pour cold water on your spirit, why not go to your desk right now and get off an order? Yes, you could go to your bookstore and that might be faster, but it would mean a lot to me if you were to drop me a note saying,

> "Dear Dr. Lovett, I want to use my health for the Lord Jesus. I sense the Spirit's call to be a witness for Him. If you have a plan for helping believers witness at their shyness level and easing up the ladder, I'm interested. Please send me a copy of **WITNESSING MADE EASY** and bill me. Thanks for helping us give our best to the Lord."

In His precious name,

Signed _____

Address _____

City _____

State, Zip _____

TWO BOOKS BY DR. LOVETT TO KEEP YOU PHYSICALLY FIT FOR THE MASTER'S SERVICE

No. 546

JOGGING WITH JESUS

Exercise is essential to keep your body fit for the Master's use. This book shows how to enjoy the benefits of jogging and at the same time **develop a glorious relationship with the Lord.** Every Christian should set aside time for the Lord in these busy days— and **jogging with Jesus** is a great way!

(112 pages, paperback, illustrated)

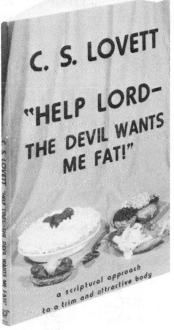

SOME QUESTIONS?

1 **Can everyone expect to be healed of every illness?**

The answer—NO. While I have laid out some of the laws and mechanics for triggering the computer, there are several things which can block the healing process:

a. **Lack of faith.**

I probably didn't need to say this, it's so obvious. It should be apparent to everyone that merely learning the techniques set forth in this book will not bring healing. A person must BELIEVE the scene he projects onto the conscious screen. The LAW OF BELIEF is itself a vital healing law. If a person violates that law, there can be no healing. The computer will **not** carry out the HEALED IMAGE unless the owner truly believes what he sees on that screen. There are those who simply cannot bring themselves to this kind of belief. The worse the illness, the harder it is to use the law of belief.

> **NOTE.** If you have an illness that brings considerable pain, it is hard to behold the healed image in your imagination and say . . . "I believe the pain is gone, my body is now perfectly sound." It takes a high degree of faith to do this. The nice thing about faith, however, is that it can go where reason cannot follow. A person must bring his faith to the necessary level or the computer will not activate. It takes total confidence in God's healing laws plus an awareness of His healing presence to reach this point. Yet it can be done. Once the needed level of faith is reached, the computer has the power to execute the healing order, and heal ANY emotionally induced illness.

b. **Divine intervention.**

While visiting in Switzerland, a tourist came upon a shepherd and his flock of sheep high up on a mountainside. The tourist's attention was drawn to a poor sheep bleating in pain. It couldn't get about. It's leg was broken. When the tourist asked the shepherd about it, he said:

"I broke it myself. It was the only way I could keep the little dickens from wandering off. We shepherds have to do this from time to time. We find that after we break a sheep's leg and nurse it back to health, it gets so attached to us it will come instantly when we call it. After that we have no more trouble with it."

Sometimes it's like that with us and the Lord Jesus. An illness strikes. That illness draws us closer to the Lord. In kindness the Lord **overrules the healing mechanism** so that the affliction remains. The result is closer and sweeter communion with our Savior. Finally we become so conditioned to our new relationship with Him, that we follow His leading most eagerly. I don't think God does this very often, but I'm sure there are times when He does.

● We definitely know this was the case with the apostle Paul. He had an ailment which he labeled as a ''thorn in the flesh, a messenger of Satan sent to buffet me . . . '' (II Cor. 12:7). Three times he sought healing from the Lord. But each time the Lord said—''NO!'' The specific reply was, ''My grace is sufficient for thee.''

Paul understood. He knew God's thinking. Behind that affliction was the fact that Paul had been ''caught up to the third heaven,'' and in that paradise ''heard unspeakable words which it is not lawful (natural law) for a man to utter'' (II Cor. 12:2,4). It was because of the abundance of revelations that God permitted Paul

271

to have this affliction. It kept him from becoming puffed with pride and getting the big head. The apostle appreciated that God had dealt with him this way. He acknowledged that the Lord had stayed his healing, "lest I should be exalted above measure."

> **NOTE.** If you have such an experience, or receive an astonishing revelation, gift, or power, you might expect God to also give you what you need to keep you from glorying in yourself. If you get sick or fall victim to some humbling disease—and are unable to use the healing laws for deliverance—then you might assume the Lord is dealing with you to keep you from foolish pride. Personally, I feel such instances are rare. It seems that God does NOT intervene except in the most unusual cases. Therefore DON'T let Satan deceive you into thinking you can't have healing because you've had some sort of vision or manifestation. It would have to be something as remarkable as Paul's heavenly excursion for that to be the case. We can expect the healing laws to hold firm, with recovery certain if we meet the conditions.

c. **Lack of nutrition and exercise.**

We must give the computer what it needs to do the job. The body is made of food. There are certain foods (nutrients) which are absolutely necessary. Without them the computer cannot produce the healing you want. True, it can rob nutrients from other parts of the body, but that is not the right way to get well.

Exercise is also vital to the computer. Unless the capillaries are open, it cannot deliver the necessary nutrients to the cells in the distressed area. We violate God's law when we do not work our body enough to keep the supply lines open. In an emergency, of course, the computer could force the capillaries to open and heal. But who is able to bring EMERGENCY faith or feeling to his computer? Generally it takes a crisis to do that.

❷ What should be the attitude of the Christian who is not healed?

Suppose you have faithfully disciplined yourself to do the healing exercises for six months. As far as you can tell you have met all the conditions. You are sure you have the faith necessary for triggering the computer, yet there is no sign of any change in your body. Let's also assume that the cause of your illness is also unknown. What should be your attitude now? It is summed in four words . . .

"PRAISE THE LORD ANYHOW!"

NOTE. The Christian is unique. He alone can give thanks for tribulation. He can accept sickness and suffering, knowing his whole life is in God's hands anyway. He knows the Lord is able to make ALL THINGS work together, including his sickness (Rom. 8:28). Ah, but notice I said ACCEPT. That is a significant word. It is not the same as RESIGNING yourself to an illness. The Christian should NEVER resign himself to sickness. Resignation is negative and passive. It means the person has given up all struggle against the illness. God doesn't want that. Christians are able to accept illness because they know God can turn the most tragic experience into a blessing.

The Christian who resigns himself to sickness usually becomes resentful. He feels sorry for himself, thinking God has dealt unfairly with him. You know what this does to his joy. Yet the Word of God tells all of us to "REJOICE" in tribulation (I Peter 4:13; II Cor. 6:10). A believer can ACCEPT sickness, praise God for it—and still NOT GIVE UP on the healing laws. Who knows, in time the sickness itself may bring forth the very fruit which makes healing possible. That is, the illness could cause the CHANGES a person needs to make in order for him to be healed. There should always be hope when it comes to healing.

273

If you are not healed after six months, and the doctors can do nothing for you, DON'T GIVE UP. Ask God for wisdom. Assume He has a purpose in the illness. He may reveal it to you and then you could go to work with Him in making changes in your life. In time you may find you have met the conditions and the "miracle" will occur. Even though you should suffer for years, you can still be sure it is God's intention that you should be well (III John 2). He does not delight in our sicknesses.

> **NOTE.** There is no greater testimony to the glory of the indwelling Christ than to see a Christian radiantly accept suffering as from God. No one else can do this. It is actually a GREATER MIRACLE than healing. It takes supernatural power. The unsaved have no way to accept suffering joyously. For them, this one life on earth is all they have. To be denied any part of it, through an affliction, is a terrible loss. They may try to shrug it off as a "bad break," but it is still suffering without hope. When medical science tells the unsaved man it can do nothing for him, he feels cheated. He thinks he's been robbed of his chance to get the most out of life. For those out of Christ, suffering is an incomprehensible mystery. For the believer, however it is an opportunity to glorify Jesus in a startling way. The reward for showing off the glory of the Lord in this fashion just has to be great.

❸ Can unsaved people use this approach to healing?

The answer is YES.

God's laws are not solely for the benefit of the Christian. The Lord Jesus revealed that in His sermon on the Mount. In one place He said the Father, "makes His sun to rise on the evil and the good, and sends rain on the just and the unjust" (Matt. 5:45). God's laws are for the operation of the universe and the maintenance of the animal kingdom. There is no partiality whatsoever. There is no respect of persons with God.

The healing laws are universal. The AUTOMATIC healing principle operates throughout nature. Every creature, our animal bodies included, enjoys the benefits of automatic healing. The healing laws function in all of us. It doesn't matter whether the person is a Christian or not. Everyone has a computer. And since the computer is activated by the LAW OF BELIEF, it can be used by anyone able to believe what he sees on the conscious screen. There are those who trigger the computer and get well who know nothing of God's laws.

I've mentioned the witch doctor. He can produce healings. He does it by getting his patient to BELIEVE he is going to get well. But medical doctors do the same. If what they say leads a patient to BELIEVE he is going to recover, the healing process is often triggered. Doctors are used to this. When a patient comes back telling of an amazing recovery, the physician shakes his head, "I don't understand it, but I'm glad for your sake." In the back of his mind he has written it off as "placebo effect," or some unresolved mystery of nature.

NOTE. The Christian Science and Science of the Mind people are in a different category. They know about the laws and how to use them. Of course they know nothing about salvation and the indwelling presence of Jesus. Neither do they have the Spirit of God to coach them. If they did, they would not explain God as a Universal Mind to whom all are linked through the unconscious. When you read their books, you see that they are completely in the dark when it comes to true knowledge of the things of the Spirit. But they have discovered the healing laws and possess a degree of proficiency in using them. Unfortunately they point to the healings as proof

275

of their doctrines. This, of course, deceives those who do not know the Word of God.

While God's laws are for everyone, the Christian has a huge advantage over the non-Christian. His personal friend is the Author and Teacher of those laws. This is the big edge. But in no way does it mean that God is partial. He isn't. He would that all men come to Him and enjoy the same privileges. He excludes no one from this invitation. But men EXCLUDE THEMSELVES when they refuse Christ as their personal Savior. The Christian, then, experiences a number of blessings unknown to the unsaved man:

A. The Christian is aware of the Lord's presence in His life. This MOTIVATES Him to live godly in accordance with God's Word.

B. The Christian is also EMPOWERED to live a holy life. It is the work of the Holy Spirit to strengthen believers, helping them to overcome evil and live the life that makes for physical health.

C. The Christian can UNBURDEN himself on Christ. He can get on his knees before a loving Lord, Whom he knows personally, and experience forgiveness for every sin in his life. Forgiveness is powerful medicine. As the believer searches his heart before the Lord, the Spirit helps him remember BURIED things which can be brought out and dumped in God's waste basket.

The unsaved do NOT have these blessings.

NOTE. Our Great Physician is also a Great Psychiatrist. When we go to Him with our sins, He receives us warmly. There is no hint of condemnation. In this climate of TOTAL ACCEPTANCE we find it easy to bring out ALL sin that comes to mind. It seems that when we confess one sin, another surfaces. This is marvelous. We all have sins that are buried so deeply they don't come up easily. If we went to a human psychiatrist he'd probe for a year and then hand us a whopping bill. With His sweet, uncondemning Spirit, God can do the same thing for us in minutes. And when God forgives—WOW! The weight is gone. The matter is utterly removed from us. The worldly psychiatrist has no way to perform that miracle. Those outside of Christ have no way to experience the wondrous blessings of forgiveness. People in the cults are guilt ridden. They are not at peace with God or themselves. Hence they are not truly healthy even though they get healings by using the healing laws.

❹ Just how is Jesus glorified by our using the healing laws?

Dedicated Christians are bound to ask that.

On the surface it seems more godly to seek healing in prayer and expect a "miracle." But is that more godly, really? What is so godly about it? The miracle? The only reason we call it a miracle is because we don't understand what is happening. When we know the laws behind ANYTHING God does, it is no longer miraculous, but lawful. When we **don't** understand the laws we call it a miracle.

When we understand God's laws, healing is no longer so mysterious. The question then is, does it ROB God of His glory for us to understand something like this? It would be most strange if it did, for then God's glory would depend on our IGNORANCE. We'd be saying that it honors God more for us to know nothing of His laws so that everything He does appears as miraculous.

Now I know some Christians would rather have it that way. They prefer to keep all of our dealings with God on a miraculous, mysterious basis. That way they feel that what occurs will more likely be of God and less of man. I appreciate their loyalty to God, but it is not the way of our heavenly Father to base His glory on the ignorance of His people. It's true that God does conceal things, but it is also His pleasure to reveal. In fact, it seems to me that one of the reasons He hides things, is that we might have the joy of discovering them.

NOTE. Even though we understand the laws and use them for healing, who gets the credit? The Lord. It is still His GIFT to us, a gift which has come by lawful means. They are **His** laws. What kind of a glory would it be that disappeared when God's people learned HOW it was that God blessed them lawfully? We work to earn money for our daily bread, yet we thank God at mealtime for providing the food. He didn't lower the food through the roof to place it on the table before us. Are we any the less thankful because we know HOW our food came to us? Does it reduce His glory for us to work WITH HIM in the process? We thank Him as sincerely as if it had appeared as did the manna in the wilderness. So we observe this: it is not the MEANS which brings glory to God, but the PRAISE of His people. God is glorified by the testimony of His people regardless of the METHOD He uses to bless them.

Here's a man just out of the hospital. His family meets him to take him home. He's still so weak they must help him into the car. The surgery was successful and now he's going home to await the new strength sure to come. Now WHO healed this man? The Lord? Of course. And just as surely as if he had stood before an evangelist. The MEANS is different, but that's all. In either case there is NO GLORY for Jesus unless the healed man GIVES IT TO HIM. Until a healed person gives Christ the credit, there is no honor for Jesus. In both cases God has used men. One was a doctor, the other an evangelist.

5 What is the significance of the New Testament practice of laying hands on the sick?

In the 28th chapter of Acts we find Paul shipwrecked on the island of Malta. While on this island, he laid hands on a man and he was healed. It occurred while Paul was a guest in the home of Publius, the magistrate of the island. It so happened that Publius' father was stricken with Maltese fever while Paul was in the house. This is a loathesome disease accompanied by dysentery. Paul went to the man as he lay sick with the fever and prayed for him. Then he laid his hands on the man and he was healed (vs.8).

Now why the hands? What part does the laying on of hands play in healing? It serves the same purpose as the EVANGELIST'S TOUCH in a healing meeting. It helps the sick person RISE in faith. The touch of another person can be dramatic, especially if you think you are going to receive something from him. Just one little touch can escalate a person's feelings sky high. And with those feelings, the hope that something will happen.

Now when Paul came into the man, what was the first thing he did? He PRAYED for him. How would you have liked to have been there to hear what the apostle said to Jesus in behalf of this man? Wouldn't that be exciting? Well, the man was there. He heard Paul talking to Jesus. He heard everything Paul said. It couldn't help but kindle wonder and hope within. Then Paul laid his hands on him. That touch must have been electrifying after hearing those words of prayer. His faith jumped to the place where he could be healed.

I have watched this happen numbers of times in the course of calling on the sick. I am thinking now of a certain man who suffered terrible head-aches. When I would come to his home, he was usually in bed, his head pounding so badly he didn't want to talk to people. Yet he hoped for help from a man of God. On this occasion he was in particular agony. I didn't touch him. I prayed for him first, conscious that he was looking for help in every word I said to the Lord. Then I reached over and laid my hand on his forehead. Instantly the pain departed. He was so thrilled. The first words on his lips were, "Praise the Lord, it's gone!"

NOTE. Some teachers think a special gift from God is imparted by the imposition of hands. I do not. If this were so, it seems to me, EVERYONE on whom the heal-ing evangelist laid hands would be healed. But this isn't the case. It is my opinion that ANY Christian can lay hands on a sick person and bless the sufferer by causing his faith to rise. If the act is preceded by a prayer which proves the ministering Christian is **really close to Christ,** the sick person is bound to have hope. When he hears the believing Christian ASK GOD for his healing, antici-pation stirs in the victim's heart. When the touch is felt, the sick man's faith can't help but rise. I do agree that the Holy Spirit uses the touch to PICTURE God's personal interest in the sick. And that touch, along with the Spirit's witness, can crystallize a person's faith to the place where it triggers his computer. The speed with which he is healed depends, of course, on the amount of emotion present.

Since the touch does add emotion to the scene, it can be significant.

❻ Were there different types of healings in the New Testament?

There were two types of "miraculous" healings in the days of Jesus and the apostles—COMMAND healings and FAITH healings. Beyond that, the automatic healing principle was operative then as it is now. People recovered from illnesses in those days just as they do in our time. The healing principle has served the animal kingdom from the beginning.

But we're interested in those which have been classed as miraculous. We can observe both COMMAND and FAITH healings in the New Testament.

a. **Command healings.**

JESUS RAISING JAIRUS' DAUGHTER FROM THE DEAD

281

Throughout Jesus' earthly ministry we find numerous cases where He healed people with the WORD OF AUTHORITY. No faith was needed on the part of the sick person. Here's Jairus' daughter. She died (Luke 8:49-56). Yet Jesus called her back from the dead with the word of authority. The same was true for the son of the widow at Nain (Luke 7:11-16).

In another place the Scriptures speak of Jesus' authority over illness.

> **"And when evening had come, they brought to Him many who were demon-possessed; and He cast out the spirits WITH A WORD, and healed ALL who were ill in order that what was spoken through the prophet Isaiah might be fulfilled, saying, 'He Himself took our infirmities and carried away our diseases'"** (Matt. 8:16-17 NAS).

The Lord Jesus demonstrated that He was THE HEALER by exercising authority over demons and disease. Not only did demons obey His command, but so did the BODIES of the sick. Consider the healing of the nobleman's son. Jesus was miles away from the sick lad when He said to the father, "Go thy way, thy son liveth" (John 4:50).

We further notice how the Lord Jesus DELEGATED this same word of authority to His disciples:

> **"And He called the twelve together (Judas included) and gave them power and authority over all the demons, and to heal diseases, and He sent them out to proclaim the Kingdom of God and to perform healing"** (Luke 9:1-2).

> **. . . and again:**

> **"Now after this, the Lord appointed seventy others and sent them two and two ahead of Him to every city and place where He Himself was going to come . . . and the**

282

seventy returned with joy, saying, 'Lord, even the demons are subject to us in Your Name'" (Luke 10:1, 17).

See how Jesus GAVE His healing authority to His disciples? By means of this delegated authority they were able to COMMAND both physical (diseases) and mental (demons) healings. With this kind of authority NO FAITH was necessary on the part of the sick. The COMPUTERS of the sick were under the direct authority of the disciples, and the DEMONS indwelling them had no choice but to come out on command. Healings performed by the WORD OF AUTHORITY are of a different order than those triggered BY FAITH. The word of authority was used **at will.**

Peter exercised COMMAND authority after Pentecost. We see it in action when he ORDERED the paralized Aeneas to rise up from his sick bed (Acts 9:34) and also when he SUMMONED Dorcas back from the dead (Acts 9:40).

PETER SUMMONING DORCAS BACK FROM THE DEAD

NOTE. Command healings would be a sensation today. Can you picture the amazement of doctors should a Christian with this kind of authority pass through a hospital emptying it of its sick and dying! The command healings of the New Testament established that Jesus was still alive and working through His servants. They proved the baby church was of divine origin. It was not easy for Jews to accept the fact that Judaism had been REPLACED by a fellowship of fishermen and convincing miracles were needed. But when people saw the apostles doing the SAME MIRACLES that Jesus did, it was proof that He was not dead, but alive and working THROUGH His disciples. The COMMAND HEALINGS were proof that He had come back to BE IN His people as promised (John 14:18).

© Linda Lovett 1979

THE FIRST SIX DAYS OF CREATION

● Command healings are performed by the WORD OF AUTHORITY. It is the same authority that said, "Let there be light, and there was light!" All God has to do is SPEAK—and things which do not as yet exist, leap into being. His is the CREATIVE Word. Our universe is a manifestation of that Word. God framed this world out of things we cannot see (Heb. 11:3). At this moment, the Lord Jesus is upholding the entire physical creation "by the WORD of His power" (Heb. 1:3). His is the voice of creation. This means that those healings performed by the WORD of the Lord in no way depended on the condition of the person's body. The power for healing was EXTERNAL and not in the body itself.

This is why Jesus could SPEAK and the dead Lazarus come forth from the tomb. It was NOT a matter of Lazarus' computer getting the message and summoning his body to action. His computer was dead. His body had already started to decay. This was a CREATIVE miracle, clearly supernatural. It was of the same order as the stilling of the storm and the feeding of the five thousand. Not only did the Lord perform such healings, He also delegated it to His apostles. Peter used it to summon the dead Dorcas back to life. Paul used it when he restored young Eutychus to life after he had fallen dead from a third story window (Acts 20:9).

b. **Faith healings.**

Then there were those who came to Jesus BELIEVING He could heal them. Their faith was often mingled with superstition, but that didn't make any difference. The **needed** faith was there. When word got out that Jesus was in a certain place, the people gathered bringing their sick with them. In village after village, the people laid their sick in the streets, "entreating Him that they might just touch the fringe of His cloak; and as many as touched it were cured" (Mark 6:56). This is faith healing and it took place in all the towns where Jesus went.

> **NOTE.** This was also true of the apostle Peter. He witnessed many faith healings. As the new church mushroomed into existence, the Lord began adding large numbers to the fellowship. The church was in great favor and the crowds held the chief apostle in great esteem, "to such an extent that they even carried the sick out onto the streets, and

285

laid them on cots and pallets, so that when Peter came by, at least his shadow might fall on them" (Acts 5:15). This occurred right after the Ananias and Sapphira affair so that there was great fear upon the church. People looked on God's leaders with awe. In such a situation FAITH HEALINGS were easily accomplished. All a person had to do was believe he would be healed by Peter's shadow. Then, as soon as the shadow fell on him, his faith sent his computer into action. Of course this was superstition, but it was mingled with enough faith to trigger the healings.

Remember the woman who had been hemorrhaging for twelve years? It made her an outcast. Having heard that Jesus The Healer was in the vicinity, she was desperate to get to Him. She worked her way through the crowd mobbing Him and reached out her hand. It came in contact with the tassle of His robe. This was a forbidden act, but she did it anyway—by faith. In her heart she had said, "If I may but touch His garment, I shall be whole" (Matt. 9:21). Yes, this was pure superstition, but she did it BY FAITH. Her faith expressed itself superstitiously. Even so, the woman was healed. Her hemorrhaging stopped IMMEDIATELY, even before Jesus said a word to her.

Then Jesus called out—"Who touched Me?" (Luke 8:45). Obviously this was NOT a command healing. The Lord gave NO command. The woman was healed by her own faith. It climaxed as she gripped His robe and triggered her computer. It happened just as she **believed** it would. Can we be sure of this interpretation? Jesus settles that question. He said to her, "Go in peace, daughter; YOUR FAITH has made you whole" (vs. 48). She was healed by the faith-method.

NOTE. The Lord said something else on this occasion that was striking, "I am aware that power has gone out of Me" (vs. 46). Now that is precious. It tells us that the healing stream (healing program) goes forth from God AUTOMATICALLY. When people exercise the faith for healing, it is still God's power that does the work. Even though we use the healing laws, the power behind those laws IS THE LORD. So in every case where a person is made whole by faith it is the Lord Who heals. Now what this woman did with her hand, we do with our minds. She touched His garment to trigger her computer, we use the conscious screen. The woman invoked the very same laws we do. Only the method of climaxing her faith was different.

Are you ready for something really wild? When Paul was at Ephesus, a city FILLED WITH SUPERSTITION, people were healed simply by coming in contact with his sweat cloths and aprons. Now the apostle used these in his trade as a "tentmaker." It was hard work for he had to fashion items with goats hair cloth and leather. Sweat bands were worn about his head. In the East, these bands are called "handkerchiefs."

Now the people believed that if they could simply touch one of these bands or his leather apron, they would be healed. Touching them was the means which caused their faith to rise. So these items were carried to the sick so that they could touch them. When they did, they were healed. The physical contact was sufficient to crystallize their faith and trigger their computers. This was out and out faith healing. It is the same principle used in many evangelistic healing meetings today. Sure it was superstition. But faith, even though cloaked in superstition, will still activate the unconscious computer. God's laws have to work regardless of how ridiculously one goes about using them. It is God's integrity that makes them valid, not our cleverness or clumsiness in using them.

NOTE. The same day the hemorrhaging woman was healed, two blind men staggered along behind the crowd trailing Jesus. They tried desperately to get to Him. They believed

He could heal them. Finally, in spite of their blindness they managed to get in front of Him. Their persistence was evidence of their faith. Jesus took note of their faith and said to them, "Do you believe I am able to do this?" When they assured Him they did, He touched their eyes. There was nothing in the touch itself, but their SUPERSTITION demanded it. The moment His hands contacted their eyes, their faith climaxed and their computers went to work. Then the Lord spoke the words which tell us this was NOT a command healing . . . 'Be it done unto you ACCORDING TO YOUR FAITH!' (Matt. 9:29). This was faith healing. There was NO command from Jesus. Even though it was wrapped in superstition, these two men were clearly healed by their own faith. God was pleased to use the touch-method since THEY believed it was necessary.

7 **How about healing in the church?**

James says:

> **"Is there any sick among you? Let him call for the elders of the church and let them pray over him, anointing him with oil in the name of the Lord. And the prayer offered in faith will restore the one who is sick and the Lord will raise him up, and if he has committed sins, they will be forgiven him."**
>
> —James 5:14,15.

First of all observe the oil. This was the common remedial agent in those days when medical science was in its infancy. The term "anoint," as it was used in this case, meant to MASSAGE. Therefore James was NOT suggesting that medical help was unnecessary. To the contrary, he said get the best. Massaging with oil was the best medical help available in those times. Still, he is also saying, we must NOT depend on medical help alone.

Now note the elders. They were not called upon

because of the rank or official position in the church, but because of their godly walk and spiritual gifts. They were able to DISCERN God's working in a person's life. They could sense what God was trying to do in the victim's life through sickness and counsel him. Sometimes there was a particular sin connected with the illness and a discerning elder could guide the afflicted believer in making his confession.

NOTE. The elders were godly people who could be trusted. They could be depended upon to keep a confidence. That's why they were appointed to their jobs. When a man confessed his deepest secrets to an elder, he knew they were safe. He knew he would not be betrayed. People reading these passages in James should note the connection between the elders and the practice of confession. They were especially trustworthy. Modern readers are apt to seize the principle of confession and go running off to ANY brother. This can be dangerous. Confession should be made ONLY to those whom it is proven they will keep your confidence. They should also be people, who, like the elders above, are able to discern God's working so as to SEE the connection between the sickness and the afflicted man's sin. The succeeding verses affirm the truth of this.

"Therefore confess your sins one to another and pray for one another, so that you may be healed. The effective prayer of a righteous man can accomplish much" (James 5:16).

● Confession is a marvelous resource of the living church—or should be. In many places this wonderful exercise is no longer encouraged. The incidence of mental and nervous breakdowns among Christians could be reduced if this practice were reinstituted. The believer who can open his heart to a godly brother (elder) receives instant relief and help through prayer.

Now unclean minds, those that are filled with worry, anger, pride, lust, and a critical spirit, are sick. Those are spiritual sicknesses. Those who gossip, for example, do not realize they are ill, but they are. Every such illness is eventually reflected in the body. Consequently when confession is made to a "righteous" brother, one who is steadfast in prayer, the illness is discharged. If the victim repents, that is, actually turns from the evil, healing can come. Sometimes very fast.

In studying this healing passage in James, the particular thing to note and emphasize is FORGIVENESS. That is the vital element in healings that occur in the church. It is forgiveness that brings the healing. Why? Forgiveness is SPIRITUAL healing. The man who is forgiven—and knows it—experiences relief and well being at the mental level. If the release is complete, and by that I mean, if he actually turns from the sin so that he does not accrue further guilt, this new spiritual health will be reflected in his body.

> **NOTE.** In this book we have dealt with the amazing relationship between our MINDS and our BODIES. When the image of God is spiritually sick, his body tries to REFLECT his mental attitude. The person who is distressed and feels "mean" in his mind, can expect those destructive feelings to take their toll somewhere in his body. He can become physically ill as a result of his spiritual sickness. But when the mind is RELIEVED of guilt (forgiven) and he TURNS from the sin, (so that new guilts do not replace the old ones), his new health is reflected in the body. This is why it takes a WISE counselor to handle confessions. It is not enough to LISTEN to the sordid details of a confession. The elder must be skilled in coaching a victim in turning from his sin and teach him WHY it is necessary. Only then will he be motivated to do it.

8 What about fasting today?

We don't hear much about fasting today as a way to strengthen one's closeness to Christ. Yet a fast "unto the Lord," is one of the most spiritual things a person can undertake. Such a fast is one where the eating of food is secondary to occupation with Christ. Modern society is geared to the EASY life, not one of abstinence or self-denial. It seems almost unnatural to deny yourself food when you live in a land that is dedicated to stuffing itself with anything it wants—simply because it can afford it. To deny one's self anything is hard in our day.

NOTE. Fasting is a spiritual weapon which the devil does not want in the hands of God's people. He trembles when believers mean business for Christ to the point where they are ready to forego food in order to become intimate with Him. Yet when we look at the giants of the Bible; men such as Moses, David, Elijah, and Daniel, we find they all sought God with fasting. The devil has worked hard to keep modern Christians from rediscovering its power. Those who fast regularly and seek the Lord during that time, testify that after the third day their spiritual sensitivity soars dramatically. They find themselves able to spend long hours in prayer, enjoying the Lord's presence in a way that is not otherwise possible. Even protracted times of prayer are a rarity today, let alone going without food to sharpen your spiritual appetite. God is apparently ready to listen to people who are more interested in Him than food.

© Linda Lovett 1975

JESUS FASTED FORTY DAYS AND FORTY NIGHTS
IN THE WILDERNESS

• When our Lord Jesus was led of the Spirit in the wilderness to be ''tempted of the devil.'' He fasted forty days and forty nights (Matt. 4:1,2). He had just been baptized by John the Baptist where it was confirmed from heaven that He was the Son of God. Whatever clues or foregleams He had before that time, as He worked at His carpenter's bench, were suddenly confirmed in that moment. He needed time to adjust to the revelation and let the significance of it be tested. That's why He was led into the wilderness.

The account reads that He afterwards ''became hungry.'' We may assume that He did not become thirsty, that He drank water during the time. The body can go for forty days without food and suffer no damage at all, but it cannot go more than a few days without water. There is nothing to indicate that God supernaturally intervened to cancel His thirst as He did in the case of Moses (Ex. 34:28). So we must assume His fast was from food only. The apostle Paul, we may note, fasted for three days without food and water after he was saved on the Damascus Road (Acts 9:9).

• On one occasion, when the Lord's disciples found themselves powerless to cast out certain demons, they went to the Master about it. ''This kind,'' He said, ''goeth not out but by fasting and prayer'' (Matt. 17:14-21). Fasting has a way of detaching us from the material things of this world and fixing our focus on God. The finite world fades from view as we center our thoughts wholly on Jesus. When a man gets to the place where he prefers fellowship with Jesus to food, he finds it brings a release of faith which won't come otherwise. In those moments he is able to trust God for things which would be impossible as long as his vision was clouded by temporal longings.

NOTE. There's no way for me to estimate the number of readers who would be interested in fasting as a spiritual weapon or resource. I am not qualified to say more than I have. I have never used fasting for deliverance or for revelation. Perhaps that is to my shame. But I do mean to look into it. I have a handbook that deals with the spiritual side of fasting in a nice way. It is **God's Chosen Fast,** by Arthus Wallis. It is a 120 page paperback and sells for $1.25. It can be ordered from the Christian Literature Crusade, Fort Washington, PA 19034. My interest in fasting has been concerned with the benefit it brings the body, particularly as it detoxifies the body.

Fasting detoxifies the body.

When next you visit your doctor, look at the certificates hanging on his wall. Among them you will find the Hippocratic Oath. When your doctor received his M.D. degree, he took that oath. But what he perhaps doesn't know or has forgotten is that the author of that oath made a very arresting statement over 2500 years ago. "Fasting is the cornerstone of body healing." Wouldn't it be something if the medical profession got around to rediscovering that proposition? Now Hippocrates did not get that bit of wisdom out of a book. He observed it from watching the behavior of the human body during an illness.

> **NOTE.** When people are sick, it is the natural impulse of the body to detoxify itself with an enforced fast. We simply don't feel like eating when we're sick. And we shouldn't. The computer shuts down the digestive system in order to deploy the body forces against the illness. No animal eats while sick or injured. All creatures (our animal bodies included) fast when there is something physically wrong. During the fast, the body lives on surplus fat. At the same time it continues to work like an incinerator, burning up the waste and decaying tissues of the body. Some of those wastes have been stored in the various organs for years. Without the owner knowing it, some parts of his body can actually be impaired because of collected

294

wastes. As the body is gradually detoxified through fasting, many of the organs return to their ORIGINAL CONDITION.

Can fasting be dangerous? Sure, if a person fails to observe certain cautions. There are some important things to know before you even consider a fast. Diabetics, for example, should not consider fasting without first checking with their doctors. Also, there is a lot to learn about the way to begin and end a fast. The person who has never fasted must not start off with a long fast. The body has to get used to going without food—**by degrees.** Most people break themselves into fasting by starting off with one day fasts and gradually increasing the span. Finally, they get to the place where they can go a week or longer.

Coming off the fast is even more critical than starting. There are only certain things that should go into your stomach after it has been shut down for a long period of time. If you feel God's witness in the idea of fasting, then be sure to get a couple of books on it and read up on the subject before you start. There are some vital rules to follow. Observe them and fasting is not dangerous at all. A healthy body, one that is fairly well nourished can go for several weeks without food and suffer no damage to good cells. All that is consumed is surplus. When the body starts to use up good cells, you get hungry again. That's how you know to end the fast.

9 Can the devil heal?

In his book, **I Talked With Spirits,** Victor Ernest says, "Every seance with which I am familiar has healing meetings." He then goes on to describe the action which takes place in such a meeting:

"Usually the medium touches the affected areas, moving

his hands down over the area of pain and then quickly removes them. The action is completed with a snap of the hands and wrists, as though the pain were actually being withdrawn." (Page 82).

After reading this book, and knowing what you do now, you can see how a person could indeed get well in such a meeting. If he really believed the spirits could heal, the touch of the medium would have the same effect as the touch of the ''healing evangelist.'' In a seance, the emotional build up is tremendous. The anticipation of seeing or hearing spirits mounts by the minute. In time, a person's feelings can reach a high pitch. Therefore the SAME LAWS which produce healings in an evangelistic meeting can also produce them in spiritist seances.

> **NOTE.** We surely don't want to be so naive as to think we could discover and use the healing laws, and the "prince of this world," couldn't. Of course he knows of them. He USES them continually to accomplish his evil purposes in people. In fact, he uses them in reverse. That's how he makes people sick. He plants destructive thoughts in their minds. People embrace these thoughts and feed them. In time their bodies become sick. It stands to reason that Satan knows these laws, and has no trouble teaching them to his workers. It is easy to lure people into the cults with promises of healing and seeing the supernatural. Men love the supernatural. We can be sure that Satan is the author of many healings. And his particular delight is using them to deceive and confuse the child of God. More than one Christian has been fooled by Satan's supernatural powers, and more specifically his ability to COUNTERFEIT some of the things found in God's Word.

● As we move into the end of the age we are going to see many ''healings'' and wonders as the devil seeks to counterfeit the signs expected to attend the coming of the Lord. Just before Jesus comes again, Satan, himself, will appear on the scene in a human body, claiming that he is God (II Thess. 2:3,4). He will even have forerunners heralding his coming. The signs will be so convincing that those of God's people who do not know better, will be deceived. There will be great confusion among the Christians, particularly those who are not saturated with the Word of God.

⑩ WHAT MUST A PERSON DO TO STAY HEALED?

1. Discipline his thought-life (as unto the Lord).
2. Eat nutritious food.
3. Exercise regularly.

If he will do those things
. . . he will keep the healing God gives him via the computer.

The law of health written in our members guarantees good health—if we cooperate with it. That has been the purpose of this book. I have sought to show you HOW to align yourself with that law. **I have NOT given you all of the healing laws. I don't know them.** But I have shared those that I do know. The nice thing about it is that they can all be proved in clinical situations. These laws work. Use them as I have described and you will be blessed with healing. It is the nature of laws to do their job when we meet the conditions. These cannot fail because the God behind them cannot fail. So expect your healing.

We've come to the end. May God use this book to draw you closer to Jesus and bring you the health you desire for His sake. Your healing will come as a GIFT from the Lord. Though you have learned the laws and the techniques for using them, the blessing is from God. It is HE Who has healed you. So when you tell others of your healing, make sure Christ gets the credit. He is the Healer, the only Healer.

 Now you can do something for me. When you receive your healing, would you write and tell me about it? I would appreciate it very much. And if the Lord reveals something unusual about healing as you work with the laws, would you also pass that on to me? It will help in refining the book for future editions. Also, if the story of your healing brings definite glory to Jesus, would you allow me to share it with our readers? I never use anyone's testimony without his permission. Here's why I want permission to use your testimony. There might be a reader who hasn't quite the faith he needs to trust in God's laws. Your testimony might be just what the Holy Spirit needs to give him a boost. If you'll do that, I promise to use your testimony in a way that brings the most honor to our Lord Jesus Christ.

"PRAISE THE LORD!"

298

INSTRUCTIONS

for the three
affirmation cards
on page 301

On page 301 you'll find three cards containing prayer affirmations. Use them in connection with the healing technique set forth in your text, **Jesus Wants You Well!** Cut out the cards and plan on carrying a different one on your person for a week at a time. Inserting it in a plastic tract holder will keep it neat and handy.

As soon as you start the healing plan, Satan will begin attacks, trying to keep your mind focused on the illness. He seeks to stir up two powerful emotions— worry and fear. He knows that thinking about a sickness can trigger those emotions which in turn will reinforce your illness if allowed to persist. Let Satan's attack be a signal to make an affirmation to the Lord.

The instant he moves your mind to your illness, reach for your card. If you are alone, read your affirmation to the Lord—ALOUD. The exact words don't matter. You can use them at first, but once you get the hang of it, you'll be making up all sorts of prayer affirmations of your own.

Don't get discouraged even if you have to do this 30 or 50 times a day. The devil will give up before you will. You have the Holy Spirit to help you. Satan has nothing but his ego to help him and he can't take rejection for very long. Everytime he backs off, visualize yourself as healed. . .do your best to BELIEVE it. . .and then thank God for it.

AFFIRMATION CARD ① ①

"Dear Lord, the devil wants me to think about the illness, but I'm letting his attack remind me of your healing program. I praise you, right now, for your healing presence within me. I know that you are using the blood stream to bring new material to every cell, nerve, tissue, and fiber in my body. My _____ was designed to be perfect. I can picture it as brand new. It's great to trust in your healing laws and believe the scenes on the screen. Thank you Lord Jesus, that we can reprogram the computer together."

AFFIRMATION CARD ② ②

"Lord Jesus, thank you for your healing presence. I know you want me well. The promises of your Word and your healing laws, dear Lord, are more real than the symptoms of any disease. I'd rather trust in your laws than believe in sickness. I know that believing what I SEE on the screen is a terrific way to exercise faith in your Laws. Therefore, I affirm that your power is rebuilding my body right now according to the law of health written in my computer. I can SEE myself as healed and thank you for it."

AFFIRMATION CARD ③ ③

"Lord Jesus, according to your laws, the creative power of my blood stream is so great, I get a new body every 11 months. How can an organ remain diseased in the face of all this power when you want me well? I thank you that right now your healing power is at work all over my body, rebuilding every tissue and organ. I can SEE myself perfectly healed and affirm that it is your power, O Lord, that is doing the work. Thank you, Jesus!"